UNLOCK

BASIC SKILLS

Sabina Ostrowska
with Jennifer Farmer

CAMBRIDGE
UNIVERSITY PRESS

CAMBRIDGE
UNIVERSITY PRESS

University Printing House, Cambridge CB2 8BS, United Kingdom

One Liberty Plaza, 20th Floor, New York, NY 10006, USA

477 Williamstown Road, Port Melbourne, VIC 3207, Australia

4843/24, 2nd Floor, Ansari Road, Daryaganj, Delhi – 110002, India

79 Anson Road, #06-04/06, Singapore 079906

Cambridge University Press is part of the University of Cambridge.

It furthers the University's mission by disseminating knowledge in the pursuit of education, learning and research at the highest international levels of excellence.

www.cambridge.org
Information on this title: www.cambridge.org/9781316636480

© Cambridge University Press 2017

This publication is in copyright. Subject to statutory exception and to the provisions of relevant collective licensing agreements, no reproduction of any part may take place without the written permission of Cambridge University Press.

First published 2017

20 19 18 17 16 15 14 13 12 11 10 9 8 7 6 5 4 3 2 1

Printed in the United Kingdom by Latimer Trend

A catalogue record for this publication is available from the British Library

ISBN 978-1-316-63648-0 Unlock Basic Skills Teacher's Book with Downloadable Audio and Video
ISBN 978-1-316-63649-7 Unlock Basic Literacy Teacher's Book with Downloadable Audio
ISBN 978-1-316-63645-9 Unlock Basic Skills Student's Book with Downloadable Audio and Video
ISBN 978-1-316-63646-6 Unlock Basic Literacy Student's Book with Downloadable Audio

Cambridge University Press has no responsibility for the persistence or accuracy of URLs for external or third-party internet websites referred to in this publication, and does not guarantee that any content on such websites is, or will remain, accurate or appropriate. Information regarding prices, travel timetables, and other factual information given in this work is correct at the time of first printing but Cambridge University Press does not guarantee the accuracy of such information thereafter.

CONTENTS

Your guide to *Unlock Basic Skills*		4
Teaching tips		6
STARTER UNIT	The basics	13
UNIT 1	Meeting people	19
UNIT 2	People and things	32
UNIT 3	University life	43
UNIT 4	Different countries	56
UNIT 5	Work	69
UNIT 6	Food and health	83
UNIT 7	Places	96
UNIT 8	Spending	105
UNIT 9	Technology	122
UNIT 10	Free time and fashion	134
Acknowledgements		160

YOUR GUIDE TO UNLOCK

UNLOCK BASIC SKILLS UNIT STRUCTURE

The units in *Unlock Basic Skills* are carefully scaffolded so that students build the skills and language they need throughout in order to be successful in the final speaking and writing tasks.

UNLOCK YOUR KNOWLEDGE | Introduces Learning Objectives for the unit and encourages discussion around the theme of the unit with inspiration from striking visuals.

LISTENING AND READING 1
LISTENING AND READING 2
LISTENING AND READING 3 | Provides information about the topic, introduces new vocabulary and grammar in context, and practises listening and reading skills. Where relevant, this section also includes a focus on sound and spelling or a pronunciation feature which will further enhance listening and speaking comprehension.

WATCH AND REMEMBER | Features engaging and motivating video which recycles the language learned in Listening and Reading 1–3 and extends the vocabulary.

LANGUAGE FOCUS | Practises the vocabulary and grammar from Listening and Reading 1–3, focuses on functional language for speaking, and prepares students for the final speaking and writing tasks.

ACADEMIC LISTENING AND SPEAKING | Features an academic listening text that practises listening skills and acts as a model for the final interactional speaking task that uses the skills and language learnt over the course of the unit. It includes a Critical Thinking section that prepares students for speaking.

ACADEMIC READING AND WRITING | Features an academic reading text, practises reading skills and acts as a model for the final writing task that uses the skills and language learnt over the course of the unit. It includes Academic Writing Skills and a Critical Thinking section that prepares students for writing.

OBJECTIVES REVIEW | Allows students to evaluate how well they have mastered the skills covered in the unit.

WORDLIST | Includes the key vocabulary from the unit and space for notes.

These lessons give students the opportunity to use all the language and skills they have learnt in the unit. Students practise the unit's main Learning objectives.

UNLOCK BASIC RESEARCH

- Developed in collaboration with pre-A1 teachers at a number of universities so we can be sure our material is relevant, engaging and effective
- 👁 Informed by Cambridge's expert language research into the words students use and the words they should be using to provide the syllabus they need

UNLOCK BASIC SKILLS AND LANGUAGE

- Combines listening, speaking, reading and writing to provide extra support for pre-A1 students as they begin to learn English
- Prepares students for the final speaking and writing tasks through well-scaffolded lessons
- Gives extra language support where students need it most with NOTICE and REMEMBER boxes

UNLOCK BASIC CRITICAL THINKING

- Provides an introduction to critical thinking to support students as they take their first steps to academic success
- Based on Bloom's Taxonomy to ensure students develop a range of thinking skills

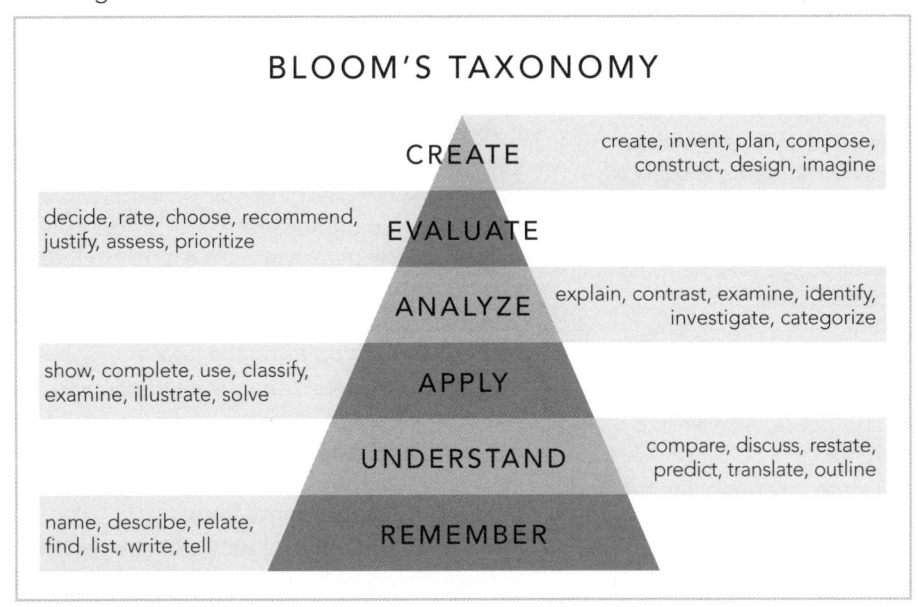

BLOOM'S TAXONOMY

- **CREATE**: create, invent, plan, compose, construct, design, imagine
- **EVALUATE**: decide, rate, choose, recommend, justify, assess, prioritize
- **ANALYZE**: explain, contrast, examine, identify, investigate, categorize
- **APPLY**: show, complete, use, classify, examine, illustrate, solve
- **UNDERSTAND**: compare, discuss, restate, predict, translate, outline
- **REMEMBER**: name, describe, relate, find, list, write, tell

UNLOCK BASIC WATCH AND REMEMBER

- Provides videos in short, manageable chunks in well-staged lessons
- Recycles language from earlier in the unit to provide students with extra exposure and practice
- Provides opportunities to extend unit vocabulary

> "The quality of the video is great!"
> Megan Putney, Dhofar University, Oman

TEACHING TIPS

1 Meeting the needs of pre-A1 students

The combined skills approach

For pre-A1 students the acquisition of new language items is the starting point for development of any language competency. To develop skills evenly, students need to focus on all aspects of new language – associating the sounds of English with the written form. *Unlock Basic Skills* takes a combined-skills approach in order to best support pre-A1 students. Each lesson and unit of *Unlock Basic Skills* builds from language input and practice to more extended skills work.

Literacy

For pre-A1 students from a non-Roman alphabet background, learning English presents a number of specific challenges. *Unlock Basic Skills* has been designed to provide support for all of these challenges.

- Audio support is provided for all new lexis and all Reading material on the page.
- Awareness of word and sentence boundaries is developed through the step-by-step approach to language presentation and reading skills.
- Regular NOTICE features are included, drawing attention to punctuation and other features of written language.
- Regular activities focus entirely on punctuation.
- Written records of new vocabulary alongside visual representations of meaning are always visible on the page, giving students security of correct word forms for reference in written tasks.
- REMEMBER boxes provide students with the written records of the language they need for more extended productive tasks.
- Tasks which require students to produce new structures in writing are staged so that students have the opportunity to focus on the meaning and form of the lexis, before being asked to reproduce it in writing.
- The amount students write is carefully limited and gradually extended throughout the course. See the Writing section for more details.

Unlock Basic Literacy can be used in conjunction with *Unlock Basic Skills* and follows the same syllabus with the aim of developing literacy. *Unlock Basic Literacy* focusses specifically on the needs of Arabic L1 beginners and offers full support for your students in developing literacy.

Introduction to Critical Thinking

Even at a very low level of language proficiency, students can be familiarized with the ways in which they can plan for more extended writing and speaking activities. In the Academic Reading and Writing and Academic Listening and Speaking lessons, *Unlock Basic Skills* presents students with models for Speaking and Writing and frames for generating ideas, such as tables, notes, ideas maps, charts, etc. Students use lower order thinking skills (remember, understand, apply) to relate a frame to a model. Then students use lower and higher order thinking skills (analyze, evaluate, create) to prepare their own ideas for the Academic Writing or Academic Speaking tasks.

2 Communicating with pre-A1 students

Learning objectives in the pre-A1 classroom

Learning objectives are motivating to students because they give them a clear way to measure their progress, and give individual activities within a lesson a clear sense of purpose. *Unlock Basic Skills Student's Book* provides a list of Learning objectives at the beginning of each unit. In addition there is a matching checklist at the end of each unit. The *Unlock Basic Skills Teacher's Book* provides lesson-by-lesson Learning objectives which can be used both at the beginning and end of each lesson.

- **Communicating Learning objectives**

Learning objectives tend to be expressed in language which will not yet be familiar or comprehensible to your students. If you speak the students' L1, you could translate the objectives and write them on the board.

If you cannot or do not wish to use L1 in the classroom, you could use the following procedure:

Write the examples of the target language only on the board and demonstrate what students will learn as follows. Read each objective aloud in English as you do so.

Vocabulary sets: Show the flashcards briefly and point to the examples on the board.

Punctuation: Circle examples of the punctuation on the board.

Listening and reading: Use gestures to communicate the skills whilst indicating the text or the script in the Student's Book.

Speaking: Use a symbol such as a speech bubble and connect it with the target sentences and structures on the board. You can also provide an oral model of any exchanges.

Critical thinking: For more extended or specific speaking and writing tasks, you may wish to point out any frameworks such as ideas maps or survey questions in the Student's Book.

Writing: Say: *Write*, and write the target structures on the board.

Academic Writing: Circle or underline any features of the written words you will focus on, such as pronouns and linking words, on the board.

- **Measuring progress**

Monitoring at every stage of the lesson is the key to recognizing how well students are progressing with their objectives. You can also round off each lesson and unit with an objectives review. Encourage students to reflect on the objectives and communicate to you how confident they feel about each objective. You could use a sliding scale on the board, for example:

very well   not very well

Gauge the students' feelings regarding each objective, and assure students they will get the opportunity to review and practise any areas they are not yet confident in in future lessons.

There are also Review tests, which are designed to be used after the students have completed each unit of the Student's Book. Each Review test checks students' knowledge of the key language areas taught in the unit and practises the Literacy, Sound and Spelling, Pronunciation and Writing Skills from the unit. Go to esource.cambridge.org to download the printable Review tests and the Review test audio.

Wordlists

The Student's Book features unit-by-unit wordlists which can be used during lessons or at home. The wordlists are found at the end of each unit and are composed of the new vocabulary which students have practised in the unit. There are many ways that you can work with vocabulary. For example, you could encourage the students to learn the new words by setting regular, informal reviews and spelling tests. You could also ask the students to choose, e.g. five words from the unit vocabulary to learn. The wordlists are in alphabetical order, but you can also ask students to focus on particular topic groups of words, e.g. colours or clothes. At the end of each unit, make sure students practise the new words and a selection of words from previous units. Use these lists as a way of focusing your students on the key language in the unit.

At the back of the Student's Book on pp. 210–213 there is also an extensive glossary section with the unit-by-unit wordlists. There is space in the glossary for students to write the words in their own language. Alternatively, they could practise writing the words in English.

Communicating instructions and demonstrating activities in the pre-A1 classroom

Grading your language

It is important not to overwhelm students with language in the classroom. Be particularly aware of common phrasal verbs in your speech. For example, instructions such as '**Pick up** your book.' and '**Get up** and **walk around**.' are unlikely to be understood without demonstration.

Use the simplest, most familiar language you can to communicate with students, but do not grade your language so that it is unnatural. For example, if you are asking questions about a picture, 'Where is he going?' will be understood through the meaning of the content words (where, he, go) – students do not need to be familiar with the present continuous to understand this. This Teacher's Book provides examples of language you can use for particular situations.

Non-verbal communication

Your role as the teacher in the pre-A1 classroom is perhaps more central than at other levels. In addition to reading rubrics aloud, it is important that you demonstrate activities. In general, the following non-verbal techniques can be helpful. Always accompany these with the spoken words.

- Use gestures and props such as books and headphones to communicate rubrics such as: *read, write, listen, do not write, do not speak*, etc.
- Use culturally appropriate gestures and/or facial expressions to accompany phrases such as *That's right. That's not right. What's this? Which one? Is this yours? Whose is this? What's wrong with this sentence? Is this right or wrong? Work in pairs. Work in a group of three.* etc.
- Use gestures or clapping to communicate language points such as contractions, intonation, and word and sentence stress.
- Use symbols on the board to communicate Right (✓), Wrong (✗), Same (=), Different (≠), Ask me a question (❓), Say / Tell me / Describe (◯), etc.

Use the examples in each activity in the Student's Book to demonstrate the procedure for each activity. Model the activity by miming doing the example and pointing out relevant sources of information on the page, such as vocabulary sets and grammar tables students can refer to.

Setting up speaking activities with a model is particularly important. If you like, you can take on the role of both students, changing where you are standing to indicate different speakers. Alternatively you can demonstrate the full activity with a student.

Concept checking

Checking understanding of new lexis with pre-A1 students can seem challenging. However, as new language is often very concrete in meaning, it can actually be a more straightforward task at this level. You can use the following techniques:

Images, flashcards and realia What's this? What are these? Is this (a tree)? Is he old? Is it busy?

Questions (go to work) Do I go to work on Thursday? (Yes) Saturday? (No) Do I go to work in the evening? (No).

Substitution drills (See the section on Drilling in Teaching Pronunciation, below.)

Controlled practice exercises (on the board as a class, or monitoring as students work individually)

In general, it is recommended that you prepare a way to check the meaning of new language before lessons.

⊙ Common student errors

Throughout the Teacher's Books there are boxes which tell you about typical errors your students may be prone to (depending on their L1). These are informed by the Cambridge Learner Corpus, a bank of official Cambridge exam papers. The highest frequency errors made by students have been included, allowing you to work on these in a remedial way, should you notice these errors occurring as you monitor.

3 Teaching skills

Listening

Students who aim to study at university will need to develop sub-skills to help them orient themselves to extended listening. The listening texts in *Unlock Basic Skills* provide students with practice in the different listening sub-skills, and also provide topic-related vocabulary, structures and functional language needed for the Speaking task. In the Academic Listening and Speaking lessons, the Academic Listening provides a complete model for the Speaking task.

Listening in *Unlock Basic Skills* is supported by transcripts on the page as is suitable for pre-A1 students. Academic Listening is not transcribed and offers students an opportunity to consolidate the Listening Skills they have practised across the unit in a more challenging way.

Speaking

Students work towards the Speaking task throughout the unit by learning grammar, vocabulary and functional language relevant for the task, and then by listening to a model of the activity. Students use lower order thinking skills (remember, understand, apply) to relate a notes frame or other visual organizer to the model. Then students use lower and higher order thinking skills (analyze, evaluate, create) to prepare their own ideas for the Speaking task.

Unlock Basic Skills includes two types of Speaking task – presentational and interactional. In the presentational tasks, students will be required to give a short presentation or monologue on a familiar topic. The interactional tasks require students to role-play or interact with others in the class. Sometimes tasks are a combination of these formats.

Conducting feedback on extended speaking

During the Speaking tasks, note examples of good and flawed language use. After the Speaking task, use this to feed back to students. Write the examples you noted on the board and encourage students to identify their own utterances, and, if necessary, correct them. Deal with meaning of correct new language use which may not be familiar to all members of the class. Praise more complex language used accurately and also those who correct themselves. Do not criticize the students who cannot correct their mistakes, but point out the sections of the Student's Book where this language can be reviewed.

Additional Speaking tasks

There is an additional Speaking task for every unit on pages 149–155 of this Teacher's Book. This can be used as extra practice to be prepared at home or done in class. You could use this as part of an end-of-unit test/evaluation.

Reading

Students who aim to study at university will need to develop sub-skills to help them orient themselves to extended reading. The reading texts in *Unlock Basic Skills* provide students with practice in the different reading sub-skills, and also provide topic-related vocabulary, structures and functional language needed for the end-of-unit Speaking and Writing tasks. In the Academic Reading and Writing lessons a text of a real-world genre is provided, offering students an opportunity to consolidate the Reading Skills they have practised across the unit in a more challenging way.

Reading in *Unlock Basic Skills* is supported by audio as is suitable for pre-A1 students who come from non-Roman L1 backgrounds. If literacy is not an issue for your students, use the procedures in these sections without the audio. This will provide a more appropriate level of challenge for your students.

Writing

Students work towards the Writing task throughout the unit by learning grammar, vocabulary and academic writing skills such as linking, punctuation and spelling relevant for the task. They meet a model for the writing in the Academic Reading and Writing lesson, and use lower order thinking skills (remember, understand, apply) to relate a notes frame or other visual organizer to the model. Then students use lower and higher order thinking skills (analyze, evaluate, create) to prepare their own ideas for the Writing task.

Unlock Basic Skills is designed for students who will not yet be proficient in writing. The amount students write is carefully limited and gradually extended throughout the course, from letters and numerals in the Starter Unit, to words and sentences. By the end of the course, students link clauses in compound sentences with *and* and *but*, and link consecutive sentences with *also*. Academic writing tasks provide a frame within which students can complete more extended writing tasks securely.

Additional Writing tasks
There is an additional Writing task for every unit on pages 149–155 of this Teacher's Book. This can be used as extra practice to be prepared at home or done in class. You could use this as part of an end-of-unit test/evaluation.

Research projects
There is an opportunity for students to investigate the unit topic further in the Research projects which feature at the end of each unit of this Teacher's Book. These are optional activities which will allow your students further practice of critical thinking and written and spoken presentation skills as they source information, analyze, and present on a particular aspect of the unit topic.

4 Teaching pronunciation
Unlock Basic Skills features Sound and Spelling, Pronunciation for Speaking, and Pronunciation for Listening.

Sound and Spelling
Students focus on common spellings of individual sounds and variations in the way individual letters and combinations of letters are pronounced. Focusing on these common sound and spelling relationships is helpful for accurate reading and writing, as well as listening and speaking.

Pronunciation for Speaking
Word stress Using word stress accurately is key to intelligibility. Focusses on word stress in multi-syllable words are regularly included.
Main stress Using main stress accurately is important for intelligibility. Varying the main stress in a sentence can significantly affect meaning. *Unlock Basic Skills* includes a regular focus on main stress in questions and statements.

Pronunciation for Listening
Sentence stress Focusing on sentence stress helps students develop their ability to listen to English. By understanding that only stressed syllables in content words are fully pronounced, they can tune in to the language of other speakers – especially native speakers – more easily.

Drilling
Drilling refers to activities in which the same thing is repeated several times in order to practise it. Drilling new language is important to expose students to the sounds of new language, focus on accuracy in a very controlled practice, and build confidence with both the form and the sounds in subsequent practice and communicative use.

Simple drills
To conduct a drill, model the target language or play the audio and encourage the students to repeat it. Choose individual students to repeat the words and then encourage the whole group to repeat. You may wish to break down longer phrases into chunks, e.g. fruit / vegetables / fruit and vegetables / eat fruit and vegetables. Focus on word and sentence stress by clapping or punching the air on stressed syllables. With sounds that your students find particularly difficult, model the phoneme then the word, for example /fr/ /fruit/.

Substitution drills
Substitution drills are a useful technique for practising longer sentences and structures in a very controlled manner. Drill a sentence, for example, *I like driving at weekends.* and then call out a variant of one part of the sentence, e.g. 'He'. The students replace *I* with *He* in the sentence and make any other grammatical changes, *He likes driving at weekends.* In the beginning, choose the same variant part to change e.g. the subject (*I, He, We You, Ahmed, My father*). As students grow more familiar with the activity, you can vary other parts of the sentence e.g. *walk in the park* (He likes walking in the park at weekends.), *not like* (He doesn't like walking in the park at weekends.).

5 Using the video in the classroom
The Watch and Remember sections in *Unlock Basic Skills* are based on videos which are carefully edited to be accessible to pre-A1 students. The videos consolidate the learning the students have done in the unit so far in a new, real-world context. The lessons are scaffolded to help you exploit the videos to their full potential. There are also many different ways you could use the video in class.

Lead-in You could play the video without the sound and encourage students to name and note down the places and things they see. Then play the video with the sound and students can see what they were right about and what was unexpected.

Checking answers You could use the subtitles for checking answers, rather than going through the key yourself. It may be necessary to pause the video to give adequate time for students to check.

Fluency and language review You could follow up the activities in the lesson by playing the video without the sound. Books closed. Students recall what was said during each part of the video.

Language accuracy You could use the video scripts to create gap fills, gapping grammar words only. Students complete the gaps and then watch the video and check their answers.

Reading comprehension You could copy the audio script and cut it up into sections. Students read and place the sections in order before watching.

6 Lead-ins and Optional activities

Throughout the teaching notes in this Teacher's Book are Lead-ins and Optional activities. Some of these activities are very flexible and can be used with a wide range of language. The instructions for this type of activity are included below.

Flashcards

Some of the Lead-ins and Optional activities require flashcards, a very useful teaching tool with pre-A1 students. All of the flashcards needed for the activities have been provided for you at esource.cambridge.org to print out and use.

Flashcard contents

Set	Topic
0.1	Numbers 0–10
0.2	Alphabet
0.3	Instructions
0.4	Numbers 11–20
0.5	Sound and Spelling Starter
0.6	Greetings
1.1	Personal details 1
1.2	Countries
1.3	Personal objects 1
1.4	Personal details 2
2.1	Family
2.2	Personal objects 2
2.3	Numbers 20–100
2.4	Academic Reading and Writing pre-teaching
3.1	University subjects
3.2	Days of the week
3.3	Adjectives 1
3.4	Time
4.1	Adjectives 2
4.2	Pronouns
4.3	Adjectives 3
5.1	Jobs
5.2	Phrases 1
5.3	Phrases 2
5.4	Months
6.1	Food and drink
6.2	Phrases 3
6.3	Phrases 4
6.4	Feelings
7.1	Places 1
7.2	Places 2
7.3	Places 3
7.4	Directions
8.1	Personal objects 3
8.2	Calendar
8.3	Frequency
8.4	Spending
8.5	Currencies
8.6	Big numbers
9.1	Phrases for technology 1
9.2	Phrases for technology 2
9.3	People
9.4	People Singular vs Plural
10.1	Free time activities 1
10.2	Free time activities 2
10.3	Clothes
10.4	Colours

Extra cards for *Unlock Basic Literacy* only and extra cards for *Unlock Basic Skills* only

Learning styles and motivation

Including a variety of activities in your lesson planning to suit different student styles can be a great way to keep all the members of the class motivated. Regularly changing the pace and focusing attention away from the book will make learning more engaging and less predictable. Most students respond to several styles, so the following activities will be suitable for all classes (providing they are suitable for your teaching context).

Flashcard activities

Team pelmanism

Shuffle each set of flashcards but keep them separate. Divide the class into two groups, Group A and Group B. Give each group a set of cards. Ask a student from Group A to hold up a card. Group B students should find the matching card and hold it up. You may wish to give a time limit of 10 or 15 seconds. If Group B are correct, they win the cards. If not, the teams put the cards back in the pile. Then Group B hold up a card and Group A try to find the matching card. The group with the most cards at the end of the game is the winner.

Sound and spelling

Hold up the cards one by one. Elicit the letter(s) you are focusing on, e.g. *b*, the sound /b/ and the word /bus/. If you like you could show the matching word card to confirm students' answers. This activity can be used as a competitive team game. Award a point for each correct answer.

Slow reveal

You will need something to cover cards with, such as a large folder.

Books closed. Hold up the first card behind the folder so that students cannot see it. Slowly pull the card out to your right, so that students can see a little bit of the picture and perhaps the first letter. Encourage students to guess the words on the card. Slowly reveal more and more of the card until a correct answer is given. Award the card to the student who guessed correctly and repeat for all the cards in the set.

TEACHING TIPS

Team spelling test
Go through the flashcards and review each vocabulary item orally by asking students to name the places they see. Students work in small groups. Ask each group to choose one student to be their writer. Tell the writers to write the numbers, (e.g. *1–12* or however many items you are testing) on a page in their notebook. Tell students they are going to look at the cards and write the words. Remind students to include any small grammar words, e.g. *a/an* or prepositions.

Display the flashcards one by one. Remember to note down the order you show them in. Students work in their groups to name the things they see and write the words. Groups swap notebooks. Write the answers on the board. Tell each group to check another group's answers – giving one point for the correct word and one point for the correct spelling. The team with the most points wins.

Chain sentences
Display a single flashcard. Elicit the words and then display a second flashcard next to it. Elicit the first structure which brings the two words together (e.g. *a school and a university*). Display a third flashcard and elicit a chain (e.g. *a hospital, a school and a university*). Now repeat the sequence with one, two and then three flashcards, but elicit the chains of items from the students. Now show a fourth flashcard on its own, and elicit the whole chain. (This is a memory game as well as focusing on the vocabulary and structures in the lesson). Continue for the whole set of flashcards. If no student can remember the sequence, support them by quickly flashing up a flashcard.

Then move on to structure 2. Shuffle the flashcards to keep the activity cognitively challenging. Repeat the procedure above. Finally move on to structure 3.

Alphabet vocabulary
Books closed. You will need one or more sets of alphabet flashcards (enough to give each group of three students five cards). Take out the Xs and the Zs. Demonstrate the activity. Write the letter *c* on the board and look around you. Say: *something in the university, c* /k/ … . If students do not volunteer ideas, say: *Classroom!* Elicit at least one idea from the students (e.g. *computer, chair*). Divide the class into groups of three and give each group five cards. Tell the group they need to think of something in the university that begins with each letter they have and write it down. The group that finishes first will be the winner. Monitor and help as necessary. When a group finishes, check their list.

Other activities

Alphabet categories
Write the categories on the board. Concept check these by giving an example and then eliciting two more examples. Write these on the board.

Tell students you are going to call out a letter of the alphabet, and they should think of something in each category which begins with that letter. Demonstrate the activity with the first letter in the list. Only use letters with examples which have been included in the course so far (i.e. the ones in the list). However, accept any valid words the students give you.

When you have worked through all the letters, elicit sentences with the words on the board. If possible with the set, elicit individual sentences which use words from more than one category.

Alphabet memory game
To review the words that students have learned so far, play an alphabet memory game. Write the alphabet on the board and model the game; for example, point to A and say: *apple*; then indicate a student and the letter B on the board, elicit a word starting with B, e.g. *bag*; Elicit a chain of words, *apple, bag* … . The next student has to repeat the words heard so far and add a new word starting with the next letter of the alphabet, e.g. *apple, bag, computer*. Continue around the class in this way. Keep the chain going as long as possible. If students cannot remember the chain, you could prompt them, or start from the next letter in weaker groups.

Aural dictation
Ask students to number the lines in their notebooks (for the number of sentences in the activity). Encourage students to listen carefully. Read the first sentence from the activity box in the unit aloud. Say: *Listen and write*. Read each sentence aloud at a normal speed. Do not pause between words. Repeat each sentence twice, or three times if the sentence is long, or the class is weaker.

When students have written all of the sentences, write the sentences on the board. Students check their own answers, or swap notebooks and check each other's answers. Remind them to check punctuation as well as spelling.

Aural dictation (contractions)
Review the contracted form and full written form of a contraction you are going to use on the board. Point to the contraction and say: *Listen*. Point to the full form and say: *Write*. Ask students to number the lines in their notebooks (for the number of sentences in the activity). Encourage students to listen carefully. Read the first sentence from the activity box in the unit aloud. Read each sentence aloud at a normal speed, with normal sentence stress.

Do not pause between words. Repeat each sentence twice. Monitor and check that students are attempting to write full forms.

When students have written all of the sentences, write the sentences on the board. Students check their own answers, or swap notebooks and check each other's answers. Remind them to check punctuation as well as spelling.

Aural gap fill

Encourage students to listen carefully. Read the first sentence from the activity box in the unit aloud, replacing the underlined words with a pause. If you like, you could count on your fingers to show there is a missing word. Ask students to raise their hands if they can say the whole, complete sentence. Repeat the sentence if necessary. Continue the activity with the remaining sentences one by one. You could ask students to write down the missing words rather than say the sentences aloud. With strong classes, you can ask individuals or teams to write the whole sentences.

Running dictation

Make several, enlarged copies of the texts and label them clearly if different students are looking at different texts. Display these in different places around the class, away from where the students are sitting. Students work in pairs or groups of three. One student goes to the printed text and memorizes a few words or a sentence. Then they come back to their group and dictate the text. The other student(s) write down the words they hear. To set up the activity, demonstrate doing this on the board with a student as the writer (if it is appropriate in your context). Set a time limit, for example, ten minutes. Tell students to swap roles (writer and runner) every 2–3 minutes.

When the time is up, groups swap papers. Give out the correct texts to each group and ask them to check the accuracy of the writing and award a mark out of ten.

Mingle

Mingling activities are used to practise a variety of exchanges. Here is an example with questions. Ensure students know what question they are to ask by checking with individuals. Encourage students to stand up and walk around the classroom. Demonstrate this type of mingling activity the first time you use it by joining in for the first couple of turns. Encourage students to circulate using hand gestures. Knock on your desk. Students stop, say hello, and ask their question to one nearby student. The other student replies and asks their own question. When you knock on the desk again, they say goodbye and walk around again. Knock on the desk again, and they stop and speak to a new student.

Alternative to mingling: If mingling activities are not appropriate for your context, ask students to sit in groups in a circle and speak to the person to their left. Then change direction. Then swap seats.

Classroom messages

If students are spread out in the room, ask them to move. They should be close enough to the student next to them to lean over and speak quietly to them. If there is room in your classroom, the students could sit in a circle or a long line.

Speak quietly to one student so that the other students cannot hear. Say a simple, familiar sentence, e.g. *How are you?*. Encourage the student to repeat the same sentence very quietly to the next student, and so on. Monitor closely but do not correct students unless they have not understood the activity. When all the students have passed on the message, ask the last student to tell you the sentence they heard. Write this on the board and ask the first student if it is correct. Correct any mistakes as a class. Repeat the activity with the sentences in the activity box in the unit. You may change the order so that that the last student is now the first one.

False information

Students make changes to the material they are working on to create two or three false pieces of information amongst the true information. Students then read this aloud to a partner, a group or the whole class. The other students tell them which information was not true.

STARTER UNIT THE BASICS

Learning objectives

- Recognize and say basic introductions – *Hello. I'm … Hi. I'm …*
- Recognize and write the numerals 0–10
- Understand basic classroom instructions – *Look. Read. Listen. Write. Point. Say.*
- Recognize and write the English alphabet (lower and upper case)
- Recognize and say consonant and vowel sounds
- Gain awareness that individual vowels make more than one sound
- Recognize the written forms of numbers 0–10

See p. 6 for suggestions on how to use these Learning objectives in your lessons.

Lead-in

You will need enough blank pieces of paper to give one to each student. Put these on students' desks before the class.

Write your name on the board. Say your name and indicate you are introducing yourself. Repeat your name and encourage individual students to repeat it back to you. Focus on one student and elicit their name. Indicate that the student should write their name on a piece of paper, fold it, and display it on their desk. Choose students at random and elicit their names, encouraging them to write and display them.

GREETINGS

1 🔊 0.1 Focus on the photographs. Say: *Listen and read*. Cup your ear when you say *listen* and demonstrate reading using a book when you say *read*. Play the audio. Drill the dialogue by reading it out sentence by sentence, pointing to the text in the speech bubbles and encouraging students to repeat after you. See p. 9 for advice on drilling. With an all-male group, you could change the names in the dialogue to boys' names.

NOTICE

Say *I* and indicate yourself. Focus on an individual student and say *you*. Repeat with several students.

Focus on the NOTICE box. Point out each picture and say the words *I* and *you*. Focus on the dialogue in Exercise 1. Read each speech bubble aloud, pointing at each word as you say it. Demonstrate underlining *I* and *you*. Indicate that students should underline these words in the speech bubbles. Monitor and then go through the dialogue to check answers (I'm Manal. / I'm Lucy. Nice to meet you. /Nice to meet you, too.).

2 Demonstrate the exercise with a student. Focus on the speech bubbles on the left and say *Hello. I'm* (your name). Focus on the speech bubbles on the right and encourage the student to reply *Hi. I'm* (their name). Continue with the remaining speech bubbles. Students work in pairs and practise the dialogue. Monitor and correct pronunciation.

Ask students to close the book. Students work in new pairs and say the dialogue from memory.

NUMBERS

3 🔊 0.2 Focus on the numerals (not the written numbers). Demonstrate looking and pointing as you say numbers 0–3 in the book. Play the audio. Ask students to say the numbers. Repeat as necessary and then drill the numbers.

4 🔊 0.3 Write the numbers *3* and *4* on the board. Say: *Listen* and cup your ear and then say: *Circle* and demonstrate circling with a pen. Say: *Four*. Circle 4 on the board.

Focus on the completed example in the book. Say: *Three*. Play the audio for students to listen and circle the numbers. Play the audio again if necessary. Students work in pairs and check their answers. Monitor and encourage students to say the number they circled. Go through answers on the board as a class.

Answers
7 9 0 10 2 4 6

5 Focus on the row of dots (not the written numbers). Elicit the number of dots (five) from the class. Choose individual students at random and elicit the remaining numbers. Demonstrate the exercise with a student. Say: *Five* and encourage them to say the next number in the sequence (one). Respond with the next number, speeding up a little and encouraging the student to do the same. Students work in pairs and say the numbers. Monitor and check for accuracy and pronunciation.

UNL**O**CK BASIC SKILLS TEACHER'S BOOK 13

THE ALPHABET

6 🔊 0.4 👤👥 Write the lowercase alphabet on the board. Check students' current knowledge of the names of the letters by pointing at them in sequence and trying to elicit the names. If students seem to know the names of the letters already, point at individual letters and see if they can name them.

Focus on the lowercase alphabet in the book. Demonstrate pointing as you say the letters. Play the audio and encourage students to point as they listen. Students say the letters. Drill the alphabet with the class by pointing to the individual letters on the board.

> **Optional activity**
>
> You will need enough sets of printable Flashcards 0.2 for each group of four students. Go to esource.cambridge.org to print the flashcards. There are two cards for *a* (*a* and *a*). Only give students the card with *a*.
>
> Shuffle each set of flashcards. Divide the class into groups and give each a set of cards. Ask students to arrange the flashcards in order on their desks. Monitor and help as necessary. Quickly go through answers as a class by asking students to hold up the cards one at a time as you say the letters. Point out any errors.

> **NOTICE**
>
> The aim of this NOTICE box is to draw attention to the letters with common sounds in their names. Focus on the NOTICE box. Say the first line of letters. Cup your ear and say the letters again. Then say /eɪ/ and point to line 1. Say the second line of letters. Cup your ear again. Say /iː/ and point to line 2. Repeat lines 1 and 2 and elicit the sounds /eɪ/ and /iː/. Say line 3 and elicit the sound /e/. Continue with the remaining lines (4 /aɪ/ 5 /əʊ/ 6 /juː/ 7 /ɑː/). Students work individually and practise saying the letters in their sound groups. Monitor and correct any errors.

7 🔊 0.5 👤👥 Write: *a w t u* on the board. Say: *Listen* and cup your ear and then say: *Circle* and demonstrate circling with a pen. Say: *w*. Circle *w* on the board.

Focus on the completed example in the book. Play the audio for students to listen and circle the letters. Play the audio again if necessary. Students work in pairs and check their answers. Monitor and encourage students to say the letter they circled. Go through answers on the board as a class.

> **Answers**
> 2 e 3 l 4 c 5 o 6 m 7 e

> **Optional activity**
>
> With stronger groups only. Write the grid from Exercise 7 on the board.
>
> If appropriate in your context, invite a student up to the board. Say: *w*. Encourage the student to circle the letter (or circle yourself). Continue with the letters *e l c o m e*. Encourage the class to guide the student (or yourself) at the board. Ask: *What does it say?* Read the word. Use gestures to indicate that there is a word hidden horizontally in the letters. Elicit the answer *welcome* and write it on the board.

CLASSROOM INSTRUCTIONS

8 🔊 0.6 👤 Write: *read* and *listen* on the board. Mime reading using a book. Say: *Read* and point to the word on the board. Show headphones or cup your ear. Say: *Listen* and point to the word on the board.

Focus on the pictures in the book and point to the words. Play the audio. Drill the vocabulary and check understanding. See pp. 7 and 9 for advice on concept checking and drilling.

Demonstrate the next part of the exercise with a student. Point to a picture and encourage the student to say the correct word. Then encourage the student to point at a picture, and say the correct word or phrase yourself. Students work in pairs. Monitor and correct any errors.

9 🔊 0.7 👤 Say: *Listen and read.* Mime listening and reading to show you are doing two things at the same time.

Focus on sentences 1–3 in the book and play the audio. Encourage students to point to the words as they hear the phrases. When the audio finishes, point out photographs a–c for matching. Focus on the completed example. Say the phrase and ask students to repeat. Play the audio again. Students work individually and match the instruction to the correct photograph. Go through answers as a class by pointing at each photograph and encouraging students to say the words.

> **Answers**
> 2 a 3 c

THE ALPHABET

10 🔊 0.8 👤👥 Write the uppercase alphabet on the board. Check students' knowledge of the names of these letters by pointing at individual letters and eliciting a response.

THE BASICS STARTER UNIT

Focus on the alphabet in the book (upper and lower case together). Demonstrate looking and pointing as you say the letters. Play the audio and encourage students to point as they listen. Students say the letters.

> **Optional activity**
> You will need printable Flashcards 0.2. Go to esource.cambridge.org to print the flashcards.
> **Team pelmanism**: See p. 10 for the procedure.

11 🔊 0.9 Focus on the completed example. Say: *Listen* and cup your ear, then say: *Circle* and demonstrate circling with a pen. Say: *A H K*. Mime circling the letters in the book. Play the audio for students to listen and circle the letters. Play the audio again if necessary. Students work in pairs and check their answers. Monitor and encourage students to say the letters they circled. Go through answers on the board as a class. Point out that the answers in each line all have the same sound (1 /eɪ/ 2 /iː/ 3 /e/ 4 /aɪ/ 5 /juː/).

> **Answers**
> 2 R U Z
> 3 F P N
> 4 E Y V
> 5 Q U W

12 🔊 0.10 Focus on the photographs and the acronyms. Play the audio and point to each acronym. Encourage students to listen and repeat. Point to a photograph and encourage a student to say the acronym. Then encourage the student to point at a photograph and say the correct acronym yourself. Students work in pairs and continue pointing to photographs and saying the correct acronyms. Monitor and correct any mistakes with vocabulary or pronunciation.

NUMBERS

13 🔊 0.11 Focus on the row of numerals (not the written numbers underneath them). Count upwards from 1 and check students' existing knowledge by eliciting the numbers 1–20 as far as possible. Demonstrate looking and pointing in the book as you say the numbers 1–3. Play the audio and encourage students to say the numbers (16, 17, 19, 11, 15, 13). Repeat as necessary and then drill the numbers 11–20 only. Point out the word stress on numbers with *-teen* by clapping your hands on the last syllable.

14 🔊 0.12 Write: *1* and *11* on the board. Say: *Listen* and cup your ear and *circle* and demonstrate circling with a pen. Say: *Eleven*. Circle *11* on the board.

Focus on item 1 in the book. Point out the completed example. Play the audio for students to listen and circle the numbers. Play the audio again if necessary. Students work in pairs and check their answers. Monitor and encourage students to say the number they circled. Go through answers on the board as a class.

> **Answers**
> 12 3 14 6 15 18

15 🔊 0.13 Focus on the photographs and the numerals. Elicit the numbers (8, 18, 4, 14).

Play the audio. Students listen and read. Drill the sentences. Point at the photograph of the schoolboy. Students read the sentences aloud. Say: *He is eight. Yes or no?* Use a questioning tone and culturally appropriate gestures to communicate *yes or no*. Elicit the answer (yes). Point at the picture of the 18-year old and say: *He is eight. Yes or no?* Elicit the answer (no). Continue with the pictures in this way, saying different ages, some correct and some incorrect.

> **NOTICE**
> Focus on the NOTICE box. Point out each picture and say the words *he* and *she*. Indicate a student in the classroom and say to the rest of the class *He/She* (depending on gender). Say: *I* and indicate yourself. Focus on one student and say: *you*. Then indicate another student in the classroom and say to the class (not the individual student) *He/She* (depending on gender). Focus on the photographs in Exercise 15 and point to each one and elicit: *He/She*. Read each sentence aloud while pointing at each word in the book as you say it. Demonstrate underlining *He* and *She*. Indicate that students should underline these words in the sentences in Exercise 15. Go through the answers on the board as a class. (He is eight. He is eighteen. She is four. She is fourteen.)

16 🔊 0.14 Focus on the photographs and elicit: *He/She* for each one. Focus on the numerals on each photograph and elicit the correct numbers. Play the audio for students to listen. Ask students to say the sentences. Demonstrate the exercise with a student.

Focus on the speech bubble on the left and say: *He is 16*. Focus on the speech bubble on the right and encourage the student to reply: *She is 17*. Students work in pairs. Monitor and correct use of *he/she* and correct numbers. Go through answers as a class.

SOUND AND SPELLING: CONSONANT SOUNDS

> **Common student errors**
>
> The following consonant sounds are not distinct in Arabic: /p/–/b/ (*pill/bill*); /f/–/v/ (*fan/van*); /k/–/g/ (*classes/glasses*). Students find it difficult to discriminate between these sounds and this leads to spelling errors.
>
> The consonant sounds /l/–/r/ (*lot/rot*) are not distinct in Japanese. Students find it difficult to discriminate between these sounds and this leads to spelling errors.

17 (0.15) Focus on the photographs only, indicating that students should cover the letters in bold and words. Working line by line, elicit as many of the things in the photographs as you can. Now focus students on the letters in bold and words. Play the audio for students to look at the letters, listen to the audio, and repeat.

Go through the letters and words on each line. Point at the first photograph and say: /b/ *bus*. Point at the second photograph. Elicit: /k/ *coffee* from the class. Elicit the remaining letters and words from the class.

18 (0.16) Demonstrate the exercise by saying *karate* and pointing to the correct photograph in Exercise 17. Repeat for *queen*, *yacht*, *doctor* and *salad*. Play the audio. Students work individually and point to the correct photographs. Monitor and check that students can follow the audio. If students are finding this difficult they could work in pairs, or you could read out the script slowly yourself, to give students more time.

Demonstrate the next part of the exercise with a student. Point to a photograph and encourage a student to say the word. Then encourage the student to point at a photograph, and say the word yourself. Students work in pairs. Monitor and help as necessary. Note any difficulties with pronunciation of individual words and drill these separately.

> **Answers**
>
> radio, queen, nine, message, palm, bus, doctor, four, zero, salad, taxi, jeans

19 (0.17) Draw a basic outline of a bus on the board and write _us. Say: *us* /ʌs/. Point at the space before the letter *u* and elicit the letter *b*. Write the *b* and say: *bus*.

Focus on the table in the book. Play the audio. Students work individually and complete the exercise. Go through answers on the board as a class.

> **Answers**
>
> 2 bus 3 salad 4 jeans 5 doctor 6 lemon
> 7 gas 8 message

> **Optional activity**
>
> You will need printable Flashcards 0.5. Go to esource.cambridge.org to print the flashcards.
> **Sound and spelling:** Follow the procedure on p. 10.

SINGULAR AND PLURAL NOUNS

20 (0.18) Focus on the photographs. Point at the doctor and say: *One or two?* (one). Say: *A doctor*. Point at the photograph of two doctors and say: *One or two?* (two). Say: *Two doctors*. Focus on the photographs and play the audio. Encourage students to point to the correct photograph as they hear the phrases.

Write: *two doctors, three salads, four coffees, ten lemons* on the board. Ask: *How many …?* about each phrase, communicating your meaning by counting on your fingers. Each time students answer with a number, repeat it and add the plural noun. Circle the plural *-s* on the board. Drill the pronunciation of the phrases on the board.

> **NOTICE**
>
> Write: *a coffee* on the board. Ask: *One or two?* (one). Repeat with *a salad* and *a lemon*. Focus on the NOTICE box. Point out the = sign. Say: *a is one. A salad is one salad*.

21 Focus on the photographs and encourage students to count the items. Read item 1 and demonstrate the exercise by circling the correct answer with your finger in the book. Students read and circle. Students check their answers in pairs. Go through answers as a class.

> **Answers**
>
> 1 taxis 2 a coffee 3 a yacht 4 doctors

22 🔊 0.19 👥 👤 Indicate a student and say: *I need a pen, please?* Stress *please*. When you get a pen, take it and say: *thank you*. Repeat with another student and ask for a book. Write: *please* and *thank you* on the board. Drop a pen on the floor and say: *I'm sorry!* Students then look at the pictures. Play the audio. Students listen and read. Encourage students to follow the text by pointing at the words in the book. Drill the phrases.

23 🔊 0.20 👥 Focus on the two photographs. Ask: *What are these?* (lemons / a salad). Play the audio for students to listen. Demonstrate the exercise with a student. Point out the REMEMBER box. Approach the student and say: *Four lemons, please.* If it is appropriate for your context, hold out your hands to receive the lemons. When they mime handing you the lemons, say: *thank you*. Then swap roles. Encourage the student to ask you for some lemons (any number). Students work in pairs and act out the short dialogues for each photograph. If acting a dialogue out is not appropriate in your context, ask students to remember what the people said and write it on the board.

DAY AND TIME

24 🔊 0.21 👥 Focus on the picture. Say the four new words and point to the relevant part of the picture. Play the audio and then drill the new words as a class. Point to the different sections of the picture and elicit the new words from the class. Demonstrate the next part of the exercise with a student. Point to a part of the picture and encourage the student to say the word. Then encourage the student to point at another part of the picture and say the word yourself. Students work in pairs. Monitor and correct any mistakes.

25 🔊 0.22 👥 Focus on the pictures and elicit which part of the day they illustrate. Point to the clocks on each picture and ask: *Morning or afternoon?*, etc. Play the audio for students to listen and read. Then drill the greetings. Check understanding if necessary. See p. 7 for advice on concept checking.

26 👥 Focus on the pictures and elicit which part of the day they illustrate. Demonstrate the exercise with a student. Point to a picture and encourage a student to say the greeting for the time of day. Then encourage the student to point at a picture, and say the greeting yourself. Students work in pairs. Monitor and correct any mistakes.

| Answers

2 Good morning. 3 Good evening. 4 Good afternoon.

SOUND AND SPELLING: VOWELS

> ⊙ **Common student errors**
>
> The biggest spelling problems for Arabic L1 students are with vowels. Focusing on teaching the English vowel system with these students (rather than focusing on irregular sound and spelling relationships) is helpful for Arabic L1 beginners.
>
> Turkish L1 students have difficulties with long versus short vowels in pronunciation. They tend to shorten the vowels, e.g. *leave* /liːv/ becomes *live* /lɪv/.
>
> See p. 148 for advice on how to help students with **Vowel sound** errors.

27 🔊 0.23 👤 Write: *gas, hat, bag* on the board. Point at each of the words and ask: *Which letter is the same?* (a) Underline the 'a's. Model the phoneme /æ/ and then say the first word: *gas*. Repeat the process for each of the words.

Say the phonemes /æ/ /e/ /ɪ/ /ɒ/ /ʌ/ corresponding to each letter and ask students to repeat. Focus on the letters in bold and the words. Play the audio for students to listen and repeat the words. Monitor and correct any errors with the phonemes by modelling the sounds again and then the words including the sounds for students to repeat.

28 🔊 0.24 👤 👥 Write: *hat, hot, hut* on the board. Say the vowel sound and then the word for each: /æ/ hat, /ɒ/ hot, /ʌ/ hut. Say: *Listen* and cup your ear and *circle* and demonstrate circling with a pen. Say: *hot*. Circle *hot* on the board.

Focus on the completed example in the book. Play the audio for students to listen and circle the words. Play the audio again if necessary. Students work in pairs and check their answers. Monitor and encourage students to say the words they circled. Go through answers on the board as a class. Drill all the words in each row.

| Answers

2 ten 3 bag 4 cap 5 red 6 pet

29 👥 Draw a basic outline of a bus on the board and write: *b_s*. Say: /b/ /s/. Point at the space before the letter *s* and elicit the letter *u* (or the phoneme /ʌ/ and then the letter). Write the *u* and say: *Bus*.

Focus on the words with missing letters and the photographs in the book. Elicit all the words from the class. Correct any errors with pronunciation. Students work in pairs and complete the exercise. Monitor and help students by modelling words they are stuck on. Students work in pairs and check their answers with the words on p. 16. Go through answers on the board as a class.

> **Answers**
>
> 2 t<u>a</u>xi 3 d<u>o</u>ctor 4 c<u>o</u>ffee 5 s<u>a</u>lad 6 l<u>e</u>mon
> 7 v<u>i</u>deo 8 m<u>e</u>ssage

30 🔊 0.25 👤 The aim of this exercise is to understand that vowel letters can represent different sounds in words. Write: *gas* and *palm* on the board. Say the words aloud. Circle *a* in both words and repeat the two words. Then say the two sounds of *a* (/æ/ and /ɑː/). Elicit if they are the same or different (different).

Write: *hat, taxi, radio* on the board. Underline the *a* in each word. Say each word aloud. Ask: *Which one is different?* Elicit that *radio* is different. Write a tick ✓ next to *hat* and *taxi* and a cross ✗ next to *radio*.

Focus on the vowel in bold in each row in the book. Then focus on the completed example. Play the audio for students to complete the exercise. Play the audio again for students to listen and check. Go through answers as a class, drilling all the words.

> **Answers**
>
> 2 coffee ✓ hello ✗ doctor ✓
> 3 you ✗ bus ✓ sun ✓
> 4 seven ✓ ten ✓ evening ✗
> 5 nine ✗ video ✓ big ✓

1 MEETING PEOPLE

UNLOCK YOUR KNOWLEDGE

👤 Focus on the map of the world. Ask: *Where are we?* Indicate that you are talking about the group and the country you are in now. Students find the country on the map. Elicit the name in English and write it on the board. Model the correct pronunciation. If possible, elicit the spelling. Write the country on the board. Point out the capital letter. With an international group ask individuals: *Where is your country?* and ask students to point to it on the map.

Focus on question 2. Read it aloud. Ask students to say the name of their country. Assist students with their country names in English.

LISTENING AND READING 1

Learning objectives

- Understand basic introductions – *What's your name? My name is …*
- Spell out names – *How do you spell that? M-u-r-a-t*
- Use capital letters on first names correctly – *Murat*
- Introduce yourself and spell out your name – *My name's Murat. M-u-r-a-t.*
- Gain awareness of the sounds of the letter *e* – *English, spell, hello, meet*

See p. 6 for suggestions on how to use these Learning objectives in your lessons.

Lead-in

Alphabet vocabulary Follow the procedure on p. 11.
Topic: Students' names

PREPARING TO READ

1 👤👥 Focus on the first vertical line of capital letters. Encourage students to call out the letters one by one. Then focus on the first vertical line of lowercase letters. Encourage students to call out these lowercase letters. Say: *Match* and point from one side to the other as you do so.

Point out the completed example by tracing the line from *A* to *a*. Students work individually to complete the exercise and then compare their answers in pairs. Students say the letters.

Answers
A a B b E e M m N n T t U u Y y

READING FOR GENERAL UNDERSTANDING

2 🔊 1.1 👤👥 Focus on the photographs. Ask students to listen and read. Play the audio. Encourage them to follow the text by pointing in the book at each speech bubble as they hear it. Ask: *What's his name?* (Murat), *What's her name?* (Ameena). Write these names on the board. Say: *How do you spell that?* and spell out the names as a class. Drill the dialogue by reading it out sentence by sentence and encouraging students to repeat after you. As you read, point to the text in the speech bubbles. See p. 9 for advice on drilling.

Demonstrate the next part of the exercise with a student. Focus on the speech bubbles on the left and say: *What's your name?* Focus on the speech bubbles on the right and encourage the student to reply *I'm Murat*. Continue with the remaining speech bubbles. Choose a different student to demonstrate each dialogue. Students work in pairs and practise the dialogue. Monitor and correct mistakes.

ACADEMIC WRITING SKILLS

3 👤 Focus on the names. Point out the example and underline the capital letter again. Students work individually and underline the capital letters in the names. Go through answers as a class.

Optional activity

You will need a list of 21 common first names in your region. With an international class use a mix of international names.

Demonstrate with an example first. Call out a name. Elicit the first letter of the name. Write the capital on the board. Students work in pairs and write the numbers 1–20 on a piece of paper. Write numbers 1–20 on the board as well. Say: *1* and the next name on the list. Encourage pairs to write down the capital letter of each name. Students swap their answers with another pair and check their answers. Go through answers as a class.

LISTENING FOR KEY INFORMATION

4 (◀)) **1.2** 👤👥 Write your name on the board. Erase some letters leaving a gap where the letters were. Indicate listening by cupping your ear and spell your name aloud. Write the missing letters on the lines.

Focus on the photographs and the names in the book. Encourage students to guess what the names are, but do not tell them if they are correct at this time. Play the audio. Students work individually, listening and writing the missing letters. Students work in pairs and check their answers. Then students practise spelling the names aloud. Demonstrate by pointing at the first name in the book and saying: *How do you spell that?* Elicit the spelling. Students work in pairs and practise asking and answering with the names. Monitor and correct mistakes.

Answers
Mariam   Rafael   Yasemin

NOTICE
You will need three names your students will know which include double letters, e.g. Lee, Anna, Debbie.

Focus on the NOTICE box and the name Ameena. Say: *How do you spell that?* Say: *A-M-double E-N-A*. Write the name on the board and underline the double e. Say: *double e*. Write your example names on the board and elicit the double letters from the class.

SOUND AND SPELLING: e

5 (◀)) **1.3** Focus on the words. Ask: *Which letter is in all of the words?* (e). Play the audio for students to listen and repeat. Model the phoneme /e/ and then say the first word: *Hello*. Ask: *Can you hear /e/?* Help students to understand the question by cupping your ear and using culturally appropriate gestures to indicate *yes* or *no*. Repeat with each of the words *spell* (yes) *meet* (no) *English* (no). Elicit the sounds that double e makes in *meet* /iː/ and the single e in *English* /ɪ/. Play the audio again for students to listen and repeat. Correct any errors with the phonemes /e/, /iː/, /ɪ/.

SPEAKING AND WRITING

6 👥 Point out the REMEMBER box and read through the phrases as a class. If necessary, drill the phrases, using the names of students in the room. Demonstrate the exercise with a student. Say: *Hi! What's your name?*

Encourage the student to respond. Say: *How do you spell that?* Demonstrate writing the name on the first name card. Point out the capital letter on the name you wrote. Students work in small groups and spell their names for each other. Monitor and check spelling and capital letters.

LISTENING AND READING 2

Learning objectives
- Understand information on contact cards – *phone number, name, email address*
- Ask for other people's contact details – *What's your phone number?*
- Understand and say phone numbers – *0544 343 009*
- Give other people's details – *His name is Abdullah. Her phone number is 0873 590 321.*
- Use capital letters and full stops in sentences.

See p. 6 for suggestions on how to use these Learning objectives in your lessons.

Lead-in
Write the heading *Names* on the board. Then write the names of students in your class on the board, one name at a time, letter by letter. Stop after each letter you write and encourage students to guess the name. If a student gives you the correct name, ask the rest of the class to spell out the remaining letters. Say: *How do you spell that?* Include some names with double letters, if possible, and remind students of the correct way to spell these out: *double (letter)*.

VOCABULARY: ID

1 (◀)) **1.4** 👤👥 Focus on the contact cards. Say: *Read and listen*. Play the audio. Encourage students to follow the text by pointing in the book at each line on each contact card as they hear it. Focus on the icons and text in 1–3. Read the words and phrases in the central column aloud. Point out the completed example by tracing the line from the person icon to *name* in the central column and then to *Jenny Baker* in the right-hand column. Then point at Jenny Baker's ID card and the information there. Students work individually and then compare their answers in pairs. Go through answers as a class. Remember to teach that both *phone number* and *number* are the same in *What's your number? What's your phone number? My number is … My phone number is …*.

20   UNLOCK BASIC SKILLS TEACHER'S BOOK

MEETING PEOPLE UNIT 1

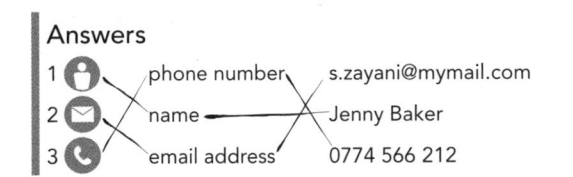

Answers
1 phone number — 0774 566 212
2 name — Jenny Baker
3 email address — s.zayani@mymail.com

> **NOTICE**
> Focus on the NOTICE box. Read it out as a class. Give students a minute to read the information. Students practise saying Jenny and Sultan's phone numbers.

LISTENING FOR DETAIL

2 🔊 1.5 Focus on Leyla's two phone numbers. Point out the completed example. Play the audio for students to listen and underline the correct numbers. Play the audio again if necessary. Students work in pairs and check their answers. Monitor and encourage students to say the number they underlined. Go through answers as a class.

> Answers
> 2 0774 902 154 3 0714 332 503

READING FOR DETAIL

3 Focus on Leyla's contact card in Exercise 1. Read the first sentence in Exercise 3 aloud. Say: *Yes or no?* in a questioning tone. Elicit the correct answer (yes). Students work individually, looking at the contact cards in Exercise 1 and circling *Yes* or *No* for each sentence.

Students work in pairs and check their answers. Go through answers as a class. Point to each piece of information on the correct contact card and read the sentence. Students say *yes* or *no*.

> Answers
> 2 No 3 No 4 Yes

> **Optional activity**
> **Aural dictation** Follow the procedure on p. 11.
> 01751 367 816
> 0191 230 1441
> 01793 996 990

GRAMMAR: POSSESSIVE ADJECTIVES

4 🔊 1.6 Focus on the photographs and the captions. Play the audio for students to listen and read. Point out *his* in the caption about Sultan and ask: *Who?* (Sultan). Say: *His name is Sultan.* Write this on the board and circle *His*. Repeat for *Jenny* and *her*. Say: *My name is* (your name). and indicate you are referring to yourself. Focus on an individual student and say: *Your name is …* Then indicate an individual student and say to the rest of the class (not the individual student): *His/Her name is …* Use the table to check understanding. See p. 7 for advice on concept checking.

5 🔊 1.7 Focus on the options under the line in sentence 1. Focus on the photograph of the male student. Say: *He or She?* (He). Read the correct sentence 1 aloud. Ask: *His or Her?* (His). Demonstrate circling the correct option under the line in the book. Play the audio. Students work individually and circle the correct options. Go through answers as a class. Then ask students to write the correct answers in the gaps.

> Answers
> 2 His 3 His 4 Her 5 Her 6 Her

ACADEMIC WRITING SKILLS

6 Write: *My name is Sara. My phone number is 0889 543 010.* on the board. Move your pen along the sentences. Say: *Stop!* where the first sentence ends and circle the full stop. Continue moving your pen along, encouraging students to say *Stop!* when you get to the final full stop. Repeat with the capital letters. Underline them.

Focus on the sentences in the book and point out the completed example. Students work individually and complete the exercise. Students work in pairs and check their answers. Use the procedure at the start of this exercise to go through the answers on the board as a class.

> Answers
> 2 <u>H</u>is name is <u>M</u>ike. <u>H</u>is phone number is 0782 822 513.
> 3 <u>H</u>er name is <u>A</u>seel. <u>H</u>er email address is aseel.w@mymail.co.uk.
> 3 (alternative answer) <u>H</u>er name is <u>A</u>seel. <u>H</u>er email address is aseel.w@mymail.co.uk.

UNLOCK BASIC SKILLS TEACHER'S BOOK 21

> **⊙ Common student errors**
>
> **Punctuation:** Arabic L1 and Turkish L1 students frequently omit full stops or use a comma where they should use a full stop. Here is an example of this error:
>
> *My name is Ali, I am from Turkey I am a student, my teacher is Mrs Akalay*
>
> See p. 148 for tips on how to help students with **Punctuation** errors.

WRITING

7 Focus on the gapped sentences. Say: *Write about you*. Demonstrate writing about yourself on the board. Write: *My name is* (your name). Elicit the next word: *(My) phone number is …* Say again: *Write about you*. Students work individually and complete the sentences with information about themselves. If students do not want to give their personal information, they could create new phone numbers and emails. Point out the capital letters in each sentence and in the names on the board. Students swap books with another pair and check each other's writing for correct capital letters.

SPEAKING AND WRITING

8 Point out the REMEMBER box and read through the sentences as a class. Check understanding by asking the questions and eliciting the correct responses. If necessary, drill the questions and sentences again. Demonstrate the exercise with a student. Say: *What's your name?* Encourage the student to respond. Say: *What's your phone number?* Demonstrate writing the information in the correct places in the book. Elicit: *his/her* for each of the sentences. Students work in groups of three, taking turns to ask and answer the questions and complete the sentences. Monitor and help as necessary. Put students into new groups of three. Students tell each other about the students they wrote about.

LISTENING AND READING 3

> **Learning objectives**
>
> - Name six countries – *Japan, Turkey, Mexico, the UK, Saudi Arabia, India*
> - Talk about nationality using the verb *be* – *Where are you from? I'm from Mexico. He's from India.*
> - Talk about occupation using the verb *be* – *I'm a student. She's a teacher.*
> - Read and understand forms and ID cards – *first name, family name, country*
> - Write about nationality and occupation using the full form of *be* – *I am a student. He is from Turkey.*
>
> See p. 6 for suggestions on how to use these Learning objectives in your lessons.

> **Lead-in**
>
> Use the map of the world on Student's Book pp. 20–21. Display the map in a large format on the board, if possible. Point to a country you think your students will know the name of. Point to another country. Elicit the names and write them on the board. Give students two minutes working in small groups to name as many countries as they can in English. If you wish, you could allow students to use dictionaries here. Students work in new groups and compare their lists.

VOCABULARY: COUNTRIES

1 🔊 1.8 Focus on the map. Point at each flag and trace the line to the country on the map. Ask students to listen and read. Play the audio. Encourage students to follow the audio by pointing in the book at each country's name as they hear it. Drill the names of the countries. See p. 9 for advice on drilling. If any students' country is not on the list, elicit the name and write it on the board.

Demonstrate the next part of the exercise with a student. Point to a flag and encourage a student to say the country's name. Then encourage the student to point at a flag and say the country's name yourself. Students work in pairs. Monitor and correct any errors.

PRONUNCIATION FOR LISTENING

2 🔊 1.9 Write these three stress patterns and country names on the board with bubbles above the vowels (●● Turkey ●● Japan ●●● India). Say: *Turkey*, clapping on each syllable. Clearly emphasize the stressed syllable by clapping harder for extra impact.

22 UNLOCK BASIC SKILLS TEACHER'S BOOK

MEETING PEOPLE UNIT 1

Repeat for Japan and India. Encourage students to join you saying the words and clapping the syllables.

Play the audio for students to listen and repeat.

> **Optional activity**
>
> Write the names of some countries that your students know the names of, e.g. America, Brazil, England, Portugal, Oman, Bahrain.
>
> Say the name of a country. Count the syllables together as a class. Mark these on the words with small bubbles, e.g.
>
> • • • •
> America
>
> Say the name again, making sure to add stress to the stressed syllable. You may wish to clap again with weaker groups. Point at the bubbles and elicit the stressed syllable. Mark this with a big bubble.
>
> • ● • •
> America
>
> Repeat for several countries, eliciting the number of syllables and the stressed syllable each time.

ACADEMIC WRITING SKILLS

3 Point at India on the map in Exercise 1. Write: _ndia on the board. Point at the space and elicit the letter *i*. Write capital *I* and say *India*.

> **NOTICE**
>
> Focus on the NOTICE box, point out the highlighted capital letters at the beginning of each country name. Allow students a minute to read the NOTICE box.

Focus on the words with missing capital letters. Students work individually and complete the exercise. Go through answers as a class.

> **Answers**
>
> Saudi Arabia Mexico the UK Japan Turkey

LISTENING FOR KEY INFORMATION

4 1.10 Focus on the sentences, the photograph and the options. Say: *Turkey or Mexico?* Point out the completed example. Tell students they are going to listen and circle the answers. Play the audio. Students work individually and circle the correct options. Play the audio again and check the answers with the class as you listen. Drill: *Where are you from?*

> **Answers**
>
> 2 India 3 Japan 4 Turkey 5 the UK 6 Saudi Arabia

SPEAKING

5 Ask students at random around the class: *Where are you from?* Elicit full answers: *I'm from* (their country). Encourage students to ask you and then each other. Encourage them to speak to a number of other students. With an international group you could ask them to stand up and move around the classroom, asking and answering. Monitor and correct pronunciation as necessary.

PREPARING TO READ

6 1.11 Focus on the photographs. Play the audio and point to the words in the text. Check understanding by pointing to yourself. Say: *a teacher or a student?* Ask an individual student: *a teacher or a student?* Drill the new words (a teacher, a student) and then the sentences in the book. Make sure students say the article (*a*) before the nouns.

SCANNING FOR KEY INFORMATION

7 1.12 Focus on the ID cards. Point out that there is one ID card for a student and one for a teacher. Check understanding of *First name* and *Family name*. Use your name as an example. Write it on the board and show which one is your first name and which is your family name. To check understanding, elicit more examples of students' first names and family names from the class.

Focus on the sentences. Point out the options in the sentences and the completed example. Tell students to read and circle the answers. Students work individually and check their answers in pairs. Play the audio and go through answers as a class.

> **Answers**
>
> 2 Saeed 3 Saudi Arabia 4 teacher 5 Jackson 6 the UK

GRAMMAR: VERB *BE*

8 1.13 Focus on the table and play the audio for students to listen and read. Point out *am* and *is*. Say: *I am a teacher*. Indicate an individual student and say: *He/She is a student*. Elicit different sentences following the structures in the table, e.g. *I am from Japan. He is from Japan. She is from Japan.* Write the new sentences on the board.

UNLOCK BASIC SKILLS TEACHER'S BOOK 23

> **NOTICE**
>
> Write: *I'm a student.* on the board. Circle and say: *I'm.* Then write: *I am a student.* underneath. Point at *I'm* and encourage students to say the word. Then point at *I am.* Say: *Say I'm. Write I am.* Repeat for *She's* and *She is*, *He's* and *He is*.
>
> Focus on the NOTICE box in the book. Allow students a minute to read the NOTICE box.

> **◉ Common student errors**
>
> **Punctuation:** Arabic L1 students frequently write *I'am* instead of *I'm* or *I am*.
>
> Write: *I'am Anna. I'm Anna. I am Anna.* on the board. Write one cross and two ticks on the board to indicate that one sentence is incorrect. Elicit from students which sentence is incorrect (*I'am Anna.*).

> **Optional activity**
>
> **Aural dictation (contractions):** Follow the procedure on p. 11
> 1 I'm from Mexico. (I am from Mexico.)
> 2 She's a student. (She is a student.)
> 3 He's from Turkey. (He is from Turkey.)
> With students who are not able to write full sentences yet, dictate only: *I'm, He's, She's.*

9 🔊 1.14 Focus on the options under the line in sentence 1. Focus on the pronoun *I*. Say: *am or is?* (am). Listen and read the correct sentence 1 aloud (I am a student.). Demonstrate circling the correct option under the line in the book. Play the audio. Students work individually and circle the correct options. Go through answers as a class. Then ask students to write the correct answers in the gaps.

> **Answers**
> 2 is 3 is 4 am

WRITING

10 Focus on the gapped sentences. Say: *Write about you.* Demonstrate writing about yourself on the board. Write: *I am a teacher.* Elicit the words to complete the gaps in the next line (*am, your country*). Say again: *Write about you.* Students work individually and complete the sentences with information about themselves. Students swap books and check each other's writing for correct use of *am* and spelling.

SPEAKING AND WRITING

11 Students work in pairs. Focus on the gapped sentences. Say: *Write about your partner.* Say: *He is a student.* Demonstrate writing the sentence in the first line of the yellow box labelled 'Your partner'. Elicit the question: *Where are you from?* Ask a student where they are from. Say: *He/She is from (student's country).* Demonstrate writing the sentence in the second row in the box. Monitor and check use of capital letters with names, countries and at the beginning of each sentence. Students swap books and check each other's writing.

WATCH AND REMEMBER

> **Learning objectives**
>
> - Understand basic introductions – *My name is Saif. I'm from Riyadh. I'm a teacher.*
> - Understand information on ID cards – *phone number, first name, family name*
> - Practise countries and cities – *Ankara, London, Mexico, Saudi Arabia*
> - Practise asking where people are from and answering – *Where are you from? I'm from Riyadh, in Saudi Arabia.*
>
> See p. 6 for suggestions on how to use these Learning objectives in your lessons.

> **Lead-in**
>
> Ask students where you and they are from.
> Ask: *Where am I from? Where are you from?*

PART 1

In Part 1, three characters introduce themselves.

BEFORE YOU WATCH

1 Check students understand the words *country* and *city*. Elicit which country is in photograph c (the UK). Point out the capital letters in the country names. Students work individually and match.

2 🔊 1.15 Play the audio for students to listen and check their answers in Exercise 1. Go through answers as a class. Students work individually and write the country names under the photographs. Monitor and check students' handwriting. Drill the pronunciation of the countries. See p. 9 for advice on drilling.

> **Answers**
> 2 b 3 a

WATCH

3 ▶ 👤 Focus on the video stills and the names in the sentences and ask students to guess who each character is. Students watch Part 1 and choose the correct options. Go through answers as a class.

> **Answers**
> 2 a student 3 a teacher

In stronger classes, Exercise 4 should be completed by students after watching Part 1. In weaker classes, students can watch Part 1 again and complete Exercise 4 or use the audio script at the back of the book.

4 👤 Focus on the names and countries. Point at the still of Saif (first still) and say *He is from Saudi Arabia*. Students work individually and match. Go through answers as a class.

> **Answers**
> 2 Mexico 3 the UK

AFTER YOU WATCH

5 👤 Focus on the words in the box and the sentences. Students complete the sentences with the words. Students swap books and check each other's writing. Go through answers as a class. Drill the pronunciation of *name's* /neɪmz/.

> **Answers**
> Carlos: from Elaine: meet

PART 2

In Part 2, a fourth character is introduced.

BEFORE YOU WATCH

6 (🔊 1.16) 👤 Focus on the library card and the gapped phrases. Students complete the card. Play the audio for students to check answers. Go through answers as a class.

> **Answers**
> Family, number

MEETING PEOPLE — UNIT 1

WATCH

7 ▶ 👤 Elicit the difference between *first name* and *family name* using your own first and family name as an example. Students watch Part 2 and circle the correct options. Go through answers as a class.

> **Answers**
> 1 first name 2 family name

AFTER YOU WATCH

8 (🔊 1.17) 👤 👥 Model and drill the sentences in Exercise 7, focusing on *his* /hɪz/, and the completed example in Exercise 8, focusing on *he's* /hiːz/. Model similar sentences about students in the class. Students circle the correct words and then check answers in pairs. Play the audio for students to check answers. Then they complete the sentences.

> **Answers**
> 2 His 3 He's 4 His

PART 3

In Part 3, the narrator's questions help students remember information. If you have time, play the whole video again. You can do this before or after playing Part 3.

REMEMBER

9 ▶ 👤 Students watch Part 3 and answer the questions. Students work individually and complete the sentences. Go through answers as a class.

> **Answers**
> 2 Mexico 3 teacher

MORE VOCABULARY: CITY NAMES

10 ▶ 👤 👥 Focus on the words in the box and the sentences. Students complete the sentences with the cities. Students work in pairs and check answers. Play Parts 1–3 again if required. Stop the video after *He's from Ankara, in Turkey*.

> **Answers**
> 2 Mexico City 3 London 4 Ankara

UNLOCK BASIC SKILLS TEACHER'S BOOK 25

ASK AND ANSWER

11 In groups, students practise asking and answering the question. Change groups to give them more opportunities to practise.

Optional activity

Repeat Exercise 11 using fictional names, cities and countries, if appropriate. These can be provided by you or students. If students are from the same place, this will make the exercise more interesting.

⊙ LANGUAGE FOCUS

Learning objectives

- Name study objects – a *pen*, *a pencil*, *a book*, etc.
- Ask for objects politely and respond – *Can I have a pencil, please? Here you are. No. I'm sorry.*
- Write a list of useful objects

See p. 6 for suggestions on how to use these Learning objectives in your lessons.

Lead-in

You will need printable Flashcards 1.3. Go to esource.cambridge.org to print the flashcards.

Hold up the photograph side of the flashcards one by one. Say: *Do you have a (pencil)?* Hold up your own pencil and indicate that students should show you the items they have with them in class and put them on the desk in front of them. Repeat for each of the flashcards.

With stronger classes hold up the word side of the flashcards and repeat the procedure. Again encourage students to hold up the items, if they have them. This time ask them to repeat the word after you.

VOCABULARY: STUDY OBJECTS

1 🔊 1.18 Focus on the photographs of study objects. Ask students to listen and read. Play the audio. Encourage students to follow the audio by pointing in the book at each study object as they hear it. Drill the vocabulary. See p. 9 for advice on drilling. Check understanding using real objects or Flashcards 1.3.

Demonstrate the next part of the exercise with a student. Point to a study object and encourage a student to say the correct word. Then encourage the student to point at a study object and say the correct word yourself. Students work in pairs. Monitor and correct any errors.

NOTICE

Focus on the NOTICE box. Read out the phrases as a class. Point out the use of *a* with all the objects in the pictures. Allow students a minute to read the NOTICE box.

SPEAKING

2 🔊 1.19 Focus on the photographs. Ask: *What's this?* and point to the objects in the two pictures (a pen, a book). Play the audio for students to listen and read. Encourage students to point at each speech bubble in the book as they hear it. Drill the dialogues by reading them out sentence by sentence and encouraging students to repeat after you. See p. 9 for advice on drilling.

NOTICE

Write *a pen* and *a library card* on the board. Focus on the NOTICE box and point at the words on the board. Elicit the word which is different (*your*). Erase *a* and write *your* in front of *library*. Hold up your own ID card or another object which is definitely yours. Say: *My ID card*. Give it to a student and elicit: *Your ID card*. If appropriate, pick up an object belonging to a student, and say: *Your* (name of object). Repeat with other objects. Drill the words in the NOTICE box. Focus on the speech bubbles in Exercise 2. Demonstrate underlining *a* and *your*. Indicate that students should underline these words in the speech bubbles.

LISTENING AND WRITING

3 🔊 1.20 Focus on the first photograph. Say: *What's this?* (a book). Read the first sentence in the book. Encourage students to write in the gap. Students work individually and complete the questions. Students check their answers in pairs. Play the audio and go through answers as a class.

Answers

1 book 2 ID card 3 dictionary 4 pencil 5 notebook

Optional activity

Help students to become more confident and authentic in their pronunciation by focusing on main stress in sentences. Drill these sentences, clapping on the underlined words which are stressed in each sentence.

<u>Excuse</u> me. Can I have your <u>book</u>, please?
<u>Excuse</u> me. Can I have your <u>student ID card</u>, please?
<u>Excuse</u> me. Can I have a <u>dictionary</u>, please?
<u>Excuse</u> me. Can I have a <u>pencil</u>, please?
<u>Excuse</u> me. Can I have your <u>notebook</u>, please?

See p. 9 for advice on drilling.

MEETING PEOPLE — UNIT 1

> **Optional actvity**
>
> You will need printable Flashcards 1.3. Go to esource.cambridge.org to print the flashcards.
>
> Elicit questions for each of the items on the flashcards, e.g. *Can I have your mobile phone, please?* You could make this a competitive game if you like. See pp. 10–11 for team games with flashcards.

SPEAKING

4 Focus on the REMEMBER box and read through the sentences as a class. Check understanding by approaching different students and ask for things on their desks, e.g. *Excuse me. Can I have your book, please?* Point at the first photograph of a pen. Demonstrate the exercise with a student. Say: *Can I have your pen, please?* Encourage the student to respond with *Here you are.* or *No. I'm sorry.* Divide the class into Student As and Student Bs.

Students use the appropriate role play cards to complete the exercise. Monitor and help as necessary.

WRITING

5 Focus on the sentence at the top of the list. Read it aloud. Say: *For my English class, I need …* and pick up some of the things you, as the teacher, need for the lesson and say their names. Drill the sentence: *For my English class, I need a dictionary.* Then encourage individual students to tell you things they need for class. If any answers are not things the students need, present the concept again (pick up some things you don't use in the classroom, e.g. a mobile phone, and indicate with appropriate gestures that these items do not complete the sentence). Students write their ideas and then compare them with a partner. Ask pairs to share their ideas with the class.

> **Optional activity**
>
> You will need some sticky labels or sticky notes – these will be attached to objects in the classroom.
>
> Point at an object in the classroom, e.g. a chair. Try to elicit its English name from students. If they don't know it, then write it on the board. Encourage students to point at objects around the classroom. Elicit the word from the class, or give it yourself, and write it on the board. When you have about ten objects written on the board, drill the words whilst pointing to the correct objects. Encourage students to point, too.
>
> Hand out the sticky labels to the class. Give each pair of students three labels. Demonstrate writing a word from the board on the sticky label and then sticking the label on an object. Students work in pairs, copy the words, and then attach them to an object. Monitor and check that students are copying the words correctly and labelling the correct items.
>
> Encourage students to walk around the classroom or point to objects and say the word on the labels.

ACADEMIC LISTENING AND SPEAKING

> **Learning objectives**
>
> - Understand a dialogue in which a student applies for an ID card
> - Use main stress correctly when asking questions
> - Say email addresses
> - Ask for various personal details
> - Give personal details in response to questions to complete an application form
>
> See p. 6 for suggestions on how to use these Learning objectives in your lessons.

> **Lead-in**
>
> Write the numbers 1–4 in a column down the left of the board. Ask students to write the numbers on a piece of paper or in their notebooks. Say: *1 What's your family name?* Demonstrate writing your family name next to the number 1 on the board. Encourage students to write their own family names next to 1 on their piece of paper or in their notebook. Continue with these questions:
>
> 2 *What's your phone number?*
> 3 *Where are you from?*
> 4 *What's your email address?*
>
> Students work in pairs. Ask students to look at their words together. Can they remember what you asked about? Go through answers as a class. Try to elicit the full questions you asked.

PREPARING TO LISTEN

1 Focus on the words in the first column and ask a student to read them aloud. Point out the completed example by tracing the line from *first name* to *Burak* in the book. Students work individually to complete the exercise and then compare their answers in pairs. Go through answers as a class.

> **Answers**
> 2 Bozer 3 Turkey 4 0799 011 345
> 5 b.bozer@myemail.com

USING VISUALS TO PREDICT CONTENT

2 Focus on the photograph. Read out the sentence: *Her name is Gabriela*. Point to Gabriela in the photograph. Ask: *Where is she?* (university). Read the sentences 1 and 2 and point out the options. Focus on the photograph and encourage students to circle options. Students work in pairs and make predictions.

LISTENING FOR MAIN IDEAS

3 (1.21) Play the audio for students to listen and check their answers in Exercise 2. Go through answers as a class.

> **Answers**
> Gabriela is <u>a student</u>. She needs <u>a student ID card</u>.

NOTICE

Write: *alopez@myemail.com* on the board. Circle @ and the full stop and say: at, dot. Focus on the NOTICE box in the book. Allow students a minute to read the NOTICE box.

LISTENING FOR DETAIL

4 (1.21) Focus on the sentences. Ask students to read them. Read the first sentence aloud. Say: *Yes or no?* in a questioning tone. Elicit the correct answer (yes). Ask individual students at random to read each of the other sentences. Play the audio. Students work individually and circle *Yes* or *No* for each sentence. Play the audio again if necessary. Students work in pairs and check answers. Go through answers as a class. Use the audio script on Student's Book p. 215 to show students which line the information was in. Read the script aloud. Students follow in their books and identify the relevant parts of the text.

> **Answers**
> 2 No 3 No 4 Yes 5 No

LISTENING FOR KEY INFORMATION

5 (1.21) Focus on the Student ID Card Application Form. Ask: *What does Gabriela need?* (a student ID card). Play the audio. Students listen and complete the application form with the correct information. Students then check answers in pairs. Go through answers as a class.

> **Answers**
>
> **STUDENT ID CARD APPLICATION FORM**
>
> First name: Gabriela
> Family name: Lopez
> Country: Mexico
> Phone number: 0832 556 436
> Email address: alopez@myemail.com

PRONUNCIATION FOR SPEAKING

6 (1.22) Focus on the sentences and point out the underlined words. Play the audio and clap to emphasize the stressed words (underlined). Students listen and say. Drill the main stress as a class. For advice on drilling see p. 9. Encourage students to clap with you.

NOTICE

Write: *What's your name? My first name is* (your name). on the board. Circle the question mark and the full stop. Focus on the NOTICE box in the book. Allow students a minute to read the NOTICE box.

---

28 UNLOCK BASIC SKILLS TEACHER'S BOOK

| MEETING PEOPLE | UNIT 1 |

Optional activity

Give each student in the class a number 1, 2, (NOT 3) 4, 5, 6. Focus on the questions in Exercise 6. Say: *This is your question.* and point to the numbered questions. Check understanding by asking individual students to tell you their question.

Mingle: Follow the procedure on p. 12.

Alternative to mingling: If mingling activities are not appropriate for your context, ask students to work in small groups seated.

SPEAKING TASK

7 Focus on the REMEMBER box and read through the gapped phrases as a class. Elicit variations to complete each incomplete phrase, for example:

What's your name / phone number / email address?

My name / phone number / email address is …

I'm from (Japan / India / Saudi Arabia).

Focus on the dialogue in speech bubbles. Demonstrate the exercise with a student. Say: *Hello.* Encourage the student to respond: *Hi. I need a student ID card.* Say: *Yes, of course. What's your first name?* Encourage the student to respond with their first name. Focus on the blank application form. Demonstrate writing the name there.

Divide the class into Student As and Student Bs. Students follow the relevant instructions in the book. Monitor and help as necessary. Note any errors as you monitor. When most of the pairs have finished, Student As and Student Bs swap roles. Use the notes you made while monitoring for feedback at the end of the exercise. See p. 8 for advice on conducting feedback on speaking activities.

Model answer

A: Hi.
B: Hello.
A: I need a student ID card.
B: Yes, of course. What's your first name?
A: My first name is Taner.
B: What's your family name?
A: My family name is Baran.
B: Where are you from?
A: I'm from Turkey.
B: What's your phone number?
A: My phone number is 0252 0328 730.
B: What's your email address?
A: My email is t.baran@myemail.com.

ACADEMIC READING AND WRITING

Learning objectives

- Read and understand an email from a student who needs a library card
- Critical thinking (CT): Complete detailed information on an application form
- Write your personal details

See p. 6 for suggestions on how to use these Learning objectives in your lessons.

Lead-in

Write the incorrect sentences below on the board, completing them with the information about yourself where necessary:

My number is (your name).

I am a student.

I am from Japan. (Change the country if you actually are from Japan. The sentence should be wrong.)

My email is (your phone number).

Say: *Yes or no?* in a questioning tone. Encourage students to read the sentences and tell you what the mistake is. If appropriate for your context, ask students to come to the board and write the corrections. Encourage the whole class to help with spelling and punctuation. Stronger classes could work in pairs and either write or say incorrect sentences about themselves for their partner to correct.

USING VISUALS TO PREDICT CONTENT

1 Focus on the photograph. Point to the man in the photograph. Ask: *Where is he?* (the library). Read out the two sentences in the book and point out the options. Focus on the photograph and encourage students to choose the correct options. Students work in pairs and make predictions about the reading.

READING FOR MAIN IDEAS

2 (1.23) Focus on the email. Say: *Read and listen.* Play the audio. Then students check their answers in Exercise 1. Go through answers as a class. Check understanding of the last sentence in the email: *I can come to the library on Monday.* Ask: *Where?* (the library). Use a diary or a calendar to demonstrate the question *When?* Point to the days of the week and say them in English.

Answers

a student, library card

UNLOCK BASIC SKILLS TEACHER'S BOOK 29

READING FOR DETAIL

3 Focus on the sentences. Read the first sentence aloud. Say: *Yes or no?* in a questioning tone. Elicit the correct answer (yes). Encourage students to read all of the sentences, then ask them to read the email and find the information. Students work individually and then check their answers in pairs. Go through answers as a class. Read out each sentence. Students say *yes* or *no* and show you where they found the information in the text.

> **Answers**
> 2 No 3 Yes 4 No 5 No

ACADEMIC WRITING SKILLS

4 🔊 1.24 Write the vowels on the board: *a e i o u*. Point out the completed example in the book. Ask: *What word is this?* (name). Point at the second item. Ask: *What word is this?* (country). Point at each space for a missing vowel and elicit the missing letters. (*o, u*). Allow students to check in their books. Students complete all the words with the missing vowels. Play the audio for students to listen and check their answers. With weaker classes, write the answers on the board.

> **Answers**
> 2 c**ou**ntry 3 ph**o**ne 4 **e**mail 5 b**oo**k 6 p**e**ncil 7 p**e**n 8 d**i**ct**io**nary

> ⬤ **Common student errors**
>
> **Spelling:** *Country* is in the top ten misspelled words by Arabic L1 students. These are the typical errors: *contry contre*.
>
> To focus on the problem areas in this word, you could include the exercise below in your lesson:
>
> Write these words on the board:
>
> country countr_ c__ntr_ c___tr_ c_____
>
> Focus on the first word (country). Ask students to spell it out. Then remove the complete word from the board. Ask them to spell the word out again and complete the gap in the first word with a *y* if they are successful. (If not, write the full word again and repeat the first part of the procedure.) Then remove the completed word. Continue like this with all of the gaps in the word, removing each word as you complete it.

> **Optional activity**
>
> To check students' spelling skills and their understanding of capital letters, give a short test of some of the words taught in this unit. Read these words aloud:
>
> 1 pen 2 book 3 ID card 4 Turkey 5 Japan 6 country
>
> Students listen and write in their notebooks. Students swap notebooks. Write the answers on the board. Students check each other's writing for correct spelling and use of capital letters.

CRITICAL THINKING: UNDERSTAND

5 Focus on the application form and the sentences in the student notebook. Read the first heading on the application form: *First name* and the first sentence: *My first name is …* Circle *first name* in the sentence and then point at *First name* on the application form again, and the name there, *Salim*. Demonstrate the exercise by miming writing *Salim* in the first gap. Students work individually, reading the details in the application form and completing the sentences. Students then check their answers in pairs. Go through answers as a class. Read out each sentence in the notebook. Students show you where they found the information in the application form.

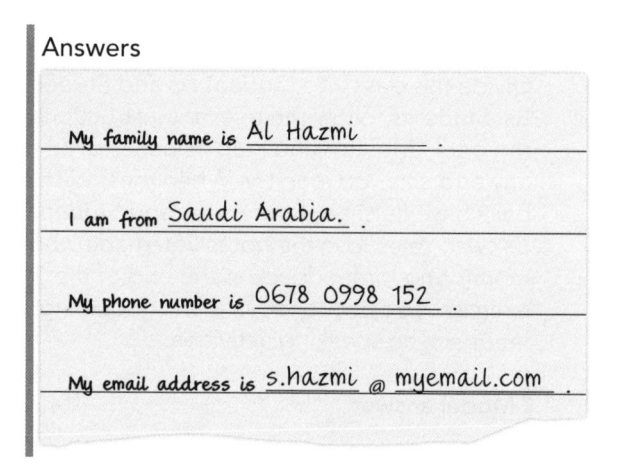

> **Answers**
>
> My family name is Al Hazmi .
>
> I am from Saudi Arabia. .
>
> My phone number is 0678 0998 152 .
>
> My email address is s.hazmi @ myemail.com .

ACADEMIC WRITING SKILLS

6 Write: *I am a student.* on the board. Circle the capital letter on *I*. Remove the sentence and write: *i am a student.* Ask: *What's wrong?* Cross out the *i* and write an *I*. Focus on the sentences for correction in the book, and point out the completed example. Students work individually and correct the mistakes by writing the missing capital letters. Go through answers as a class.

Answers

2 **I** am from **M**exico. 3 **M**y family name is **S**anchez.
4 **M**y email is r.sanchez@myemail.com.

CRITICAL THINKING: APPLY

7 Focus on the blank application form. Students work individually and complete the application form about themselves. Monitor and help with handwriting and spelling. Students swap books and check each other's writing. Remind students to check the use of capital letters.

WRITING TASK

8 Focus on the student's application form in Exercise 7 and the gapped sentences in Exercise 8. Read the first heading on the application form *First name* and the first sentence *My first name is …* . Circle *first name* in the sentence and then point at *First name* on the application form again.

Demonstrate the exercise by miming writing your first name in the first gap. Focus on the REMEMBER box and remind students when to use capital letters. Students work individually and complete the sentences. Monitor and help with handwriting and spelling.

9 Students swap books and check each other's writing. Remind students to check the use of capital letters.

Model answer
My first name is Angela.
My family name is Brown.
I am from the UK.
I am a teacher.
My phone number is 0122 389 612.
My email address is a.brown@myemail.co.uk.

MEETING PEOPLE — UNIT 1

Objectives review
See Introduction on p. 7 for ideas about using the Objectives review with your students.

WORDLIST AND GLOSSARY
See Introduction on p. 7 for ideas about using the Wordlist at the end of each unit and the Glossary at the end of the book with your students.

REVIEW TEST
See esource.cambridge.org for the Review test and ideas about how and when to administer the Review test.

RESEARCH PROJECT

Give a presentation on international names

Show the class some websites listing common male and female names in other countries. Divide the class into groups and tell them each group needs to choose one country to research. Tell them they should find ten male names and ten female names. Students could choose a country from the countries taught in this unit (but not their own country). Tell students that they should try to find similar spellings in the names, e.g.

Asif **Ar**if Han**if**

Kum**iko** A**iko** Fum**iko**

Tell students that each group will give a presentation using the names they find online. Tell students that their presentation should be 2–3 minutes long.

Allow students class time for the research, or encourage them to do this for homework. Give them class time during the next lesson to plan their presentations.

After students have given their presentations, ask questions, e.g. *Which name is your favourite? Which is the most common name?* You will need to communicate these questions carefully. See p. 6 for advice on communicating with beginners.

2 PEOPLE AND THINGS

UNLOCK YOUR KNOWLEDGE

You will need printable Flashcards 2.1. Go to esource.cambridge.org to print the flashcards. Pre-teach the vocabulary using the flashcards.

Focus on the photograph in the book.
Ask: *Where are they from?* Accept guesses from the class in L1, if necessary. Confirm when students are correct, or tell them the answer if they cannot guess (Mongolia). Ask students to find the country on the map on Student's Book p. 21.

Use the photograph to check students' existing knowledge of family vocabulary. Point at the father and say: *father*. Point to other family members. If they cannot name a family member, say the answer and move on. Focus on question 1. Read it aloud. Ask students to count the people in the photograph. Check the answer as a class.

Focus on question 2. Read it aloud. Ask students to count the people in their family and write the names on a piece of paper. Demonstrate by writing the names of your family on the board. Monitor and check students are spelling the word(s) correctly and using capital letters and lowercase letters accurately.

> **Answers**
> 1 seven 2 Answers will vary

LISTENING AND READING 1

> **Learning objectives**
> - Name members of the family – *mother, father, brother, sister, grandmother, grandfather*
> - Ask about people – *Who's this?*
> - Introduce people – *This is my mother, Mariam. This is my teacher, Mr Saeed.*
> - Use capital letters in titles correctly – *Mr, Mrs, Dr*
> - Gain awareness of the sounds of the letters *th* – *This, mother, brother*
>
> See p. 6 for suggestions on how to use these Learning objectives with your students.

> **Lead-in**
> You will need a photograph of your family to show students. Point to each person in the photograph and say their name and where they live. Do not use family vocabulary at this stage.

VOCABULARY: FAMILY

1 🔊 2.1 Focus on the family tree.
Ask: *What is this?* (a family). Ask: *Is it my family?* (no). Point to Ahmed. Say: *This is Ahmed's family.* Play the audio for students to listen and read. Encourage them to follow the audio by pointing in the book at each person in the family tree as they hear the word. Drill the family vocabulary. See p. 9 for advice on drilling.

Demonstrate the next part of the exercise with a student. Point to a person in the family tree and encourage a student to say the correct word. Then encourage the student to point at a person in the family tree, and say the correct word yourself. Students work in pairs. Monitor and correct any errors.

2 🔊 2.2 Focus on the sentences, the photographs, and the family tree in Exercise 1. Read the first sentence in Exercise 2. Point at Ahmed in the family tree and then the matching photograph in Exercise 2. Ask: *Is this Ahmed?* (yes). Say: *Read and listen.* Play the audio. Students work individually, reading the sentences and writing a tick or a cross in each tick box. Students work in pairs and check answers. Go through answers as a class.

> **Answers**
> 2 ✓ 3 ✓ 4 ✓ 5 ✓ 6 ✓ 7 ✓

> **NOTICE**
> Write: *Who's this?* on the board. Circle and say: *Who's.* Then write: *Who is this?* underneath. Point at *Who's* and encourage students to say the word. Then point at *Who is.* Say: *Say Who's. Write Who is.*
>
> Focus on the NOTICE box in the book. Allow students a minute to read the NOTICE box.

| | | PEOPLE AND THINGS | UNIT 2 |

LISTENING FOR DETAIL

3 (♦) 2.3 Focus on the names in the right-hand column and read them as a class. Say: *I'm Ahmed. This is my mother, Rana.* Point at the completed example. Play the audio for students to complete the exercise and then compare answers in pairs. Go through answers as a class.

> **Answers**
> 2 Yusuf
> 3 Hasan
> 4 Sara
> 5 Sena
> 6 Tariq

> **Optional activity**
> Focus students on the spelling of family words. Write this letter grid on the board:
>
> | f | r | o | t | n | h |
> |---|---|---|---|---|---|
> | b | a | s | h | e | r |
> | m | i | t | d | e | n |
> | s | o | n | h | d | r |
>
> Draw an arrow from left to right above the grid. Students find four family words going from left to right. Indicate that they can join letters vertically, horizontally or diagonally. Complete one word as a class (start with f in the top left and connect letters to find *father*). If appropriate in your context, you could invite a student up to the board to connect the letters. Encourage the class to guide the student (or yourself) at the board. Erase the lines and repeat for *mother*, *brother* and *sister*.

SOUND AND SPELLING: *th*

> **◉ Common student errors**
> The consonant sound /ð/ (mo*th*er) does not occur in Japanese. Students find it difficult to produce this sound and this leads to spelling errors. This is a typical error:
> *zen* (then).

4 (♦) 2.4 Focus on the words. Ask: *Which two letters are in all of the words?* (th). Students underline the letters. Play the audio for students to listen and repeat. Model the phoneme /ð/ and then say *mother*. Play the audio again. Students listen and repeat the words. Correct any errors with the phoneme /ð/. Ask students to underline *th* in the sentences in Exercise 2.

SPEAKING

5 Focus on the family tree in Exercise 1. Point to Ahmed and say: *Who's this?*. Point to Ahmed's mother and say: *Who's this? This is his mother.* Write: *This is his mother.* on the board. Underline *his* and point to the photograph of his mother and say: *This is …* Then point to Ahmed and say: *his …* and then point to the photograph of his mother and say: *mother.* Check understanding by pointing to Ahmed and then other family members and eliciting sentences (This is his father / sister / brother etc.). Point to the photograph of Rana again. Say: *What's her name?* Elicit: *Her name is Rana.*

Focus on the speech bubbles in Exercise 5. Drill the dialogue. Students work in pairs and ask about the people in the family tree in Exercise 1. Monitor and make sure students answer in full sentences. Correct any errors.

LISTENING FOR KEY INFORMATION

6 (♦) 2.5 Focus on the photographs. Ask: *Who is a teacher?* (a and b), *Who is an English teacher?* (b), *Who is a doctor?* (c). Focus on the options and say: *Are these names or numbers?* (names). Read out the names focusing on the pronunciation of *Mrs* /mɪsɪz/ *Mr* /mɪstə/ and *Dr* /dɒktə/. Point out the tick boxes. Play the audio for students to listen and match names 1–3 with photographs a–c. Go through answers as a class.

Check understanding of *Mrs, Mr* and *Dr*. Write your family name on the board and say: *Is this my first name?* (no), *Is this my family name?* (yes). Write your correct title (*Mr, Mrs* or *Dr*) on the board and read it aloud. Repeat for names 1–3 in the book. Drill pronunciation of *Mr, Mrs* and *Dr*. Focus on your name and title. Circle the capital letters. Focus on names 1–3 and ask students to circle the capital letters. Go through answers as a class.

> **Answers**
> 1 <u>M</u>rs <u>W</u>illiams   b
> 2 <u>D</u>r <u>F</u>arrel   c
> 3 <u>M</u>r <u>E</u>rkol   a

READING FOR KEY INFORMATION

7 🔊 2.6 👤 Focus on the options under the line in sentence 1. Focus on the photograph. Say: *He or She?* (He), *Mr or Mrs?* (Mr). Say: *Listen* and read the correct sentence 1 aloud. Demonstrate circling the correct option under the line. Students work individually and circle the correct options. Play the audio for students to check. Go through answers as a class. Ask students to write the answers in the gaps. Monitor and check spelling and use of capital letters.

> **Answers**
> 2 Mrs 3 Mrs 4 Dr

8 🔊 2.6 👤 Focus on the sentences in Exercise 7. Play the audio. Drill the sentences in Exercise 7.

> **NOTICE**
> Focus on the NOTICE box. Say: *Her name is Mia Young*. Ask: *What's her first name?* (Mia), *What's her family name?* (Young). Say: *Her name is Mrs Young.*

WRITING AND SPEAKING

9 👤👥 Tell students to turn to Student's Book p. 206. Focus on the cards and read through the words. Ask students to complete the notes about their family members. Then focus on the REMEMBER box and read through the phrase as a class. Elicit variations to complete the phrase, e.g. *This is my mother, Rana. / This is my father, Hassan.*

Point at the first card. Demonstrate the exercise with a student. Say: *Who's this?* Encourage the student to respond: *This is my mother,* (mother's name). Students work in pairs and take turns asking and answering questions about the cards. Monitor and help as necessary.

LISTENING AND READING 2

> **Learning objectives**
> - Talk about the names and relationships of groups of people – *We're brothers. Our names are … Their names are …*
> - Talk about the nationalities of groups of people – *We're from Saudi Arabia. They're from Japan.*
> - Talk about the occupations of groups of people – *They're teachers. We're students.*
>
> See p. 6 for suggestions on how to use these Learning objectives with your students.

> **Lead-in**
> Write the heading *People* at the top of the board. Give students oral clues to words for different types of people they have met on the course so far, e.g.
> *In your family. First letter f. He is your …* (father)
> *In the university. First letter t. I am a …* (teacher)
> *In the university. First letter s. You are a …* (student)
> *In your family. First letter b. He is your …* (brother)
> *In your family. First letter g. She is your …* (grandmother)
> Write the first letters on the board as you say them. You could give similar clues for these words: *mother, sister, grandfather, doctor*. Encourage students to call out answers, and elicit the spelling as you write the answers on the board.

USING VISUALS TO PREDICT CONTENT

1 🔊 2.7 👥 Focus on the photographs. Encourage students to tell you what they see. Focus on the sentences. Read sentence 1 aloud. Say: *yes or no?* in a questioning tone. Students work in pairs and circle *Yes* or *No* for each sentence. Play the audio for students to check their answers. Go through answers as a class.

> **Answers**
> 1 Yes 2 No (Mr Cole and Mrs Nolan are teachers.)

READING FOR KEY INFORMATION

2 🔊 2.7 👥 Focus on the speech bubbles. Play the audio for students to read and listen. Focus on the options below the text. Say: *Hamad and Nasser, teachers*. Say: *yes or no?* in a questioning tone. Elicit the correct answer (no). Demonstrate writing a cross (✗) in the box. Students work individually, reading the texts and writing a tick or a cross in each tick box.

Students work in pairs and check their answers. Go through answers as a class. Read out each piece of information and underline it in the text.

> **Answers**
>
> | Hamad and Nasser | ✗ teachers ✓ students |
> | --- | --- |
> | | ✗ from the UK |
> | Mr Cole and Mrs Nolan | ✓ teachers ✗ brothers |
> | | ✗ from Saudi Arabia |

34 UNL⌀CK BASIC SKILLS TEACHER'S BOOK

PEOPLE AND THINGS — UNIT 2

NOTICE

Point to yourself and say: *I'm a teacher.* Indicate an individual student in the classroom and say to the rest of the class (not the individual student): *He/She* (depending on gender). *He's/She's a student.* Write: *I'm a teacher. He's a student.* on the board. Circle *a* and ask: *How many?* about each sentence (one, one).

Now focus on two students. Ask: *A student or students?* (students). Then indicate the two students and say to the rest of the class (not the two students): *They're students.* Write this on the board. Underline *They're* and circle the plural *s*.

Write: *We're students.* on the board. Speak to the two students and say: *I'm a teacher.* Elicit: *We're students.* by pointing at the words on the board. Repeat a few times. Check that students have understood by focusing on individuals and pairs around the class.

Focus on the NOTICE box in the book. Point out the first photograph and say: *How many?* (one). Point at the second photograph and say: *How many?* (three). Focus on the speech bubbles in Exercise 2. Read each sentence aloud while pointing at each word as you say it. Demonstrate underlining *I'm*, *We're* and *They're*. Indicate that students should underline these words in the speech bubbles in Exercise 2. Monitor and help as necessary.

GRAMMAR: VERB *BE*: *WE* AND *THEY*

3 (♪ 2.8) Focus on the pictures and the speech bubbles. Play the audio for students to listen and read. Encourage students to follow the text by pointing to each speech bubble as they hear it. Drill the sentences from the table. See p. 9 for tips on drilling.

NOTICE

Write: *We're students.* on the board. Circle and say: *We're.* Then write: *We are students.* underneath. Point at *We're* and encourage students to say the words. Say: *Say We're. Write We are.* Repeat for *She's a teacher.* and *He's from Japan.*

Focus on the NOTICE box. Allow students a minute to read the NOTICE box.

● Common student errors

Verb agreement: Arabic L1 and Turkish L1 students frequently fail to make the verb *be* agree with the subject. For Arabic students, these errors almost certainly occur because there is no equivalent in their L1. Because this error occurs with the Present simple tenses, it needs particular attention at beginners' level. Here are some examples of this error type:

The brothers is very different.

Jeans is the best clothes to wear.

The people is lovely.

See p. 148 for tips on how to help students with **Verb agreement** type errors.

---

4 (♪ 2.9) Focus on the options under the line in sentence 1. Focus on the photograph on the left in Exercise 5. Say: *How many?* (two), *I or We?* (We). Demonstrate circling the correct option under the line. Students work individually and circle the correct options answers. Play the audio for students to check. Go through answers as a class. Ask students to write the correct answers in the gaps. Monitor and check students' spelling and use of capital letters.

> **Answers**
> 2 We 3 They 4 They

Optional activity

Aural dictation (contractions): Follow the procedure on p. 11.
1 We're from Mexico. (We are from Mexico.)
2 They're students. (They are students.)
3 We're teachers. (We are teachers.)
4 They're from Turkey. (They are from Turkey.)

LISTENING FOR KEY INFORMATION

5 (♪ 2.10) Focus on the two photographs and speech bubbles. Point out the options in the speech bubbles. Play the audio. Students work individually, listening and circling the correct words. Play the audio again for students to check. Go through answers as a class.

> **Answers**
> Our <u>teacher</u> is Mrs Moreno.
> Our <u>university</u> is in Mexico.
> They are <u>students</u>.

GRAMMAR: *OUR* AND *THEIR*

6 (♪ 2.11) Point to yourself and say: *I'm a teacher. My name is* (your name). Then indicate an individual student in the class and say to the rest of the class: *He/She* (depending on gender). *He's/she's a student. His/her name is* (student's name). Write: *I'm a teacher. My name is* (your name). *He's a student. His name is* (student's name). on the board. Circle *I*, *My*, *He* and *His*.

Now focus on two students. Then indicate the two students and say to the rest of the class (not the two students): *They're students.* Write this on the board. Then write: *Their names are* (students names connected with *and*).

Write: *We're students. Our names are (students' names).* on the board. Speak to the two students and say: *My name is …* Encourage them to say: *Our names are …* by pointing at the words on the board. Repeat a few times.

Check that students have understood by focusing on individuals and pairs around the class, indicating students should respond (*My name is … Our names are …*) or asking the rest of the class to respond (*His/Her name is … Their names are …*).

Focus on the table in the book. Play the audio for students to listen and read. Drill the sentences. See p. 9 for tips on drilling.

7 (◆) 2.12 Focus on the options under the line in sentence 1. Focus on the sentence: *They are students.* Say: *We or They?* (They), *Our or Their?* (Their). Read sentence 1 aloud. Demonstrate circling the correct option under the line. Students work individually and circle the correct options. Play the audio for students to check. Go through answers as a class. Ask students to write the correct answers in the gaps. Monitor and check students' spelling and use of capital letters.

| Answers
| Their   Our   Our

WRITING AND SPEAKING

8 Focus on the REMEMBER box and read through the phrases as a class. Elicit variations to complete the phrases, e.g. *Our names are (various names). We are (students / teachers / from Saudi Arabia, etc.).*

Focus on the sentences. Point at the gaps in the sentences. Students work in pairs and complete the gaps. Monitor and check students' spelling and use of capital letters. Students swap and check each other's writing. Then students work in groups of four, made up of two pairs. Each pair says their sentences to the other pair.

LISTENING AND READING 3

| Learning objectives
|
| • Name a number of common possessions – *television, computer, car, camera, bag, mobile phone*
| • Ask about possessions – *How many (mobile phones / cars) do you have?*
| • Write numbers – *one, two, three, four, five,* etc.
| • Form regular plurals – *mobile phones, bags*
| • Use main stress in sentences with numbers – *I have one car. I have five cameras.*
| See p. 6 for suggestions on how to use these Learning objectives with your students.

| Lead-in
|
| **Alphabet memory game** Follow the procedure on p. 11.

VOCABULARY: MY THINGS

1 (◆) 2.13 Focus on the photographs of objects. Play the audio for students to listen and read. Encourage students to follow the audio by pointing at each study object as they hear it. Drill the names of the objects. See p. 9 for advice on drilling. Check understanding using Flashcards 2.2. Go to esource.cambridge.org to print the flashcards.

Demonstrate the next part of the exercise with a student. Point to an object and encourage a student to say the correct word. Then encourage the student to point at an object and say the correct word yourself. Students work in pairs. Monitor and correct any errors.

READING FOR NUMBERS

2 Remind students of the way we form regular plurals with *s* using some classroom objects. Hold up two books. Elicit the phrase: *two books.* Continue with other objects. Focus on the photographs. Count the items in each photograph (5, 8, 1, 6). Write the written numbers next to each number on the board (e.g. *five, eight,* etc.). Point at the sentences and demonstrate underlining the written numbers.

Focus on the options under the line in sentence 1. Demonstrate circling the correct option under the line. Students work individually and circle the correct options.

36   UNLOCK BASIC SKILLS TEACHER'S BOOK

PEOPLE AND THINGS UNIT 2

3 (2.14) Focus on the sentences in Exercise 2. Play the audio. Go through answers as a class. Ask students to write the correct answers in the gaps. Monitor and check students' spelling. Drill the sentences. See p. 9 for advice on drilling. Check understanding of *How many … do you have?* by asking students about things on their desks (pens, books, etc.).

Demonstrate the next part of the exercise with a student. Focus on the speech bubble at the top of Exercise 2 and say: *How many cameras do you have?* Point to the photograph and sentence 1 in Exercise 2. Encourage the student to reply: *I have five cameras*. Students work in pairs and practise the exchanges. Monitor and correct pronunciation.

> **Answers**
> 2 bags 3 car 4 computers

> ⦿ **Common student errors**
>
> **Noun form:** Arabic L1 and Turkish L1 students frequently fail to form regular and irregular plurals. Here are some examples of this error type:
>
> I met him <u>two week</u> ago.
>
> In <u>these shop</u> you can find meat shop.
>
> I got <u>a lot of present</u>.
>
> **Wrong verb:** Arabic L1 students overuse the verb *be* instead of *have* for possession. Here are some examples of this error type:
>
> My family <u>is</u> two cars.
>
> My house <u>is</u> one bedroom.
>
> The farm <u>is</u> nice land and animals.
>
> See p. 148 for tips on how to help students with **Noun form** and **Wrong verb** errors.

ACADEMIC WRITING SKILLS

4 (2.15) Write the vowels on the board: *a e i o u*. Point out the completed example 1. Ask: *What number is this?* (one). Point at 2. Ask: *What word is this?* (two). Point at the gap in word 2 and elicit the missing letter (*o*). Students work individually and complete the numbers with the missing vowels. Play the audio for students to check their answers. Students could then check answers in the Starter Unit p. 12. With weaker classes, write the answers on the board. Ask students to say the numbers.

LISTENING FOR KEY INFORMATION

5 (2.16) Focus on the options under the line in sentence 1. Say: *Listen and circle*. Demonstrate circling the correct option under the line. Play the audio. Students work individually and circle the correct options. Play the audio again for students to check. Go through answers as a class. Ask students to write the correct answers in the gaps. Monitor and check students' spelling.

> **Answers**
> 2 six 3 three 4 five 5 four

> **Optional activity**
>
> **Spelling test:** Follow the procedure on p. 11. Written numbers *one* to *ten*.

PRONUNCIATION FOR SPEAKING

6 (2.17) Focus on the questions and point out the underlined words. Point out the response in the speech bubble above the exercise. Play the audio and clap or make an appropriate hand movement to emphasize the stressed words (the objects in the questions and the numbers in the answers). Drill the main stress as a class. See p. 9 for advice on drilling. Encourage students to clap with you. Play the audio again for students to listen and repeat.

Focus on the pictures and elicit the answers to the questions. Encourage students to form full sentences with *I have*. Students work in pairs and ask and answer the questions using the pictures. Demonstrate the exercise with a student in weaker classes. Monitor and check for correct pronunciation.

> **Answers**
> 1 I have two cars.
> 2 I have three cameras.
> 3 I have four televisions.
> 4 I have five bags.
> 5 I have one computer.

SPEAKING AND WRITING

7 Focus on the REMEMBER box and read through the phrases as a class. Elicit variations to complete the phrases, e.g. *How many (various objects) do you have? I / We have (number) (various objects)*.

Focus on the survey. Point at the photographs. Demonstrate the exercise with a student. Ask: *How many mobile phones do you have?* Elicit a response from the student using a full sentence (e.g. *I have two mobile phones.*). Demonstrate writing *two mobile phones* on the line. Point out that you have written the full number, not just the numeral. Students work in pairs and conduct the survey, taking turns to ask questions. Monitor and check the following: plurals when asking and answering questions, full numbers, and plural objects when writing. Some students may not own any of the objects. Help them to answer by writing *I don't have any* (plural object, e.g. *mobile phones*) on the board. The other student should write *zero* (*mobile phones*). When students have finished, take class feedback on any interesting answers. Ask students to swap notebooks and check each other's writing.

WATCH AND REMEMBER

Learning objectives

- Understand information about people and families – *His grandmother is sixty-six years old*
- Understand information about possessions – *cars, televisions, cameras, mobile phones*
- Practise saying family members – *son, daughter*
- Practise asking about family members and possessions – *How many sisters/cameras do you have?*

See p. 6 for suggestions on how to use these Learning objectives in your lessons.

Lead-in

Ask students to tell you about their families and their ages. If necessary, provide a model to help students.

PART 1

In Part 1, Hachiro (from Japan) introduces his family and talks about how many cars they own. Students check their understanding of key family words and do a listening exercise based on the video.

BEFORE YOU WATCH

1 Focus on the photographs and the words below. Say: *Match*. Students match the photographs. Students work in pairs and check their answers.

2 (2.18) Play the audio. Students listen and check their answers in Exercise 1. Drill the pronunciation, paying specific attention to the /ð/ sound in the middle of each word. Students write the words on the lines. Monitor and check students' writing.

> **Answers**
> a grandmother b mother c brother

WATCH

3 Students read the sentences and predict the answers. Students watch Part 1 and check their predictions. Go through answers as a class.

> **Answers**
> 1 brother 2 grandfather 3 grandmother

AFTER YOU WATCH

In stronger classes, Exercise 4 should be completed by students after watching Part 1. In weaker classes, students can watch Part 1 again and complete Exercise 4 or use the audio script at the back of the book.

4 Tell students to try and remember the information from the video. Students work individually, reading the sentences and completing the gaps. Students work in pairs and check their answers. In weaker classes, play Part 1 again or use the audio script on Student's Book p. 215. Go through answers as a class.

> **Answers**
> one, My, is, old

PART 2

In Part 2, three more characters are introduced. They talk about some of the objects that they own.

BEFORE YOU WATCH

5 Focus on the photographs and the phrases below. Say: *Match*. Students match the photographs.

6 (2.19) Play the audio. Students listen and check their answers in Exercise 5. Drill the pronunciation of /z/ sounds in plural nouns. Students write the phrases on the lines. Monitor and check students' writing.

> **Answers**
> a two cars b three televisions c one computer

PEOPLE AND THINGS — UNIT 2

WATCH

7 Students watch Part 2 and choose the options. Go through answers as a class. Ask students how they could have guessed the answer to question 3 before watching (no *s* on *bag*, so it is singular).

Answers
1 the USA 2 a student 3 one

AFTER YOU WATCH

8 Students complete the sentences with the words in the box. When checking answers, ensure that students put the word stress in the correct place, i.e. com*pu*ter, *cam*era.

Answers
1 camera 2 mobile phone 3 computer

PART 3

In Part 3, students remember key information from the lesson.

REMEMBER

9 Students watch Part 3 and complete the sentences. If students find this hard, provide clues about what kind of information is needed (numbers). Go through answers as a class.

Answers
1 one 2 three 3 two

MORE VOCABULARY: FAMILY

10 Focus on the words in red in the NOTICE box. Elicit the definition for each word, or explain if the meaning is unknown. Focus on the names and family vocabulary. Say: *Match*. Students work in pairs. Go through answers as a class.

Answers
2 son 3 father 4 mother

ASK AND ANSWER

11 In groups, students practise asking and answering the question. Change groups to give them more opportunities to practise.

Optional activity

Extend Exercise 11 by asking students to present their partner to the rest of the class, e.g. *Ahmed has one sister. She is eighteen years old. He has two televisions.*

LANGUAGE FOCUS

Learning objectives

- Say and write the numbers 1–100
- Ask about age of people and objects – *How old is your father? How old is your mobile phone?*
- Talk about age – *one year old, three years old*
- Discriminate between -*teen* and -*ty* numbers – *thirteen/thirty, fourteen/forty*

See p. 6 for suggestions on how to use these Learning objectives with your students.

Lead-in

You will need printable Flashcards 2.3. Go to esource.cambridge.org to print the flashcards.

Team pelmanism: Review the numbers 0–20 using Flashcards 0.1 and 0.4. Then follow the procedure on p. 10.

VOCABULARY: NUMBERS 11–100

1 (2.20) Write the vowels on the board: *a e i o u*. Focus on the numerals 11–19. Elicit the words from the class. Point out the completed example in the book. Ask: *What number is this?* (fourteen). Point at 16. Ask: *What number is this?* (sixteen). Point at the gap and elicit the missing letter (i). Students complete all the numbers with the missing vowels. Students check their answers in Starter Unit p. 15. With weaker classes, write the answers on the board. Play the audio for students to listen and repeat the numbers.

NOTICE

Write the following on the board: *16 six_ _ _ _ 17 seven_ _ _ _ 18 eight_ _ _*. Focus on the NOTICE box and read the numbers. Elicit the spelling of the highlighted letters. Ask students to spell out the words on the board (all the letters, not just -*teen*) and write as they say them. Drill the words, stressing -*teen*.

2 (2.21) Focus on the numerals and written numbers (20–100 only). Ask students to listen and read. Play the audio. Encourage students to point at each numeral as they hear it. Drill the numbers. See p. 9 for advice on drilling. Check recall using Flashcards 2.3. Go to esource.cambridge.org to print the flashcards.

Play the second part of the audio (21–29). Students listen and point.

Point to a numeral and encourage a student to say the correct number. Then encourage the student to point at a numeral and say the correct number yourself. Students work in pairs. Monitor and correct any errors.

> **NOTICE**
>
> Write these numbers (without hyphens) on the board: *twenty seven, twenty nine*.
>
> Focus on the NOTICE box and point out the highlighted hyphen. Say: *This is a hyphen.* Complete the hyphens in the numbers on the board. Check understanding by eliciting more numbers from students and, if appropriate, inviting them to the board to write the numbers. (If it is not appropriate, ask students to dictate the words to you, using the word hyphen between the two numbers.) Encourage the whole class to help with spelling.

PRONUNCIATION FOR LISTENING

3 🔊 2.22 Write the two stress patterns on the board with bubbles above the vowels: o O thirteen O o thirty. Sound out the stress patterns using neutral sounds, e.g. *DUH-duh* for O o and *duh-DUH* for o O. Clap your hands on the stressed syllables for extra impact. Say: *thirteen*, clearly emphasizing the stressed syllable and clapping for extra impact. Repeat for *thirty*. Encourage students to join you saying the words and clapping on the stressed syllables.

Play the audio for students to listen and look. Play the audio again for students to repeat.

> **Optional activity**
>
> Ask students to write the following stress patterns in their notebooks: 1 O o
> 2 o O
>
> Dictate these numbers: 13 30 50 15 17 70 18 40 16 90. Students write the numerals next to the correct stress pattern. Do the first one together on the board. Check that students have written the following:
>
> 1 O o 30 50 70 40 90
> 2 o O 13 15 17 18 16
>
> With weaker classes, you could give them the numeral to match to the stress patterns. Write the numerals above the patterns in a random order on the board.

SPEAKING AND WRITING

4 👥 Focus on the numerals and the completed example. Elicit the correct way to say 31 (thirty-one). Students work in pairs and say the numbers. Encourage students to point at the numbers as they say them. Monitor and correct any errors. Focus on the written numbers in Exercise 2. Elicit the correct way to say 32 and write: *thirty-two* on the board. Students work individually and write the numbers. Monitor and check for correct use of hyphens. Go through answers as a class.

> **Optional activity**
>
> **Aural dictation**: Follow the procedure on p. 11.
> 41 59 67 33 97 54 100
> Strong classes could write the words. Weaker classes could write the numerals as they listen and then write the words afterwards.

LISTENING AND WRITING

5 🔊 2.23 If appropriate in your context, guess the ages of some students in the class. Say: *I am* (your age). *You are* (guess a student's age). Focus on the photographs in the book and ask students to cover the text. Encourage students to guess the ages of the people. (She is … , He is …).

Focus on the options under the line in sentence 1. Read the completed example aloud. Demonstrate circling the correct option under the line. Play the audio. Students work individually, circling the correct options. Go through answers as a class. Ask students to write the correct answers in the gaps. Monitor and check spelling and use of hyphens.

> **Answers**
>
> 2 Forty-eight 3 Fifty-seven 4 Ninety-one 5 Thirteen

READING FOR KEY INFORMATION

6 🔊 2.24 Focus on the answers to the questions. Ask a student to read these aloud. Indicate yourself and say: *Two years old?* Elicit the answer (no). Look around the classroom for something that might be two years old (e.g. a dictionary, a computer, etc.). Repeat and elicit the answer (yes). Focus on the completed example. Read the question and options aloud. Elicit: *mobile phone* from the class and demonstrate circling the answer. Students work individually, reading the questions and answers and circling the correct options. Go through answers as a class. Play the audio and drill the questions and answers as a class.

PEOPLE AND THINGS   UNIT 2

> **Answers**
> 2 grandmother 3 car 4 mother

SPEAKING AND WRITING

7 Focus on the REMEMBER box and read through the phrases as a class. Elicit variations to complete the incomplete phrases, e.g. *How old is your* (various people and objects)? (Various numbers) *years old*.

Focus on the survey. Point at the words in the box. Demonstrate the exercise with a student. If appropriate in your context, ask: *How old are you?* Elicit a response from the student: (student's age) *years old*. Demonstrate writing the student's age in the first gap. Point out that you have written the full number, not just the numeral. Students work in pairs and conduct the survey, taking turns to ask questions. Monitor and check use of question forms and spelling of numbers. When students have finished, take class feedback on any interesting answers. Ask students to swap notebooks and check each other's writing.

ACADEMIC LISTENING AND SPEAKING

> **Learning objectives**
> - Describe objects and people
> - Understand descriptions of possessions and people in photographs
> - CT: Remember information for a fact file
>
> See p. 6 for suggestions on how to use these Learning objectives with your students.

> **Lead-in**
> Write the numbers 1–5 down the left of the board. Ask students to write the numbers on a piece of paper or in their notebooks. Say: *1 How old are you?* Demonstrate writing a numeral to represent your age next to the number 1 on the board. Encourage students to write. Continue with these questions:
> 2 How old is your grandfather?
> 3 How old is your mobile phone?
> 4 How old is your car?
> 5 How old is your television?
> Students work in pairs. Ask students to look at their answers together. Can they remember what you asked about? Go through answers as a class (you / grandfather / mobile phone / car / television). Elicit the full questions you asked.

USING VISUALS TO PREDICT CONTENT

1 🔊 2.25 Focus on the photographs. Point out the name labels and say: *His name is Ercan. His name is Taner. His name is Mr Rosales.* Point to the tablet and ask: *What are they looking at?* Elicit the answer (tablet/photographs). Read out the sentences and point out the options. Focus on the photographs and encourage students to choose an option. Students work in pairs and make predictions about the listening. Play the audio for students to check their predictions. Go through answers as a class.

> **Answers**
> Ercan has <u>two</u> cars.
> Mr Rosales is his <u>teacher</u>.

LISTENING FOR KEY INFORMATION

2 🔊 2.25 Focus on the sentences. Point out the options in the sentences. Say: *Mexico or Turkey?* Encourage students to guess, but do not confirm whether they are right or wrong. Tell students they are going to read, listen, and circle the answers. Play the audio once all the way through. Students work individually and circle. Play the audio again to check the answers with the class.

> **Answers**
> 1 Mexico 2 forty 3 twelve 4 Japan

CRITICAL THINKING: UNDERSTAND

3 🔊 2.25 Focus on the fact files. Read the first heading. Focus on *Country: Japan* and ask: *Where is the car from?* Point out the capital J. Point at the empty lines and read out the headings. Remind students to use capital letters to start the names of countries. Encourage them to write numbers in full. Play the audio again for students to listen and complete the fact files. Students check their answers in pairs. Go through answers as a class on the board.

> **Answers**
> Nissan: Japan   12 / twelve
> Jaguar: the UK   5 / five

UNLOCK BASIC SKILLS TEACHER'S BOOK

CRITICAL THINKING: REMEMBER

4 You will need your own mobile phone. Find out where it was manufactured before the class.

Focus on the fact file on the left and hold up your mobile phone. Demonstrate the exercise. Write the name of the phone, the place it was made, and how old the phone is.

Ask students to complete the fact files individually. Monitor and help as necessary. If students do not know where their things are made, ask them to say the country that the company is from or where they bought the item.

PRONUNCIATION FOR SPEAKING

5 (2.26) Focus on the sentences and questions and point out the underlined words. Play the audio and clap or make an appropriate hand movement to emphasize the stressed words. Drill the main stress as a class. For advice on drilling see p. 9. Encourage students to clap with you. Ask students to read the sentences and questions aloud.

SPEAKING TASK

6 Focus on the REMEMBER box and read through the phrases as a class. Use the fact files in Exercise 4 to elicit variations to complete the phrases, e.g. *This is (my teacher, Mr Brown / my mobile phone, etc.) My (car/teacher) is from Japan. My (teacher/computer) is (forty/one) year(s) old. I have (one mobile phone).*

Demonstrate the exercise using the fact file you completed in Exercise 4. Introduce the object to the class and give some information about it, but not everything (see Model answer below). Encourage the class to ask you one more question. Students work in groups and invent the fact files. Monitor and help as necessary. Note any errors and any correct use of language which has not been covered in the course so far as you monitor. Use the notes you made for feedback at the end of the exercise. See p. 8 for advice on conducting feedback on speaking activities.

Model answers

This is my teacher. Her name is Mrs Brown. She's from the UK.
(How old is she?) She's 30 years old.

This is my mobile phone. My mobile phone is a Samsung. My mobile phone is from Korea.
(How many mobile phones do you have?) I have two mobile phones.

Optional activity

False information: Follow the procedure on p. 12. Students use their notes in Exercise 6 to give one piece of false information about each item. Other students listen and say what is false, e.g.:
My phone is a Huawei. My phone is 5 years old. (false) My phone is from China. I have one mobile phone.

ACADEMIC READING AND WRITING

Learning objectives

- Read and understand a website introduction to a university class
- Complete detailed information on a family tree
- Write personal details about their family

See p. 6 for suggestions on how to use these Learning objectives with your students.

Lead-in

You will need printable Flashcards 2.4, photographs only, which can be printed at esource.cambridge.org.
Team spelling test: Follow the procedure on p. 11.

PREPARING TO READ

1 Choose some students (of the same gender) who are friends. Say: *Is this your brother/sister?* (no). Ask: *Who's this?* Elicit the word *friend*, if possible. Write on the board: (name) and (name) are friends. Repeat the procedure with other students. Drill the sentences on the board. Point out the vowels in *friends*.

Focus on the photographs in the book. Point to the words in the box and read the gapped sentences. Ask students to read and write. Go through answers as a class.

Answers

We are <u>brother</u> and sister. We are <u>friends</u>.

PEOPLE AND THINGS — UNIT 2

USING VISUALS TO PREDICT CONTENT

2 Focus on the photographs in Exercise 3. Point out the names and say: *Her name is (Maria/Yolanda, etc.)*. Ask: *Where are they from?* Read out sentence 1 and point out the options. Focus on the photographs and encourage students to choose an option. Students work in pairs and make predictions about the reading. Students read the text in Exercise 3 and check their predictions. Go through answers as a class.

> **Answers**
> 1 sisters 2 sisters 3 Japan

READING FOR KEY INFORMATION

3 (◀) 2.27 Focus on the text. Play the audio for students to listen and read. Focus on sentences (1–5) and point out the options. Focus on the text and find the correct number for sentence 1. Demonstrate circling the correct options. Students work in pairs and find the numbers in the text in Exercise 3. Go through answers as a class.

> **Answers**
> 2 18 3 25 4 5 5 100

ACADEMIC WRITING SKILLS

4 (◀) 2.28 Write the vowels on the board: *a e i o u*. Then write: *y* on the board separately, underneath the vowels. Point out the completed example. Ask: *What word is this?* (sister). Point at word 2. Ask: *What word is this?* (friend). Point at each space for a missing vowel in word 2 and elicit the missing letters (ie). Students complete the remaining words with the missing letters. Play the audio for students to check their answers. Go through answers as a class.

> **Answers**
> 2 fr<u>ie</u>nd 3 br<u>o</u>ther 4 m<u>o</u>ther 5 f<u>a</u>ther 6 eight<u>ee</u>n
> 7 thirty-s<u>e</u>ven 8 fifty-f<u>i</u>ve

CRITICAL THINKING: UNDERSTAND

5 Focus on the notes and the family tree underneath. Point at the word *mother* in the family tree. Point at the student notes. Demonstrate writing the information about the mother in the gaps. Ask students to complete the family tree with the names and ages of the family from the notes. Students work individually and then check their answers in pairs. Go through answers as a class.

> **Answers**
>
> ```
> mother ─────────── father
> Name: Lucia        Name: Jim
> Years old: 45      Years old: 50
>
>        sister              me
>   Name: Tanya         Name: Chris
>   Years old: 15       Years old: 23
>   sister              brother
> Name: Mia            Name: Ben
> Years old: 12        Years old: 18
> ```

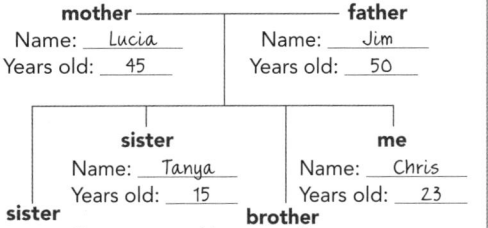

ACADEMIC WRITING SKILLS

> ⊙ **Common student errors**
>
> **Conjunctions:** English and Japanese do not have corresponding conjunctions. For example, there are 11 corresponding Japanese conjunctions for the word *and*, and Japanese conjunctions often have a number of equivalents in English. Therefore, Japanese L1 learners often have problems using conjunctions.

6 Choose two students in the class. Write: *(student's name) _____ (student's name) are friends.* on the board. Elicit the word *and*.

Focus on the completed example in the book. Read it aloud. Demonstrate circling the word *and*.

Ask students to read the sentences and circle *and*. Students work individually and then check in pairs. Demonstrate that *and* joins two things of the same kind by underlining *Mia* and *Tanya*, *sisters* and *brother*, *Maria* and *Yolanda*.

> **Answers**
> 2 I have two sisters <u>and</u> one brother.
> 3 Maria <u>and</u> Yolanda are from Mexico.
> 4 My name is Chris <u>and</u> I am twenty-three years old.

UNLOCK BASIC SKILLS TEACHER'S BOOK

> **Optional activity**
>
> Write these pairs of words on the board joined with *and*: 1 brother and sister 2 pen and pencil 3 father and computer 4 Mr and Mrs 5 students and teachers 6 Ali and book 7 five and seven 8 one hundred and car.
>
> Students work in pairs and decide which uses of *and* are correct. (1 yes 2 yes 3 no 4 yes 5 yes 6 no 7 yes 8 no). Go through answers as a class. Elicit some alternative words for the incorrect pairs.

7 (2.29) Write on the board:

Mr Brown _____ teachers.

and / are / Mrs Brown

Point at the words under the line and use appropriate hand gestures to indicate that students need to reorder the words. Elicit: *Mr Brown and Mrs Brown are teachers.*

Focus on the completed example in the book. Ask a student to read the sentence. Students work individually. Monitor and help as necessary. Play the audio for students to check. Go through answers as a class.

> **Answers**
>
> 2 Noora <u>and Fatima are</u> students.
> 3 Chris <u>and Lee are</u> my brother and sister.
> 4 Erin <u>and Rin are</u> my brothers.

CRITICAL THINKING: CREATE

8 Focus on the family tree. Ask students to work individually and complete the tree with information about their own family. Point out *Name* and *Years old*. In stronger classes, encourage students to add *grandmother* and *grandfather* to the tree. Monitor and remind students to use capital letters on names.

WRITING TASK

9 Focus on the family tree in Exercise 8 and the gapped sentences in Exercise 9. Read the first three gapped sentences. Focus on *She* and elicit which family member the sentence could be about. Ask: *Who?* and point at the family tree (mother, sister, grandmother). Demonstrate the exercise by miming writing *mother* in the first gap in the sentence. Students work individually and complete the gaps with information from their family tree. Monitor and help as necessary. If students have problems, point out the REMEMBER box.

10 Students swap books and check each other's writing.

> **Model answer**
>
> My name is Carla.
> This is my family.
> This is my mother, Anna. She is 60 years old.
> This is my father, Tim. He is 62 years old.
> I have two brothers and one sister.
> My sister is 27 years old. My brother is 20 years old.
> We are from the UK.

> **Objectives review**
>
> See Introduction on p. 7 for ideas about using the Objectives review with your students.
>
> **WORDLIST AND GLOSSARY**
>
> See Introduction on p. 7 for ideas about using the Wordlist at the end of each unit and the Glossary at the end of the book with your students.
>
> **REVIEW TEST**
>
> See esource.cambridge.org for the Review test and ideas about how and when to administer the Review test.

RESEARCH PROJECT

> **Conduct an online survey and present the results.**
>
> Show the class a website where they can create an online survey. (If this is not appropriate for your context, students could do the survey on paper.) Divide the class into groups and tell them each group needs to create a survey about things people have. Tell them they should ask four questions about one of these devices: camera, car, computer, mobile phone.
>
> Tell students that each group will give a presentation using the information they get from the survey. Let students know how long their presentations should be (2–3 minutes).
>
> Allow students class time to create the survey. They should share the survey online with their friends and family. (If this is not appropriate for your context, students could do the survey on paper around the university.) Give students class time during the next lesson to look at their results and plan their presentations. You could help them with ideas for how to present their results:
>
> *10 people have two mobile phones.*
> *20 people have one mobile phone.*
> *25 people have HP computers.*
>
> Students should give their presentations in the next lesson.

3 UNIVERSITY LIFE

UNLOCK YOUR KNOWLEDGE

Focus on the photograph and point out the questions. Ask a student to read each question aloud. Students work in groups and answer the questions. Take feedback as a class.

> **Answers**
> 1 Students and their teacher
> 2 University
> 3 Students' own answers (yes or no, age of university)

LISTENING AND READING 1

> **Learning objectives**
> - Name university subjects – *Maths, Chemistry, English, Biology, History, IT, Business, Japanese*
> - Ask about subjects people study – *What subjects do you study?*
> - Talk about subjects you study – *I study Maths, English and Business.*
> - Use capital letters in subjects correctly – *Maths, Chemistry*
> - Gain awareness of the sound of the letters *sh* and *ch* – *English, teacher, Chemistry*
> - Use commas (,) and the word *and* correctly – *I study Biology, English and Japanese.*
>
> See p. 6 for suggestions on how to use these Learning objectives in your lessons.

> **Lead-in**
>
> Write: *University* as a heading on the board. Then write these words on the board, one word at a time, letter by letter: *student, class, teacher, English*. Stop after each letter and encourage students to guess the word. If a student gives you the correct word, ask the rest of the class to spell out the remaining letters. Say: *How do you spell that?*
>
> Say: *I am an English teacher.* Write: *English teacher* on the board. Then write _____ *teacher* underneath. Explore students' knowledge of subject names in English by eliciting more kinds of teacher. You could give clues, such as drawing mathematical symbols. Here are some examples of subjects: *Maths, History, Science, Business.*

VOCABULARY: SUBJECTS

1 🔊 3.1 👥 Focus on the photographs and the subject names in the book. Ask students to listen and read. Play the audio. Encourage students to follow the audio by pointing in the book at each subject name as they hear it. Drill the names of the subjects. See p. 9 for advice on drilling. Check understanding using printable Flashcards 3.1. Go to esource.cambridge.org to print the flashcards.

Demonstrate the next part of the exercise with a student. Point to a subject and encourage a student to say the correct word. Then encourage the student to point at a subject and say the correct word yourself. Students work in pairs. Monitor and correct any mistakes with vocabulary or pronunciation.

If you wish to make this topic relevant to students already studying at university, you will need to make a list of the types of subjects they study other than English. Write them in English on the board and use realia such as timetables, subject books or photographs to deal with the meanings. Drill the pronunciation. Allow students to use these subjects in any tasks which involve personalization in this unit.

ACADEMIC WRITING SKILLS

2 👤 Point at Maths in Exercise 1. Write: *_aths* on the board. Point at the space before the letter *a* and elicit the letter *m*. Write capital *M* and say: *Maths*.

Focus students on the words with missing capital letters. Students work individually and complete the exercise. With stronger classes, ask students to cover Exercise 3 as they complete the exercise. Go through answers as a class.

> **Answers**
> 2 Chemistry 3 English 4 Biology 5 History
> 6 Business 7 IT 8 Japanese

UNLOCK BASIC SKILLS TEACHER'S BOOK   45

SOUND AND SPELLING: *sh, ch*

3 🔊 3.2 👤 Focus students on the words with missing letters and the words in Exercise 1. Students work individually and complete the exercise. Go through the answers on the board as a class. Focus on the letters (*sh, ch*) in *English* and *teacher*. Say the letters and then the sounds: *English, s-h*, /ʃ/ and *teacher, c-h*, /tʃ/. Drill the sounds and then the words.

Focus on the irregular sound of *Ch* in *Chemistry*. Say: *Chemistry. Can you hear* /tʃ/? (no). Elicit that *ch* here makes the sound /k/. Do not drill *Chemistry* again as it is not a regular sound of *ch*.

> **Answers**
> 1 English 2 teacher 3 Chemistry

LISTENING FOR KEY INFORMATION

4 🔊 3.3 👤👥 Focus on the photographs. Ask: *Are they students?* (yes). Ask: *What are their names?* (Nur, Yasemin, Paul and Marco). Focus on the four subjects in the box next to each photograph. Say: *Read* and give students a few moments to recognize the subject words. Say: *Listen and circle three subjects* and demonstrate circling three of the subjects next to Nur's photograph. Play the audio for students to listen and circle the correct words. Go through answers as a class.

Focus on the question in the speech bubble at the top of the exercise. Say: *What subjects do you study?* Drill the question. Then drill the responses (I study Maths, Business and IT., etc.). See p. 9 for advice on drilling.

Demonstrate the exercise with a student. Ask: *What subjects do you study?* Point at Nur's subjects and elicit a correct response using a full sentence from the student, e.g. *I study Maths, Business and IT.* Encourage the student to point at Yasemin's subjects and ask *What subjects do you study?* You respond, *I study History, English and Japanese.* Students work in pairs and practise the exchanges.

> **Answers**
> **Nur:** Maths Business IT
> **Yasemin:** History English Japanese
> **Paul:** English Maths IT
> **Marco:** Biology Chemistry English

LISTENING FOR KEY INFORMATION

5 🔊 3.4 👤 Focus on the sentences. Play the audio and ask students to listen and read the sentences. Point to the photographs of the people in Exercise 4. Read the example sentence aloud. Say: *yes or no?* in a questioning tone. Read the list of three subjects that students circled for Nur in Exercise 4. Elicit: *no*. Students work individually and circle *Yes* or *No*.

> **Answers**
> 1 No (Maths, Business and IT)
> 2 No (History, English and Japanese)
> 3 No (English, Maths and IT)
> 4 Yes

ACADEMIC WRITING SKILLS

6 👤 Write two subjects on the board with a gap between them: *Maths Chemistry*. Elicit the word *and*. Now write three subjects on the board with gaps between them: *Maths Biology Chemistry*. Encourage students to try to fill the first gap.

Focus on the sentences in Exercise 6. Elicit the comma (,) and the *and*. Complete the second line on the board with a comma and *and*. Tell students the name of the symbol is a comma. Drill the phrase on the board with a pause to indicate the comma.

Focus on sentence 1 and read it aloud. Demonstrate circling the comma and the word *and* in the book. Ask students to read the sentences and circle the comma and the word *and*. Students work individually. Go through answers as a class.

READING AND WRITING

7 🔊 3.5 👤 Focus students on the sentences and the photographs. Ask: *What subject is this?* and point to the photograph that represents English. Say: *I study English …* in the first sentence. Point at the next photograph and say: *What subject is this?* (Chemistry). Demonstrate writing *Chemistry* in the first gap. Students work individually and complete the sentences. Play the audio for students to listen and check. Ask individual students to read out each sentence to the class.

> **Answers**
> 1 Chemistry, IT 2 History, Biology 3 Business, Maths

| UNIVERSITY LIFE | UNIT 3 |

SPEAKING

8 Divide the class into Student As and Student Bs. Say: *Student As go to page 200. Student Bs go to page 203*. Demonstrate turning to one of these pages in the book to ensure students understand. Focus on the REMEMBER box and read through the sentences as a class. Focus on the *Your subjects* box. Ask students to read the subjects there silently.

Ask Student As to speak first by asking: *What subjects do you study?* Student Bs answer. Then students swap roles.

> **Optional activity**
>
> **Chain sentences:** Follow the procedure on p. 11.
> 1 English, Maths and Biology
> 2 study English, Maths and Biology
> 3 I study English, Maths and Biology.

LISTENING AND READING 2

> **Learning objectives**
>
> - Name days of the week – *Sunday, Monday, Tuesday, Wednesday, Thursday, Friday, Saturday*
> - Use capital letters in days of the week correctly – *Sunday, Monday*
> - Read a detailed timetable
> - Understand people giving details about their timetables
> - Ask questions with question words when and where – *Where is our English class? When is our English class?*
>
> See p. 6 for suggestions on how to use these Learning objectives in your lessons.

> **Lead-in**
>
> You will need printable Flashcards 3.1. Go to esource.cambridge.org to print the flashcards. You need the cards with photographs only.
>
> Divide the class into teams. Hold up one card. Elicit the vocabulary item (e.g. Chemistry). Hold up two cards together. Elicit the vocabulary items, (e.g. English, Chemistry). Say: *English and Chemistry*. Divide the class into two teams. Hold up the cards, two at a time. Students knock on the desk if they can remember both the subject names. Award a point for each correct answer using *and*. Deduct a mark for not using *and* or long pauses. The first team to get five points is the winner.

VOCABULARY: DAYS OF THE WEEK

1 🔊 3.6 Focus on the calendar and the days of the week. Ask students to listen and read. Play the audio. Encourage students to follow the audio by pointing in the book at each day of the week as they hear it. Drill the names of the days of the week. See p. 9 for advice on drilling.

Demonstrate the next part of the exercise with a student. Point to a day of the week and encourage a student to say the correct word. Then encourage the student to point at a day of the week and say the correct word yourself. Students work in pairs. Monitor and correct any mistakes with vocabulary or pronunciation.

ACADEMIC WRITING SKILLS

2 Point at *Sunday* in the calendar in Exercise 1. Write: *_unday* on the board. Point at the space before the letter *u* and elicit the letter *s*. Write capital: *S* and say: *Sunday*.

Focus students on the words with missing capital letters. Students work individually and complete the exercise. Go through answers on the board as a class.

> **Answers**
>
> 2 <u>M</u>onday 3 <u>T</u>uesday 4 <u>W</u>ednesday 5 <u>T</u>hursday
> 6 <u>F</u>riday 7 <u>S</u>aturday

> **NOTICE**
>
> Write: *Mon_ _ _ Tues_ _ _ Wednes_ _ _* on the board. Focus on the NOTICE box and read the days of the week. Elicit the spelling of the highlighted letters. If appropriate for your context, invite three students to the board to complete the words. If not, ask students to spell out the words on the board (all the letters, not just *day*) and write as they say them. Drill the words, stressing the first syllable.

> **Optional activity**
>
> Write the days of the week out of order on the board. Focus on *Sunday* and elicit: *Sunday*. Say: *What next?* and indicate the words on the board. Students work individually and write the names of the days of the week in order on a piece of paper or in their notebooks. Monitor and check spelling and use of capital letters. Students work in pairs and compare their answers. Students check their answers with the calendar in Exercise 1.

UNL⌀CK BASIC SKILLS TEACHER'S BOOK 47

3 👤 Focus on the timetable in Exercise 3. Focus on the words *morning* and *afternoon* on the timetable. Ask: *Is it morning now?* (your own answer), *Is it afternoon now?* (your own answer). Focus again on the timetable and the days of the week. Elicit which days are missing. Students write in the missing days. Monitor and check spelling. Stronger students could cover up the days of the week in Exercise 1. Weaker classes can use Exercise 1 for support. Go through answers with the class. Write each missing day on the board one letter at a time, eliciting the correct spelling from class.

> **Answers**
> Monday Thursday

READING FOR KEY INFORMATION

4 🔊 3.7 👤 Focus on the timetable in Exercise 3 and the subjects in Exercise 4. Say: *Read and match* pointing at the options in the right column. Students work individually, looking at the timetable and matching the classes to the correct option. Say: *Listen and check.* Play the audio. Go through answers as a class.

> **Answers**
> 1 Thursday afternoon 2 Wednesday morning
> 3 Room 24

LISTENING FOR DETAIL

5 🔊 3.8 👤 Focus on the timetable in Exercise 3 again. Point out the three gaps where there is missing information. Point at the first gap. Say: *Where is English? Listen and write.* Play the audio. Students work individually and write the room numbers in the gaps in the timetable. Go through answers as a class. Ask questions *Where is the English class on Sunday morning?* etc. to elicit the answers from the class.

> **Answers**
>
> | | Sunday | Monday | Tuesday | Wednesday | Thursday |
> |---|---|---|---|---|---|
> | **MORNING** | English Room 11 | History Room 11 | IT Room 24 | Chemistry Room 21 | Biology Room 17 |
> | 12:00–1:00 | | | | | |
> | **AFTERNOON** | History Room 13 | Chemistry Room 21 | Maths Room 13 | English Room 11 | Business Room 18 |

GRAMMAR: *WHEN / WHERE* AND *IN / ON*

6 🔊 3.9 👤 Focus on the grammar table in the book. Point out the highlighted words. Play the audio for students to listen and read. Drill the questions and answers. See p. 9 for advice on drilling. Check understanding by eliciting more possible answers to each question. Then ask more questions about the timetable in Exercise 3.

7 🔊 3.10 👤 Focus on the options under the line in dialogue 1. Read the dialogue aloud including the options and the answer to the question. Ask: *In or On?* (In), *Where or When?* (Where). Read the correct question aloud: *Where is our IT class?* Demonstrate circling the correct option under the line in the book. Say: *Read and circle.* Students work individually and circle the correct options. Play the audio for students to listen and check. Go through answers as a class. Then ask students to write the correct answers in the gaps. Monitor and check students' spelling and use of capital letters.

> **Answers**
> 2 On 3 In 4 When

WRITING AND SPEAKING

8 👤👥 Focus on the empty timetable and ask a student: *When is your English class? Where is your English class?* Elicit the day, the time of day and room number. Demonstrate writing the information in the correct columns in the book. Point out the two additional subjects (Business and Chemistry). Demonstrate thinking and writing some imaginary information about these two subjects. Students work individually and complete the timetable with their days, time, and room numbers. Monitor and check spelling and use of capitals on days of the week.

Focus on the REMEMBER box and read through the phrases as a class. Elicit variations to complete the phrases, e.g. When is your (Business) class? Where is your (Chemistry) class? On (Monday) morning. In room (12), etc.

Focus on the timetable. Demonstrate the exercise with a student. Ask: *When is your English class?* Elicit a correct response from the student (On (day) (morning/afternoon).). Students work in pairs, taking turns to ask questions. Monitor and check use of correct question forms and spelling of days and numbers. Ask students to swap notebooks and check each other's writing.

UNIVERSITY LIFE — UNIT 3

LISTENING AND READING 3

Learning objectives

- Name basic adjectives – *boring, interesting, easy, difficult*
- Understand people's opinions about subjects they study – *Biology is not boring. It is interesting.*
- Use the verb *be* with *it* – *It is interesting. It is not boring.*
- Gain awareness of sound and spelling of letter *s* in *it's* and *isn't*
- Read and write about university subjects

See p. 6 for suggestions on how to use these Learning objectives in your lessons.

Lead-in

Write the following schedule with six mistakes (shown here in bold) on the board.

sunday morning	English	Room 11
Monday **efternoon**	maths	Room 13
Tusday afternoon	It	**Rom** 9

Students work in pairs. Ask them to find the six mistakes as quickly as possible. When a pair finishes, stop the rest of the class. Ask them to tell you the six mistakes and the corrections.

VOCABULARY: ADJECTIVES

1 (♪ 3.11) Focus on the photographs. Play the audio for students to listen. Encourage students to follow the audio by pointing at each adjective as they hear it. Drill the adjectives. See p. 9 for advice on drilling.

Demonstrate the next part of the exercise with a student. Point to a photograph and encourage a student to say the correct word. Then encourage the student to point at a photograph and say the correct word yourself. Students work in pairs. Monitor and correct any mistakes with vocabulary or pronunciation.

Check understanding of these words further using the opposite adjectives. Write the word *easy* on the board and then write a cross ✗. Elicit the word *difficult*. Repeat for the other adjectives in the set.

You could also elicit some examples of subjects or other things your students find interesting, difficult, etc. However, these answers will naturally tend to be quite subjective, so it will not be a clear indicator of understanding.

LISTENING FOR KEY INFORMATION

2 (♪ 3.12) Focus on the names next to the sentences (Toki, Robert, Rashid). Read the sentence for each person aloud. Say: *Listen.* and *Write 1, 2 or 3*. Demonstrate writing a number in one of the boxes. Play the audio for students to listen and put the people in the order they appear in the audio. Go through answers as a class.

> **Answers**
>
> Rashid and Tahir 1   Toki 2   Robert 3

LISTENING FOR DETAIL

3 (♪ 3.12) Focus on the photographs in Exercise 2. Ask: *Who's this?* and point to Rashid in the photograph and his sentence in Exercise 2 (1 Rashid). Repeat for the other photographs (2 Toki, 3 Robert). Focus on the dialogue and the options next to the subject names. Say: *Listen and circle*. Demonstrate circling the word *easy* in the book. Play the audio. Students work individually, listening and circling the answers. Students work in pairs and check their answers. Go through answers as a class.

Drill the questions and answers in the speech bubbles. See p. 9 for advice on drilling exchanges.

> **Answers**
>
> 2 interesting   3 difficult

GRAMMAR: VERB *BE*: IT

4 (♪ 3.13) Write this short dialogue on the board:

What's Maths like?

Maths is interesting.

Focus on the first line in the grammar table in the book and then back on the second sentence on the board. Ask: *What's different?* and look from the board to the book. Elicit: *It*. Change the sentence on the board to *It is interesting*. Circle *Maths* in the question and *it* in the sentence and draw an arrow from *Maths* to *interesting*. Now write these sentences on the board: *Maths is interesting. Maths is not boring.*

UNLOCK BASIC SKILLS TEACHER'S BOOK   49

Focus on the second part of the grammar table and then back on the second sentence on the board. Ask: *What's different?* and look from the board to the book. Repeat the procedure above to elicit *It* in place of *Maths* in the second sentence. Underline *not boring* in the sentence. Ask: *Is Maths boring?* (no), *Is Maths interesting?* (yes). Play the audio and drill the sentences in the grammar table.

> **NOTICE**
>
> Write: *It's boring.* on the board. Circle and say: *It's.* Then write: *It is boring.* underneath the sentence. Point at *It's* and encourage students to say the word. Then point at *It is.* Say: *Say It's. Write It is.* Repeat for *It isn't interesting.*
> Focus on the NOTICE box in the book. Allow students a minute to read the information there.

> **Optional activity**
>
> **Aural dictation (contractions):** Follow the procedure on p. 11.
> 1 *It's easy. (It is easy.)*
> 2 *English isn't boring. (English is not boring.)*
> 3 *It isn't difficult. (It is not difficult.)*

5 (3.14) Focus on the options under the line in item 1. Read sentence 1 aloud including the options. Ask: *Difficult or easy?* (easy), *Is not easy or Is easy?* (is easy). Read the correct sentence aloud (*Chemistry is not difficult. It is easy.*). Demonstrate circling the correct option under the line in the book. Say: *Read and circle.* Students work individually and circle the correct options. Play the audio for students to listen and check. Go through answers as a class. Then ask students to write the correct answers in the gaps. Monitor and help as necessary.

> **Answers**
> 2 is 3 is not 4 is not

SOUND AND SPELLING: s

6 (3.15) Focus on the highlighted letters. Play the audio for students to listen and read. Play the audio again for students to listen and repeat. Write the sentences on the board and underline the words with main stress.

It'**s** *boring*. It'**s** *difficult*.
It *isn't* boring. It *isn't* difficult.

Drill the sentences and clap or make an appropriate hand movement to emphasize the stressed words. For advice on drilling see p. 9. Encourage students to clap with you.

7 (3.16) Focus on the sentences and point out the options. Say: *It's interesting.* Demonstrate circling *'s* in the first item in the book. Say: *Listen and circle.* Play the audio. Students work individually, listening and circling the correct options. Students compare answers in pairs. Play the audio again for students to check answers. Students work in pairs and practise saying the sentences. Monitor and correct errors with main stress.

> **Answers**
> 2 isn't 3 's 4 isn't

SPEAKING

> ⦿ **Common student errors**
>
> **The verb be:** Japanese L1 learners often leave out the verb *be* with adjectives, because in Japanese, adjectives can be inflected. Here are some examples of this error:
> *My English bad.*
> *Biology interesting.*

8 Focus on the REMEMBER box and read through the phrases as a class. Elicit variations to complete the question: *What's (Maths/English) like?* using different subject vocabulary.

Focus on the survey. Point out the two completed subjects and the space to write their own subject. Demonstrate writing a subject of your choice on the line. Ask students to write a subject on the line.

Demonstrate the exercise with a student. Ask: *What's English like?* Elicit a correct response from the student, e.g. *It's easy. It's interesting.* Demonstrate circling the answers in the book. Students work in pairs, taking turns to ask questions and circle the answers or to answer questions. Monitor and check students are recording their partner's answers.

READING AND WRITING

9 Demonstrate the exercise using students' answers from Exercise 8 to complete the sentences. Students work individually. Monitor and check that students are writing full forms, not contractions. Ask students to swap books and check each other's writing.

WATCH AND REMEMBER

Learning objectives
- Understand information about what people study – *I study Business/Japanese/Chemistry.*
- Understand information when and where classes take place – *It's at 9 o'clock … It's in room 42.*
- Practise talking about your own classes and what you think of them – *My class is interesting.*

See p. 6 for suggestions on how to use these Learning objectives in your lessons.

Lead-in
Write: *What subjects do you study?* on the board. In weaker classes, use Flashcards 3.1 to revise vocabulary.

Ask students to tell you or a partner about what subjects they are studying.

PART 1

In Part 1, four students talk about the subject which they are studying.

BEFORE YOU WATCH

1 Focus on the photographs and the subjects. Students work individually and match.

2 (3.17) Play the audio for students to listen and check their answers in Exercise 1. Go through answers as a class. Students work individually and write the subject names under the photographs. Monitor and check students' handwriting. Drill the pronunciation of *business* /bɪznɪs/. See p. 9 for advice on drilling.

> **Answers**
> 1 c 2 a 3 b

WATCH

3 Focus on the names in the sentences and the options. Point at the completed example. Students watch Part 1 and circle the correct answer. Go through answers as a class.

> **Answers**
> 2 IT 3 Japanese 4 Chemistry

AFTER YOU WATCH

In stronger classes, Exercise 4 should be completed by students after watching Part 1. In weaker classes, students can watch Part 1 again and complete Exercise 4 or use the audio script at the back of the book.

4 Tell students to try and remember the information from the video. Students work individually, reading the sentences and completing the gaps. Students work in pairs and check their answers. Monitor and check students' handwriting. In weaker classes, play Part 1 again or use the audio script on Student's Book p. 217. Go through answers as a class. In feedback, you could point out that *student* and *study* are in the same word family – this can be a good way to build vocabulary.

> **Answers**
> student, study, interesting

PART 2

In Part 2, the same students talk about when and where their classes take place. A professor gives information about a timetable.

BEFORE YOU WATCH

5 Focus on the pictures with the room numbers and the completed example. Students work individually and complete the gapped sentences. Monitor and check for capital letters at the start of days of the week.

> **Answers**
> 2 Tuesday, room, 56 3 Thursday, 42

WATCH

6 Focus on the sentences said by the students and the options. Students watch Part 2, read the sentences, and circle the correct options. Go through answers as a class.

> **Answers**
> 2 Monday 3 Tuesday 4 Friday

AFTER YOU WATCH

7 Focus on the timetable and the correction to the room number on Monday. Students correct any errors. If they are finding this difficult, tell them there are two more corrections and use the audio script on Student's Book p. 217. Go through answers as a class.

> **Answers**
> Tuesday: Room 22 Wednesday: Room 13

PART 3

In Part 3, students remember key information from the lesson.

REMEMBER

8 ▶ 👥 Ask students what kind of information there should be in sentences 1–4 (a subject). Students watch Part 3, answer the questions, and complete the sentences. Students work in pairs and check their answers. Go through answers as a class.

> **Answers**
> 1 Business 2 IT 3 Japanese 4 Chemistry

MORE VOCABULARY: WHAT FLOOR IS IT ON?

9 👥 Focus on the words in the box and the words with photographs. Students fill in the missing words. Students work in pairs and check their answers. Go through answers as a class. Drill the pronunciation of first, second, third and fourth. See p. 9 for advice on drilling.

> **Answers**
> 2 second 3 third 1 first

ASK AND ANSWER

10 👥 In groups, students practise asking and answering the questions. Change groups to give them more opportunities to practise.

> **Optional activity**
> Extend Exercise 10 by asking students to work in pairs again. Students compare their answers, noting the similarities and differences.

👁 LANGUAGE FOCUS

> **Learning objectives**
> - Identify and say the times of the day – *nine o'clock, seven-thirty*
> - Ask and answer questions about time – *What time is it? It's ten o'clock.*
> - Use the preposition *at* with times – *It's at 10:00.*
> - Understand when people talk about time
> - Use main stress correctly when giving time
>
> See p. 6 for suggestions on how to use these Learning objectives in your lessons.

> **Lead-in**
> Write the following times on the board. Draw rectangles around them to indicate that they are digital clock times.
> 07:00, 02:30, 17:30, 10:30, 14:30, 23:30, 20:00
> Ask about the first time: *Is it morning, afternoon, evening or night?* (morning). Elicit the correct period of the day for all the other times.
> Now explore your students' knowledge of the vocabulary area in English. Ask about the first time: *What time is it?* (seven o'clock). Do not try to pre-teach the times. Accept all answers.

VOCABULARY: TIME

1 🔊 3.18 👥 Focus on the pictures. Point out the digital clocks. Ask students to listen and read. Play the audio. Encourage students to follow the audio by pointing in the book as they hear it. Drill the sentences. See p. 9 for advice on drilling.

Demonstrate the next part of the exercise with a student. Point to a picture and encourage a student to say the correct time. Then encourage the student to point and say the time yourself. Students work in pairs. Monitor and correct any errors with vocabulary or pronunciation.

2 🔊 3.19 👤 Focus on the clocks. Ask: *What time is it?* about each one. Encourage students to answer, but do not confirm if they are right or wrong. Focus on sentences 1–4. Point out the boxes at the end of the sentences. Say: *Read, match and write the letter in the box.* Demonstrate reading and looking at the clocks and writing a letter in the first box. Students work individually, reading and matching the sentences to the clocks. Play the audio for students to listen and check. Go through answers as a class. Drill the question *What time is it?* and answers 1–4 with the class. See p. 9 for advice on drilling exchanges.

> **Answers**
> 2 D 3 C 4 B

SPEAKING

3 👥 Focus on the speech bubble. Encourage a student to ask you the question: *What time is it?* and give them the actual time. Students work in pairs and take turns to ask and answer about the clocks. Monitor and check that they use the complete expressions. In weaker classes, extend this exercise by asking students to use the clocks from Exercises 1 and 2 as well. Go through the answers to Exercise 3 orally, eliciting the times from students.

UNIVERSITY LIFE — UNIT 3

> **Answers**
> It's eight o'clock. It's eleven o'clock. It's two-thirty. It's twelve-thirty.

LISTENING AND WRITING

4 🔊 3.20 Focus on the photograph. Say: *Who are they?* (students), *What time is it?* (ten-thirty). Focus on the speech bubbles. Point out the gapped times. Say: *Listen and read.* Play the audio. Encourage students to follow the text in the speech bubbles by pointing to each word as they listen. Play the audio again and encourage students to write the missing times in the gaps. Go through answers as a class on the board.

> **Answers**
> 10:00   10:30

> **NOTICE**
> Focus on the NOTICE box. Read the questions and answers aloud. Point out the highlighted word *at*. Look at your watch or the clock on a mobile phone. Ask: *What time is it?* Write the real time on the board. Then ask: *What time is the English class?* Elicit: *at* + the real start time and write it on the board. Underline *at*. Ask about the time of different classes and elicit the full answer with *at*, e.g. *It's at two o'clock.*

PRONUNCIATION FOR SPEAKING

5 🔊 3.21 Focus on the sentences and point out the underlined words. Play the audio and clap or make an appropriate hand movement to emphasize the stressed words. Drill the main stress as a class. For advice on drilling see p. 9. Encourage students to clap with you.

LISTENING FOR DETAIL

6 🔊 3.22 Focus on the exchanges. Read the first exchange aloud. Say: *Yes or no?* in a questioning tone. Play the audio. Students work individually and circle *Yes* or *No* for each exchange. Play the audio again if necessary.

Students work in pairs and go through their answers. Then go through answers as a class. You could use the audio script on Student's Book p. 218 to show students in which line the information is. Read the script aloud. Students follow in their books and identify the relevant parts of the text.

> **Answers**
> 2 Yes 3 No

> **Optional activity**
> **Aural gap fill:** Follow the procedure on p. 12.
> 1 What time is our English class? It's <u>at</u> 5 o'clock.
> 2 When is our English class? It's <u>on</u> Monday.
> 3 Where is our English class? It's <u>in</u> room 21.
> 4 <u>When</u> is our Chemistry class? It's on Tuesday.
> 5 <u>What time</u> is our Chemistry class? It's at four-thirty.
> 6 <u>Where</u> is our Chemistry class? It's in room 4.

SPEAKING

7 Divide the class into Student As and Student Bs. Tell Student As to turn to Student's Book p. 200 and Student Bs to Student's Book p. 203. Point out the gaps in the two timetables. Focus on the Remember box and practise the phrases as a class. Tell students to sit facing each other in pairs.

Students As start by asking a question about a class and Students Bs answer giving the information from the timetable. Monitor and note any errors, especially with prepositions. Use the notes you made for feedback at the end of the exercise. See p. 8 for advice on conducting feedback on speaking activities.

Answers

	Sunday	Monday	Tuesday	Wednesday	Thursday
morning 8:00–9:30	IT	Chemistry	Business		Biology
10:00–11:30		English		Chemistry	
afternoon 1:30–3:00	Business		IT	English	

ACADEMIC LISTENING AND SPEAKING

> **Learning objectives**
> - Ask and talk about your subjects, when and where you have lessons – *When is your … class? What time is your … class? Where is your … class?*
> - Listen and identify when and where lessons take place
> - CT: Transfer information from a note to a timetable
> - Gain awareness of intonation used in *Wh* questions
>
> See p. 6 for suggestions on how to use these Learning objectives in your lessons.

UNLOCK BASIC SKILLS TEACHER'S BOOK   53

> **Lead-in**
>
> **Mingle**: Follow the procedure on p. 12.
> 1 What subjects do you study?
> 2 Where is your English class?
> 3 When is your English class?
> 4 What's English like?
> 5 What time is your English class?
>
> **Alternative to mingling**: Follow the procedure on p. 12.

PREPARING TO LISTEN

1 Focus on questions 1–4 and ask a student to read them aloud. Point out the completed example by tracing the line from *What subjects do you study?* to the correct answer in the book. Students work individually to complete the exercise and then compare their answers in pairs. Go through answers as a class. Then students work in pairs and practise the exchanges. Monitor and check pronunciation. Students swap roles.

> **Answers**
> 2 It's on Wednesday at 3 o'clock.
> 3 It's in room 16.
> 4 It isn't easy.

> **NOTICE**
>
> Write this sentence on the board: English is __ Monday __ five o'clock. Focus on the NOTICE box. Point out the highlighted prepositions and elicit these from students to complete the sentence on the board (English is on Monday at five o'clock.). Focus on the sentence in the NOTICE box again.
> Ask: *When is the class?* and elicit: *It's on Wednesday.*
> Ask: *What time is the class?* and elicit: *It's at 3 o'clock.*

2 (3.23) Focus on the gapped sentences and the prepositions in the box. Students work individually and complete the sentences with the correct prepositions. Monitor and check that students are reading carefully. Play the audio for students to listen and check their answers. Drill the sentences 1–4. See p. 9 for advice on drilling.

> **Answers**
> 1 at 2 at, on 3 on, at 4 at, on

LISTENING FOR MAIN IDEAS

3 (3.24) Focus on the photograph. Read out sentences 1–2 and point out the options. Play the audio. Students work individually, listening and circling the correct options. Go through answers as a class.

> **Answers**
> 1 students 2 Business

LISTENING FOR KEY INFORMATION

4 (3.24) Ask students to read the sentences in the notebook. Point out the options. Play the audio. Students work individually, listening and circling the correct options. Students compare their answers in pairs. Play the audio again if necessary. Go through answers as a class. Use the script on Student's Book p. 218 to go through the answers with weaker classes.

> **Answers**
>
> Amal is a <u>student</u>.
> Her Business class is on <u>Tuesday</u> afternoon at <u>1:30</u>. It's in room <u>43</u>.
> Her Business class is not <u>easy</u>.

CRITICAL THINKING: UNDERSTAND

5 Focus on the timetable. Point out the *Student name* at the top (Amal Sabry) and the completed gap next to *Day* (Tuesday). Point out the remaining gaps. Encourage students to read the timetable themselves and tell you what information is missing (a time, a subject, a room). Tell students to look at Exercise 4 and find the information they need. Students work individually and complete the timetable. Go through the answers as a class, asking students to show you where they found the information in Exercise 4.

> **Answers**
>
> **STUDENT NAME:** Amal Sabry
> **CLASS:** GH642
> **DAY:** <u>Tuesday</u>
>
> | TIME | SUBJECT | ROOM |
> | --- | --- | --- |
> | 9:00–10:30 | Maths | 35 |
> | 11:00–12:00 | IT | 24 |
> | <u>1:30</u> –3:00 | <u>Business</u> | <u>43</u> |

UNIVERSITY LIFE   UNIT 3

PRONUNCIATION FOR SPEAKING

6 ◀) 3.25 Focus on the questions and point out the highlighted words. Play the audio and clap or make an appropriate hand movement to emphasize the main stress. Drill the questions as a class. For advice on drilling see p. 9. Encourage students to clap with you.

> **Optional activity**
>
> You will need printable Flashcards 3.1. Go to esource.cambridge.org to print the flashcards. You need the sides of the cards with pictures only.
>
> Review *What is … like?* questions and the following adjectives: *interesting, boring, easy, difficult*. Write the adjectives on the board. Review the pronunciation and drill the words again if necessary.
>
> Hold up one card. Elicit the vocabulary item (e.g. Chemistry). Elicit the question: *What's Chemistry like?* Demonstrate the exercise with a student. Ask: *What's Chemistry like?* Encourage the student to answer by pointing at the adjectives on the board, e.g. *It's boring. It isn't interesting.*
>
> Divide the class into Student As and Student Bs. Students work in pairs. Hold up one card at a time. Student As ask Student Bs a question and Student Bs answer. Then Student Bs ask the question and Student As answer. Then hold up a new card. Continue with all of the subjects.

CRITICAL THINKING: EVALUATE

7 Focus on the empty timetable and ask a student: *When is your English class? Where is your English class?* Elicit the day, time of day and room. Demonstrate writing the information in the correct gaps in the book. Point out the two additional subjects (Biology and Chemistry). Demonstrate thinking and writing some imaginary information about these two subjects. Students work individually and complete the timetable with their times and room numbers. Ask students to swap notebooks and check each other's writing.

SPEAKING TASK

8 Focus on the REMEMBER box and read through the questions as a class. Elicit variations to complete the phrases, e.g. *When is your (Business) class? Where is your (Chemistry) class? What time is your Business class? What is your English class like?*

Focus on the timetable. Demonstrate the exercise with a student. Ask: *When is your English class?* Elicit a correct response from the student. Students work in pairs, taking turns to ask and answer questions. Monitor and check use of correct question intonation.

> **Model answers**
>
> **A:** When is your English class?
> **B:** On Thursday morning at 10 o'clock.
> **A:** Where is your English class?
> **B:** In room 5.
>
> **A:** When is your Biology class?
> **B:** On Thursday at 12:30.
> **A:** Where is your Biology class?
> **B:** In room 7.
>
> **A:** When is your Chemistry class?
> **B:** On Thursday afternoon at 2:00.
> **A:** Where is your Chemistry class?
> **B:** In room 10.

ACADEMIC READING AND WRITING

> **Learning objectives**
>
> - Read and identify key information in an email
> - Understand and use prepositions – *in, on, at*
> - CT: Identify key information in a note and transfer it to a timetable
> - Prepare a timetable for your own classes
> - Write about your classes saying when and where they take place
>
> See p. 6 for suggestions on how to use these Learning objectives in your lessons.

> **Lead-in**
>
> **Classroom messages:** Follow the procedure on p. 12.
> 1 *Maths is on Thursday morning.*
> 2 *History is in room 13.*
> 3 *IT isn't interesting.*
>
> Ask the last student to receive each message to write it down. Correct these sentences (if necessary) as a class.

PREPARING TO READ

1 ◀) 3.26 Focus on the photographs. Play the audio for students to listen and read. Encourage students to follow the audio by pointing in the book at each word as they hear it. Drill the words and check understanding. See p. 9 for advice on drilling.

UNLOCK BASIC SKILLS TEACHER'S BOOK   55

READING FOR MAIN IDEAS

2 🔊 3.27 👤 Focus on the email. Read out sentences 1 and 2 and point out the options. Point out the headers on the email (*From / Subject / Dear* …) and the sign off (*Dr Mohamed Khan*). Encourage students to use these to choose the correct option for each sentence. Play the audio for students to listen, read, and check their answers. Go through answers as a class. Point out or elicit the clues in the headers and sign off (*your timetable, Dear students, Dr Mohamed Khan*).

> **Answers**
> 1 a teacher 2 a timetable

SCANNING FOR KEY INFORMATION

3 👥 Focus on the timetable. Ask: *When is the IT class? Where is the IT class?*, etc. Point out the amendment of *Business* to *Maths* in handwriting. Focus on the email and read the first bulleted sentence together (Maths is on Sunday and Tuesday at 11 o'clock.). Use the headings in the timetable to show the amendment on Sunday at 11 o'clock is correct. On the timetable, point to 11 o'clock on Tuesday. Say: *Maths* in a questioning tone. Elicit that the timetable is incorrect. Demonstrate crossing out *History* and writing *Maths*. Ask students to read the email and correct the timetable. Students work in pairs and compare their answers. Go through the answers as a class, asking individual students to tell you an amendment they made to the timetable.

> **Answers**
>
> | TIME | SUNDAY | MONDAY | TUESDAY | WEDNESDAY | THURSDAY |
> |---|---|---|---|---|---|
> | 9:00–10:30 | English Room 12 | English Room 12 | English Room ~~12~~ 22 | English Room 12 | English Room 12 |
> | 11:00–12:30 | ~~Business~~ Maths Room 4 | Chemistry Room ~~8~~ 14 | ~~History~~ Maths Room 11 | Chemistry Room ~~8~~ 14 | English Room 12 |
> | 1:30–3:00 | IT Room 23 | Biology Room 8 | History Room 12 | Biology Room 8 | IT Room ~~23~~ 13 |

CRITICAL THINKING: ANALYZE

4 🔊 3.28 👥 Focus on the gapped timetable and then the handwritten notes. Ask students to listen and read. Play the audio. Encourage students to follow the audio by pointing at each word in the book. Look at the subject row of the timetable and point out the missing information. Elicit the missing subject from the class (English). Demonstrate writing this in the gap. Tell students to read and complete the rest of the timetable. Students work individually and complete the gaps in the timetable with the information from the notes. Students work in pairs and compare their answers. Go through answers as a class. Ask students to show you how they got their answers in the notes.

> **Answers**
>
> | SUBJECT | English | Maths | Chemistry |
> |---|---|---|---|
> | WHEN | Monday Tuesday 9:00 – 11:00 | Sunday Wednesday 1:00 – 3:00 | Thursday 10:30 – 9:00 |
> | WHERE | Room 16 | Room 21 | Room 9 |

ACADEMIC WRITING SKILLS

5 👤 Focus on the options under the line in sentence 1. Read the sentence aloud including the options. Ask: *When (Monday)? In, on or at?* (on). Read the correct sentence aloud (English is on Monday.). Demonstrate circling the correct option under the line in the book. Say: *Read and circle*. Students work individually and circle the correct options. Go through answers as a class. Then ask students to write the correct answers in the gaps. Monitor and help as necessary.

> **Answers**
> 2 in 3 at 4 on 5 in 6 at

> **NOTICE**
>
> Write: *English is __ Monday __ five o'clock __ room 16.* on the board. Focus on the NOTICE box. Point out the highlighted sections and elicit the prepositions from students to complete the sentence on the board. Focus on the question words in the NOTICE box again. Ask: *When is the class?* Elicit: *It's on Monday and Tuesday.* Ask: *What time is the class?* Elicit: *It's at 9 o'clock.* Ask: *Where is the class?* Elicit: *In room 16.*

UNIVERSITY LIFE   UNIT 3

🔴 Common student errors

Wrong word: Arabic L1 and Turkish L1 students frequently use the wrong preposition when talking about time and place:
- *in* instead of *on* with days of the week
- *on* instead of *in* with time periods such as morning and afternoon
- *in* instead of *at* with clock times

Here are some examples:
My class starts in nine o'clock.
I will come there in Monday.
I get up early on the morning.

CRITICAL THINKING: CREATE

6 Focus on the headings: *Name, English Timetable, When? Where?* Elicit the headings that are missing (day/time) and the information that is missing (room number). Ask students to work in pairs and complete the headings. Now encourage students to add information for three English classes. Students work individually and complete the timetable with their days, time, and room numbers. Monitor and check spelling and use of capitals on days of the week.

WRITING TASK

7 Focus on the gapped sentences and point out the prepositions. Elicit what comes after each type of preposition (*in* – room number, *at* – time, *on* – day of the week.) Focus on the students' own timetables in Exercise 6 and ask them to complete the sentences. Students work individually and complete the gapped sentences with information from their timetables. Monitor and check grammar, spelling, and the use of capital letters.

8 Students swap books and check each other's writing.

> ### Model answer
> This is my English timetable.
> My English class is on Tuesday morning at 8 o'clock in room 12.
> My English class is on Wednesday afternoon at 9:30 / nine-thirty in room 7.
> My English class is on Friday morning at 8 o'clock in room 8.

Objectives review

See Introduction on p. 7 for ideas about using the Objectives review with your students.

WORDLIST AND GLOSSARY

See Introduction on p. 7 for ideas about using the Wordlist at the end of each unit and the Glossary at the end of the book with your students.

REVIEW TEST

See esource.cambridge.org for the Review test and ideas about how and when to administer the Review test.

RESEARCH PROJECT

Conduct an online survey and present the results.

Show the class a website where they can create a survey. (If this is not appropriate for your context, students could do the survey on paper.) Divide the class into groups and tell them each group needs to create a survey about university subjects. Tell them they should ask opinions about four subjects. They can choose subjects covered in Listening and Reading 1 of this unit or other subjects they study.

Tell students that each group will give a presentation using the information they get from the survey. Let students know how long their presentation should be (2–3 minutes).

Allow students class time to create the survey. They should share the survey online with their friends and family. (If this is not appropriate for your context, students could do the survey on paper around the university.) Give students class time during the next lesson to look at their results and plan their presentations. You could help them with ideas for how to present their results:

Ten people say English is interesting.

Three people say English is easy.

Twenty-five people say Chemistry is difficult. etc.

Students should give their presentations in the next lesson.

4 DIFFERENT COUNTRIES

UNLOCK YOUR KNOWLEDGE

👥 Focus on the photograph. Ask: *What country is this?* Students work in pairs and discuss their answer. Point out question 1 and ask students to read and circle their answer. Confirm that the answer is Japan. Write the country on the board.

Point at the buildings and people and say: *What city is it?* Try to elicit *Tokyo*. Elicit more things that students associate with Japan (e.g. food: sushi, sashimi, noodles; things: robots, cars (Honda, Suzuki); technology: robots, computer games, Sony; activities: karate, judo; famous places: Kyoto, Mount Fuji). See p. 6 for advice on communicating with beginners.

Focus on question 2. Read it aloud. Students work in pairs and circle their answer. Take a class vote on whether Japan is interesting or boring. Focus on question 3. Read it aloud. Students think of three countries in English. Ask students to compare their lists in pairs. Write a few examples on the board.

> **Answers**
> 1 Japan
> 2 and 3 Answers will vary.

LISTENING AND READING 1

> **Learning objectives**
> - Describe qualities of countries – *hot, warm, cold, dry, wet, big, small*
> - Ask about countries – *What's the UK like?*
> - Give descriptions of countries – *It's cold and wet.*
> - Gain awareness of the different sounds of the letters *w* and *v* – *where, warm, television, video*
>
> See p. 6 for suggestions on how to use these Learning objectives with your students.

> **Lead-in**
> You will need printable Flashcards 1.2. Go to esource.cambridge.org to print the flashcards. You need the sides with pictures only and some sticky tack.
> Review the names of the countries taught in Unit 1. Stick the flashcards with the flags only to the board and number them 1–6. Divide the class into two teams, A and B. Tell students they need to name the country and spell the word accurately to get the cards. Ask Team A to choose a card (1–6) and name and spell the country. If they make a mistake, stop them and offer the other team the opportunity to name the country and spell the word. If the team are successful, take the card from the board and give it to them. The exercise is finished when all the cards have been awarded.

VOCABULARY: DESCRIBING COUNTRIES

1 🔊 4.1 👥 Focus on the photographs. Play the audio for students to listen and read. Encourage them to follow the audio by pointing in the book at each word as they hear it. Drill the adjectives. See p. 9 for advice on drilling. Check understanding of the new words by asking about Saudi Arabia and the UK: *Is Saudi Arabia hot?* (yes), *Dry?* (yes), *Big?* (yes), *Wet?* (no), *Small?* (no), etc.

Demonstrate the next part of the exercise with a student. Point to a photograph and encourage a student to say the adjective. Then encourage the student to point at a photograph, and say the adjective yourself. Students work in pairs. Monitor and correct any errors with vocabulary or pronunciation.

SOUND AND SPELLING: w and v

2 🔊 4.2 👥 Write: *V* and *W* on the board. Elicit the names of the letters and one example of a word for each letter (video, Wi-Fi). Point at the letters and elicit the sound. Drill the phonemes and the two example words.

The sound /w/ needs a lot of attention with Turkish students. /w/ occurs in some Turkish words, but not in the alphabet as a separate letter. Turkish students tend to confuse /w/ with /v/. Beginners may struggle to differentiate between these two sounds and pronounce /wet/ and /vet/ in the same way.

Focus on the words in the book and point out the gapped letters. Point out the completed example and elicit the word *wet*. Say: *Listen and write 'w' or 'v'*. Play the audio. Students work individually. Students check their answers in pairs. Write the answers on the board. Play the audio again. Students listen and repeat the words. Correct any errors with the phonemes /w/ or /v/. Ask students to underline the letters *v* and *w* in the words in Exercise 1.

58 UNLOCK BASIC SKILLS TEACHER'S BOOK

DIFFERENT COUNTRIES — UNIT 4

> **Answers**
> 2 <u>where</u> 3 te<u>le</u>vision 4 <u>what</u> 5 <u>video</u> 6 <u>Wi</u>-Fi
> 7 <u>e</u>vening 8 <u>warm</u>

> **Answers**
> 2 big, warm, dry 3 small, warm, wet 4 big, hot, wet

LISTENING FOR KEY INFORMATION

3 (4.3) Focus on the photographs. Ask: *What country is this?* about each picture and elicit the names of the countries, *Canada* and *Singapore*. Point to the following information in the Canada fact file: *9,984,670 km²*. Ask: *Big or small?* Elicit a response, then point to sentence 1 and demonstrate the exercise by pointing out the completed example. Read out the sentence. Point out that there are two options in sentence 2. Students work individually and choose the correct options for both countries. Play the audio for students to listen and check their ideas. Go through answers as a class.

> **Answers**
> 2 cold, dry 3 small 4 hot, wet

> **Common student errors**
>
> **Extra words:** Arabic L1 students often insert *it* into sentences where it is not needed. Here are some examples of this error type:
> *The UK it is cold.*
> *My house it is in Muscat.*
> *The concert it will be in Tripoli.*
> Build awareness of the meaning of these errors in feedback after speaking activities. Note their errors and write them on the board. Underline *it* and ask students to tell you what *it* represents e.g.,
> *The UK it is cold.* (*it* means the UK.) So this is equivalent to saying *the UK* twice: *The UK the UK is cold.*

PRONUNCIATION FOR LISTENING

4 (4.4) Focus on the sentences and point out the highlighted words. Play the audio and clap or make an appropriate hand movement to emphasize the stressed words. Drill the sentence stress as a class. For advice on drilling see p. 9. Encourage students to clap with you.

WRITING AND SPEAKING

6 Focus on the photographs. Ask: *What country is this?* about each picture and elicit the names of the countries, *Brazil* and *Saudi Arabia*. Point to the following information in the Brazil fact file: *8,515,767 km²*. Say: *Big or small?* Elicit a response, then point to sentence 1 and demonstrate the exercise by pointing out the completed example. Read out the sentence (Brazil is big.) Point out that there are two more gaps to complete about Brazil. Students work individually and answer the questions about both countries. Go through the answers as a class. Ask individual students to tell you about Brazil and Saudi Arabia.

> **Answers**
> 1 Brazil is big. It is <u>warm</u> and <u>wet</u>.
> 2 Saudi Arabia is <u>big</u>. It is <u>hot</u> and <u>dry</u>.

LISTENING FOR KEY INFORMATION

5 (4.5) Focus on line 1 of the exercise. Elicit the adjectives for each of the circled pictures (small, cold, wet). Say: *Listen and circle* and demonstrate circling the pictures in the book. Play the audio. Students work individually and listen and circle the answers. Go through answers as a class.

Focus on the speech bubbles. Read out the question and encourage students to answer. Drill the question. Use the audio to drill the dialogue line by line with weaker classes. Demonstrate the next part of the exercise with a student. Point to a country and ask: *What is Turkey like?* Encourage the student to reply using the pictures they circled: Turkey is big. It's warm and dry. Then encourage the student to point at a country, and respond yourself. Students work in pairs. Monitor and correct any errors.

7 Focus on the gapped sentences. With international classes, elicit their individual countries. Say: *My country is …* and point to the adjectives in Exercise 1. Elicit some ideas from individual students. Demonstrate writing in the gaps. Students work individually and write sentences about their own countries. Monitor and help as necessary. Students work in small groups and describe the country they wrote about.

UNLOCK BASIC SKILLS TEACHER'S BOOK

Optional activity

You will need printable Flashcards 1.2 and 4.1. Go to esource.cambridge.org to print the flashcards. You need the pictures only.

Hold up one country card and one adjective card at a time. Encourage students to make a correct positive or negative sentence about the two cards. For example:

(Saudi Arabia) (dry) *Saudi Arabia is dry.*

(Japan) (big) *Japan is not big.*

If you like, you could make this a competitive game and award points for each correct sentence. For further writing practice, ask students to write a sentence for each card combination you hold up. If you do this, remember to note the cards you showed students so you can go through the answers at the end.

LISTENING AND READING 2

Learning objectives

- Describe location and origin – *They're in Egypt. It's not from Japan. It's from Korea.*
- Use sentence stress for corrections – *It isn't in France. It's in Spain.*

See p. 6 for suggestions on how to use these Learning objectives with your students.

Lead-in

You will need printable Flashcards 4.2. Go to esource.cambridge.org to print the flashcards. You need the cards with pictures only and some sticky tack.

Review the pronouns taught on the course so far. Write: *You, He, She, It, They, I, We* on the board. Drill the words if necessary. Hold up the flashcards one by one and point to the words on the board. Elicit the correct pronoun from the students. Go through the cards a second time, this time eliciting correct sentences about each picture, using the pronouns and the verb *be*.

PREPARING TO LISTEN

1 🔊 4.6 Focus on the map of the world on pp. 20–21. Ask: *Where is India?* Elicit the location on the map. Go through the location of the following countries: the USA, Japan, Egypt, Canada. Ask students to go to p. 78. Focus on photograph d and ask: *What country is this?* Elicit: *India.* Focus on the sentence and point out the completed example. Demonstrate the exercise by pointing out the letter d on the picture and the handwritten letter d in the box.

Students work individually, reading and matching the sentences to the pictures. Students work in pairs and compare their answers. Play the audio and go through answers as a class. Play the audio again for students to listen and repeat the sentences.

Demonstrate the next part of the exercise with a student. Point to a photograph and encourage a student to say the correct sentence. Then encourage the student to point at a photograph and say the correct sentence yourself. Students work in pairs. Monitor and correct any errors.

Answers

2 c   3 b   4 e   5 a

NOTICE

Write these headings on the board: *People and things, Places*. Elicit a couple of examples for each (e.g. My mother, My computer / My university). Focus on the NOTICE box. Point out the highlighted prepositions. Point at the category *People and things* on the board and say: *In or from?* Elicit: *from.* Elicit some sentences about the things in that category, e.g. *My mother is from Turkey. My computer is from Japan.* Repeat for *Places* and *in*, e.g. *My university is in Saudi Arabia.*

READING FOR DETAIL

2 🔊 4.7 Focus on the photographs and the sentences. Point out the options in the sentences. Ask: *Turkey or Mexico?* etc. Encourage students to guess, but do not confirm whether they are right or wrong. Tell students they are going to read, listen, and circle the answers. Play the audio. Students work individually. Play the audio again and check the answers with the class as you hear them.

Answers

2 Sudan   3 Mexico   4 India

PRONUNCIATION FOR SPEAKING

3 🔊 4.8 Write: *It isn't in Saudi Arabia. It's in Turkey.* on the board. Underline the stressed words (isn't, Turkey). Say the sentence and clap or make an appropriate hand movement to emphasize the stressed words.

DIFFERENT COUNTRIES   UNIT 4

Focus on the sentences in the book and point out the underlined words. Play the audio and clap or make an appropriate hand movement to emphasize the stressed words. Drill the correct stress as a class. For advice on drilling see p. 9. Encourage students to clap with you.

Demonstrate the next part of the exercise with a student. Point to a photograph in Exercise 2 and encourage a student to say the correct sentence. Then encourage the student to point at a photograph and say the correct sentence yourself. Students work in pairs. Monitor and correct any errors.

GRAMMAR: VERB *BE* NEGATIVE

4 (◀ 4.9) 👤 Write: *I __ not from Japan. You __ not from Japan. He __ not from Japan.* on the board. Point out the gaps.

Focus on the table in the book. Play the audio for students to listen and read. Focus on the sentences on the board. Elicit the correct form of the verb *be* for each sentence. Play the audio again and drill the sentences. Encourage students to create new sentences using the words in the box.

> **NOTICE**
>
> Write: *It isn't in Saudi Arabia.* on the board. Circle and say: *isn't*. Then write: *It is not in Saudi Arabia.* underneath the sentence. Point at *It isn't* and encourage students to say the words. Then point at *It is not.* Say: *Say It isn't. Write It is not.* Repeat with *aren't* and the sentence: *They are not from India.*
> Focus on the NOTICE box. Allow students a minute to read the information there.

5 (◀ 4.10) 👤 Focus on the options under the line in sentence 1. Focus on the top photograph. Say: *Canada or the UK?* (the UK). Say: *Listen*, and read the completed example aloud. Demonstrate circling the correct option under the line. Point out the next sentence: *It ____ in the UK.*, and the options under the line. Students work individually and circle the correct options. Play the audio for students to check. Go through answers as a class. Then ask students to write the correct answers in the gaps. Monitor and check students' spelling.

> **Answers**
>
> 1 is 2 are not, are 3 is not, is

ACADEMIC WRITING SKILLS

6 👤 Write: *it is not in egypt* on the board. Ask: *What's wrong?* Move your pen on the board slowly across the sentence, encouraging students to shout *Stop!* when you get to the mistake. Elicit the corrections: *It is not in Egypt.* (two capitals and a full stop)

Focus on the sentences. Demonstrate the exercise by adding the capital letter and the full stop to the first sentence. Students work individually. Go through the answers on the board as a class.

> **Answers**
>
> 1 It is in Turkey.
> 2 It is not in the USA. It is in Japan.

SPEAKING

7 👥 Focus on the speech bubble. Demonstrate the exercise with a student. Point to the first photograph and the two names of the countries with a tick ✓ and a cross ✗ underneath. Point at the country with a cross and say: *It's from Singapore.* Ask: *Yes or no?* (no). Encourage a student to read the speech bubble (*It isn't from Singapore. It's from India.*). Students work in pairs making sentences about the photographs. Monitor and correct any errors with vocabulary or pronunciation.

Remind students that we use *in* with places.

> **Answers**
>
> 2 It isn't / is not in the UK. It's / is in the USA.
> 3 It isn't / is not in Oman. It's / is in Malaysia.
> 4 It isn't / is not in Canada. It's / is in the UK.

> **Optional activity**
>
> You will need a set of pictures with famous places/people/things/food from around the world. In weaker classes, use things and people only from the countries studied in the book so far.
>
> Divide students into groups of three. Ask them to choose one student in the group to write the answers. Display your photographs one by one. Ask: *What country is it in?* or *What country is it from?* Students work in their teams and quietly discuss the correct answer and then write it down. Allow time for students to discuss and write an answer to each question.
>
> Teams swap notebooks to check each other's answers. Go through answers as a class. The team with the most correct answers wins.

LISTENING AND READING 3

Learning objectives

- Describe qualities of cities – *clean, cheap, expensive, beautiful, new, old*
- Ask and answer about cities – *Is London expensive? Yes it is. No, it isn't.*
- Use capital letters on cities' names – *Dubai, Tokyo*

See p. 6 for suggestions on how to use these Learning objectives with your students.

Lead-in

Write: *country* and *city* on the board. Elicit examples of both by asking: *Where are we? What country? What city?* and write them under each heading. (If you are not in a city, use the photograph of Tokyo in Japan on Student's Book p. 75 for this part of the exercise.)

Go round the class one by one asking each student for either a country or a city, writing each example in the correct category on the board. Stop when each list reaches ten items.

Focus on the sound and spelling of *country* and *city*. Circle the *c* in each word and elicit the sound the letter makes in each word: /k/ *country* /s/ *city*. Drill the words. Then remove the vowels and the letter *y* and write blank lines *c_ _ ntr _* and *c_ t_*. Elicit the missing letters.

VOCABULARY: DESCRIBING CITIES

1 (4.11) You will need printable Flashcards 4.3. Go to esource.cambridge.org to print the flashcards.

Focus on the photographs. Play the audio for students to listen and read. Encourage them to follow the audio by pointing at each adjective as they hear it. Check understanding of the new words using the flashcards. Drill the adjectives. See p. 9 for advice on drilling.

Demonstrate the next part of the exercise with a student. Point to a picture and encourage a student to say the adjective. Then encourage the student to point to a picture, and say the correct adjective yourself. Students work in pairs. Monitor and correct any errors.

Common student errors

Spelling: In this unit, *beautiful* is in the top ten misspelled words by Arabic L1 and Turkish L1 students. These are the typical errors: *beatiful, beautifull*.

To focus on the problem areas in this word, you could include the following exercise in your lesson.

Write on the board:

beautiful b_autiful be_utiful bea_tiful b_ _ _tiful

Focus on the first word. Ask students to spell it out. Then erase the complete word from the board. Ask them to spell the word out again and complete the first word's gap with an *e* if they are successful. (If not, write up the full word again and repeat the first part of the procedure.) Then erase the completed word. Continue like this with all of the words with gaps, removing each word as you complete it.

The error with double *l* at the end of words may be better focused on by looking at the common spelling of the suffix in a number of words, e.g. *beautiful, wonderful, useful, helpful.*

LISTENING FOR KEY INFORMATION

2 (4.12) Focus on the photographs. Ask: *What city is this? What country is this?* and point to the photographs one at a time. Point out the boxes and say: *Write 1, 2 or 3.* Students work individually and listen and write the numbers. Go through answers as a class.

Answers

3 1 2

READING FOR DETAIL

3 (4.12) Focus on the photographs. Use the map on pp. 20–21 to check understanding of the countries Qatar and South Korea and the city names London, Seoul and Doha.

Focus on the options under the line in the sentence for photograph 1 (Seoul). Focus on the photograph. Say: *Old or new?* (old). Read the completed example aloud. Demonstrate circling the correct option under the line in the book. Students work in pairs and circle the correct options. Play the audio again for students to check their answers. Go through answers as a class. Then ask students to write the answers in the gaps. Monitor and check students' spelling.

Answers

2 expensive, clean 3 new, cheap

4 🔊 4.13 👤 Focus on the exchanges and then on the photographs in 2. Read 1 aloud: *Is Seoul old?* Say: *Yes or no?* in a questioning tone (yes). Say: *Yes, it is. / No, it isn't.* Demonstrate circling the correct option. Students work individually and circle the correct response *Yes, it is.* or *No, it isn't.* for each exchange. Play the audio for students to check their answers.

> **Answers**
> 1 No, it isn't 2 Yes, it is, No, it isn't.
> 3 Yes, they are, No, they aren't.

SPEAKING

5 👥 Focus on the photographs in Exercise 2. Point out the speech bubbles in Exercise 5 and demonstrate the exercise with a student. Students work in pairs, pointing and making sentences about the cities in the photographs. Monitor and correct any errors.

GRAMMAR: VERB *BE* QUESTIONS

6 🔊 4.14 👤 Write: *Is _ old? Yes _ is. / No _ is not. Are _ old? Yes _ are. / No _ are not.* on the board. Point out the gaps.

Focus on the table in the book. Play the audio. Encourage students to point to each word as they hear it. Then focus on the sentences on the board. Elicit possible words to fill the gaps in each sentence. For each correct suggestion, drill the questions and answers. For advice on drilling see p. 9.

Focus on the table again. Play the audio again and drill the sentences. Encourage students to create new questions and answers using the structures in the table. Then ask *yes/no* questions about students' country or city and elicit short answers.

> **NOTICE**
> Write: *No it isn't.* on the board. Circle and say: *Isn't.* Then write: *No it is not.* underneath the sentence. Point at: *it isn't* and encourage students to say the words. Then point at: *it is not.* Say: *Say No it isn't. Write No it is not.* Repeat for *No they aren't.*
> Focus on the NOTICE box. Allow students a minute to read the information there.

7 🔊 4.15 👤 Focus on the first photograph and the options under the first line in exchange 1. Read the exchange aloud including the options. Ask: *One or two places?* (one). Ask: *Is or Are?* (Is). Read the correct question aloud. Demonstrate circling the correct option under the line. Say: *Read and circle.* Students work individually and circle the correct options. Play the audio for students to listen and check. Go through answers as a class. Then ask students to write the correct answers in the gaps. Monitor and check students' spelling and use of capital letters.

> **Answers**
> 1 <u>No, it isn't.</u>
>   <u>Is</u> it big? <u>Yes, it is.</u>
> 2 <u>Are they</u> in Canada? <u>Yes, they are.</u>
>   <u>Are</u> they hot? <u>No, they aren't.</u>

ACADEMIC WRITING SKILLS

8 🔊 4.16 👤👥 Focus on the names of the cities with the missing letters and ask students to guess what all the words are (cities). Point out the completed city name and ask: *What city is this* (Dubai)? Point out the capital letter on the city name. Say: *Listen and write.* Play the audio for students to listen and write the missing letters. Students work in pairs and check their answers. Write up all the answers on the board. Go through the cities and check that students know where they are. Use the map of the world on Student's Book pp. 20–21 if necessary.

> **Answers**
> 2 <u>L</u>ondon 3 <u>D</u>oha 4 <u>M</u>exico City 5 <u>I</u>stanbul 6 <u>T</u>okyo

WRITING AND SPEAKING

9 👤👥 Focus on the photograph and elicit the name of the city (Dubai). Write this on the board. Focus on the adjectives at the end of each line and read the first (old) aloud. Write a question mark next to Dubai on the board. Elicit the question: *Is it old?* Then point out the completed example. Students work individually and write questions. Students work in pairs and check their answers. Go through the answers as a class on the board.

> **Answers**
> Is it cheap? Is it beautiful? Is it big?

10 👥 Divide the class into Student As, Bs and Cs. Tell each group to go to the correct page (Student As, p. 200, Student Bs, p. 203 and Student Cs, p. 206). Demonstrate the next part of the exercise with two students. Use one of the roleplay cards and ask the other students about your city. Elicit answers from them (Yes it is. No, it isn't.). Emphasize that there is no correct answer and they can use their own ideas. Students work in groups and ask questions about the city on their card. Monitor and correct any mistakes with vocabulary or pronunciation.

> **Optional activity**
>
> Hold up a piece of paper and write a city name (e.g. London) on the side that students can't see. Say: *This is a city.* Point at the word students cannot see. Write a question mark and all the adjectives from this unit on the board (*hot, cold, warm, big, small, new, old, beautiful, clean, wet, dry, expensive, cheap, old, new*). Encourage students to ask you questions: Is it old? (yes). Is it expensive? (yes). Say: *What country is it? Is it in …?* Encourage students to ask: Is it in the USA? The UK? Answer students using short answers. When a student guesses the city, tell them it is their turn to think of a city. Continue the exercise as a whole class or in small groups.

WATCH AND REMEMBER

> **Learning objectives**
>
> - Understand adjectives – *old, new, hot, cold, wet, dry*
> - Practise using adjectives and question words – *Where's this? Is it new?*
> - Practise talking about your own city – *I'm from Istanbul, in Turkey. What's it like?*
>
> See p. 6 for suggestions on how to use these Learning objectives in your lessons.

> **Lead-in**
>
> Write: *good, new, black* on the board. Point at the words and say: *adjectives.* Elicit more examples of adjectives. You could put students into teams. The winner is the team with the most adjectives.

PART 1

In Part 1, two people introduce the cities they live in (Doha and Mexico City) and talk about whether they are old or new.

BEFORE YOU WATCH

1 👤 Focus on the photographs and the adjectives. Ask students whether they recognize any of the places. Students work individually and match.

> **Answers**
>
> 1 c 2 b 3 d 4 a

2 (🔊 4.17) 👤 Play the audio for students to listen and check their answers in Exercise 1. Go through answers as a class. Students work individually and write the adjectives under the photographs. Monitor and check students' handwriting.

> **Answers**
>
> a old b new c big d small

WATCH

3 ▶ 👤 Focus on the sentences and the options. Students read the sentences and predict their answers. Students watch Part 1 and check their predictions.

> **Answers**
>
> 1 new 2 big 3 old

AFTER YOU WATCH

In stronger classes, Exercise 4 should be completed by students after watching Part 1. In weaker classes, students can watch Part 1 again and complete Exercise 4 or use the audio script a the back of the book.

4 👤👥 Focus on the dialogue with gaps and the words in the box. Point at the completed example and read it aloud. Students work individually and complete the gaps in the sentences. Students work in pairs and check their answers. Go through answers as a class. In weaker classes, play Part 1 again or use the audio script in Student's Book p. 218. Check students understand the use of the apostrophe and also that the final s in *Who's* and *Where's* is pronounced /z/.

> **Answers**
>
> warm Who's Where's new

64 UNLOCK BASIC SKILLS TEACHER'S BOOK

PART 2

In Part 2, three more people talk about their cities (Muscat, London and Seoul), talking in particular about the weather and important buildings.

BEFORE YOU WATCH

5 👤 Focus on the photographs and the adjectives describing weather. Students work individually and match the photograph to the adjective. Go through answers as a class (1b 2d 3a 4c). Students write the adjectives under the photographs. Monitor their handwriting and spelling.

> **Answers**
> a hot b cold c dry d wet

WATCH

6 ▶️ 👤 Focus on the cities and weather descriptions. Students predict the answers. Students watch Part 1 and check their predictions. Go through answers as a class.

> **Answers**
> 1 hot and dry 2 wet and cold 3 very cold

AFTER YOU WATCH

7 👤 Students complete the sentence using two adjectives to describe the weather in their city. You could repeat the exercise using the adjectives in Part 1 (i.e. new, old, big, small) as a way of preparing for Exercise 10.

PART 3

In Part 3, students remember key information from the lesson.

REMEMBER

8 ▶️ 👥 Focus on the words in the box and the gapped sentences. Students watch Part 3 and complete the gapped sentences with words in the box. Students work in pairs and check their answers. Go through answers as a class.

> **Answers**
> 1 city 2 Doha 3 London 4 Seoul

DIFFERENT COUNTRIES — UNIT 4

MORE VOCABULARY: PLACES

9 👤 Elicit the meaning of the words *fort* and *palace*. Use the video to illustrate the meanings if necessary. Students circle the correct options for their country. If students answer *Yes*, ask them to provide more information (e.g. its name / how big it is / if it is old or new) using the language learned before.

> **Answers**
> Answers will vary.

> **NOTICE**
> Focus on the NOTICE box in the book. Allow students a minute to read the information there. Ensure students are clear about the different spelling and pronunciation of *places* /pleɪsɪz/ and *palaces* /palɪsɪz/.

ASK AND ANSWER

10 👥 In groups, students practise asking and answering the questions. Change groups to give them more opportunities to practise.

👁 LANGUAGE FOCUS

> **Learning objectives**
> - Ask and answer about people, things and places – *What's this? Where's this? Who's this?*
> - Introduce and describe people, things and places – *This is the Taj Mahal. It's in India.*
> - Use stress correctly in questions – *What's this? Where's this? Who's this?*
>
> See p. 6 for suggestions on how to use these Learning objectives with your students.

> **Lead-in**
>
> Write the categories: *People, Places, Things* on the board. Divide the class into small groups. Ask them to write one letter and one word. Say: *People; first letter T.* Elicit: *teacher.* Write: *T teacher* on the board under *People* as an example. Now give another category and letter. Only use ideas which are covered by the vocabulary in the course. Here are some examples:
>
> People: *teacher, student, doctor, brother, sister, father, mother, grandfather, grandmother*
>
> Places: *Japan, Turkey, Saudi Arabia, India, Turkey, Brazil, Canada, library, university*
>
> Things: *book, notebook, pen, pencil, computer, ID card, car, mobile phone, etc.*
>
> After ten items, stop. Students join with another group and compare lists. Ask them to check their spelling in the book.

UNLOCK BASIC SKILLS TEACHER'S BOOK **65**

VOCABULARY: WH- QUESTIONS

1 🔊 4.18 👤 Focus on the photographs. Ask: *People, place or thing?* about each picture. Then say: *Where, what or who?* about each picture. Focus on the tickboxes and letters. Students work individually and match the question words to the pictures. Play the audio for students to check. Drill the questions. See p. 9 for advice on drilling.

> **Answers**
> 1 c 2 b 3 a

SPEAKING

2 🔊 4.19 👤 Focus on the photographs. Ask questions and elicit as many ideas as you can about the places, people and things in them. Use the target language from the lesson, as this should already be familiar to students receptively (*What's this? Where's this? Who's this?*). Do not confirm their ideas.

Focus on the questions 1–6 on the left. Encourage students to read out the questions one by one. Then focus on the answers on the right. Say: *Listen and match.* Demonstrate the exercise using the completed example. Play the audio for students to check their answers.

Now point at each photograph again and ask students the same questions. Elicit the correct answers, helping with pronunciation as necessary. Draw attention to the ph in elephant and elicit the sound /f/.

> **Answers**
> 2 Where's this?   It's in Kenya.
> 3 Who's this?   This is our driver.
> 4 What's this?   This is oud from Oman.
> 5 Where's this?   It's in Muscat.
> 6 Who's this?   His name's Abdullah.

> **NOTICE**
> Write: *Who's this?* on the board. Circle and say: *Who's.* Then write: *Who is this?* underneath the sentence. Point at: *Who's* and encourage students to say the words. Then point at: *Who is.* Say: *Say Who's. Write Who is.* Repeat for *What's this?* and *Where's this?*
> Focus on the NOTICE box in the book. Allow students a minute to read the information there.

PRONUNCIATION FOR SPEAKING

3 🔊 4.20 👥 Focus on the questions and point out the underlined words. Play the audio and clap or make an appropriate hand movement to emphasize the stressed words. Drill the main stress as a class. For advice on drilling see p. 9. Encourage students to clap with you.

PREPARING TO SPEAK

4 🔊 4.21 👤 Focus on the photographs. Say: *People, place or thing? Who, where or what?* Point out the gapped questions and demonstrate writing on the lines under the pictures. Students work individually. Monitor and check for correct use of capital W and spelling. Go through answers on the board as a class.

> **Answers**
> <u>What's</u> this?   <u>Who's</u> this?

WRITING

5 🔊 4.22 👤 Focus on the first three photographs and read the sentences under them. Focus on the gapped sentences next to the second three photographs and say: *What's missing?* Point at the gaps to communicate your meaning, then point back at the row of example sentences. Students work individually, reading the examples and writing the words. Monitor and check that students are using capital letters at the start of the sentences. Play the audio for students to listen and check. Write the answers on the board.

Welcome any variations in the answers as long as they are grammatically and factually correct.

> **Answers**
> <u>It is</u> Kerala in India.
> <u>This is</u> a sari.
> <u>Her name is</u> Srabanti.

SPEAKING

6 👥 Focus on the speech bubbles in Exercise 6. Demonstrate the exercise with a student. Point at the photograph of Srabanti in Exercise 5. Say: *Who's this?* Encourage the student to respond: *Her name is Srabanti.* Students work in pairs and ask about the people, places and things in Exercise 5. Monitor and make sure students ask full questions and answer in full sentences. Monitor and correct any errors with pronunciation or vocabulary.

DIFFERENT COUNTRIES — UNIT 4

Optional activity

You will need to mark three photographs of people, places and things you like throughout the book before the lesson.

Write: *People, Places, Things* on the board. Tell students to look in the book and demonstrate flicking through the book. Say: *Find one*, and point to the categories on the board. Say: *One person. One place. One thing.* Demonstrate finding a picture and writing down the page number. Allow some time for students to find the photographs they like. Monitor and help as necessary.

Focus on one of the photographs you found and encourage the class to ask you questions: *Where's this?* Demonstrate looking on the page and finding the answer. Give as much detail and opinion as you can, e.g. *This is Asma. She's from Oman. She is young. This is her brother. His name is Abdul Aziz.* Demonstrate the exercise with all three of your photographs. Students work in pairs and discuss the photographs they found.

ACADEMIC LISTENING AND SPEAKING

Learning objectives

- Give a presentation about a country, city and place
- Understand notes for a presentation
- Prepare notes for a presentation
- Use correct word stress on common adjectives

See p. 6 for suggestions on how to use these Learning objectives with your students.

Lead-in

You will need printable Flashcards 3.3, 4.1 and 4.3. Go to esource.cambridge.org to print the flashcards. You need the sides of the cards with pictures only.

Write all the adjectives on the board randomly:

hot, cold, big, small, new, old, wet, dry, expensive, cheap, interesting, boring, difficult, easy.

Hold up one card. Elicit the vocabulary item (e.g. *hot*). Hold up two cards for opposite adjectives together. Say: *It isn't hot, it's … .* Elicit: *cold*. Divide the class into two teams. Hold up the cards, two opposites at a time. Students knock on the desk if they can remember the names of the items and form the two sentences. Award a point for each correct answer. Deduct a mark for long pauses. The first team to get five points is the winner.

Follow up by asking pairs of students to give you an example with each pair of adjectives in the format: *__ isn't (adjective). It's (adjective).* E.g. *London isn't cheap. It's expensive.*

PREPARING TO LISTEN

1 🔊 4.23 Focus on the fact file and the photograph. Point out the labels and ask: *What country is this?* (Argentina), *Is it big or small?* (big). Read out the first sentence and point out the options. Focus on the fact file and encourage students to choose an option. Students work in pairs and make predictions about the audio. Play the audio for students to check their predictions. Go through answers as a class.

> **Answers**
> 1 big 2 city 3 interesting

LISTENING FOR KEY INFORMATION

2 🔊 4.24 Focus on the sentences and point out the options in 1. Say: *Argentina or Mexico?* (Argentina). Say: *Read, listen and circle the answers.* Encourage students to read all of the sentences then play the audio. Students work individually. Play the audio again and check answers with the class as you hear them. Go through answers as a class, using the audio script on Student's Book p. 219 with weaker classes.

> **Answers**
> 2 dry 3 beautiful 4 old 5 cold 6 clean

CRITICAL THINKING: UNDERSTAND

3 🔊 4.24 Focus students on the diagram and point out the central labels. Ask: *What country?* (Argentina), *What place?* (La Boca). Point out the words in the box and the examples. Say: *Argentina is big and hot.* Encourage students to remember what Natalia said and complete the rest of the missing words. Students work in pairs and complete the notes. Play the audio from Exercise 2 one more time for students to check their answers. Then go through answers as a class.

> **Answers**
> Argentina: dry
> Buenos Aires: city, beautiful, not expensive
> La Boca: not old

UNLOCK BASIC SKILLS TEACHER'S BOOK

CRITICAL THINKING: CREATE

4 Focus on the blank frame for making notes. Read the headings boxes first. Demonstrate writing the name of your country in the first box. Students work individually and complete the notes. Monitor and help if necessary. Give more support by focusing on each box and demonstrating with examples with weaker classes. If students are from the same city, brainstorm places in the city on the board and elicit adjectives to describe those places. Students work in pairs and swap books. They check each other's ideas and writing.

PRONUNCIATION FOR SPEAKING

5 (4.25) Write three stress patterns and adjectives on the board with bubbles above the vowels (O *big*, oOo *expensive*, Ooo *beautiful*). Sound out the stress patterns using neutral sounds, e.g. DUH for O and DUH-duh-duh for Ooo. Clap your hands on the stressed syllables for extra impact. Face the students and say: *expensive*, clearly emphasizing the stressed syllable and clapping for extra impact. Repeat for all the words in the set. Encourage students to join you saying the words and clapping on the stressed syllables.

Play the audio while students listen and look. Play again for students to listen and repeat.

SPEAKING TASK

6 You will need to give a short presentation about a city (similar to Natalia in Exercise 3). Try to choose a city that students are unlikely to choose. Model the speaking task by giving a short presentation. Use the Model example below as an example. Focus on the REMEMBER box and the questions they need to ask. Tell students to practise their presentations in pairs. Ask for a volunteer from the class to give their presentation first. Stand nearby as each student speaks and help as necessary by encouraging them to look at their notes, if they are finding the task difficult. After a student finishes their presentation, encourage other students to ask more questions about the country and city they talked about, e.g. *Is it new? Is it cheap in Dubai?*

> **Model answer**
> I'm Julia. I'm from Spain. It's big. It's warm and dry. My city is Barcelona. It's old and beautiful. It is expensive. Parc Guell is in Barcelona. It's interesting. Thank you.
> **B:** Is Barcelona small?
> **J:** No, it isn't. It's big.
> **B:** Is Parc Guell new?
> **J:** No, it isn't. It's old.

> **Optional activity**
> Ask students to add three more words, one for each of the stress patterns in Exercise 5.
> Write the stress patterns on the board. Number them 1–3. Give students the words below to match orally. Say the words in a random order (including the words from the lesson so far). Students call out which stress pattern they hear (1, 2, 3):
> oOo *expensive, computer*
> O *hot, big, cold, dry*
> Ooo *beautiful, India*

ACADEMIC READING AND WRITING

> **Learning objectives**
> - Read in detail about another country
> - Prepare a fact file about your own country
> - Expand a fact file to complete a paragraph
> - Link sentences with the pronoun *it*
> See p. 6 for suggestions on how to use these Learning objectives with your students.

> **Lead-in**
> You will need printable Flashcards 4.3, pictures only. Go to esource.cambridge.org to print the flashcards.
> **Team spelling test:** Follow the procedure on p. 11.

SCANNING FOR KEY INFORMATION

1 Focus on the photographs. Point to the Eiffel Tower and try to elicit the name. Accept any language. Say: *This is the Eiffel Tower.* Model the pronunciation /aɪfəl taʊə/ and ask students to repeat. Ask: *Is it big or small?* (big). Focus on the picture of the Louvre and try to elicit the name. Say: *This is the Louvre.* Model the pronunciation /luːvrə/ and ask students to repeat. Ask: *Is it old or new?* (old), *Is it in London or Paris?* (Paris). Focus on the sentences under the photographs. Point out the options in the sentences. Students work in pairs and circle the answers.

DIFFERENT COUNTRIES UNIT 4

> **Answers**
> This is the Eiffel Tower. It is <u>big</u>.
> This is the Louvre. It is <u>old</u>.
> Where is it? It is in <u>Paris</u>.

READING FOR DETAIL

2 🔊 4.26 👥 Focus on the sentences. Read the first sentence aloud: *Paris is a country in France*. Say: *Yes or no?* in a questioning tone. Elicit the correct answer (No, it's a city.). Encourage students to read all of the sentences, then ask them to read the text and find the information. Students work individually, looking at the text and circling Yes or No for each sentence.

Students work in pairs and go through their answers. Then go through answers as a class. Read out each sentence. Students say Yes or No and show you where they found the information in the text.

> **Answers**
> 2 Yes 3 Yes 4 No

ACADEMIC WRITING SKILLS

3 🔊 4.27 👤 Write the vowels on the board: *a, e, i, o, u*. Point out the completed example. Ask: *What word is this?* (country). Repeat with the second word (city). Point at the space for a missing vowel in word 2 and elicit the missing letter (i). Students work individually and complete the words with the missing vowels. Play the audio for students to check their answers. Monitor and check that weaker students are keeping up with the audio and checking their answers correctly. Write the answers on the board with weaker classes.

> **Answers**
> 2 c<u>i</u>ty 3 b<u>eau</u>tiful 4 w<u>a</u>rm 5 <u>i</u>nter<u>e</u>sting 6 sm<u>a</u>ll
> 7 ch<u>ea</u>p 8 exp<u>e</u>n<u>si</u>ve

CRITICAL THINKING: REMEMBER

4 👤👥 Focus on the fact file. Read the first line, and point out the completed example (country) and the words in the box. Say: *Read and write.* Students work individually and complete the headings in the fact file. Students check their answers in pairs. Go through answers as a class.

> **Answers**
> <u>country</u> : France – warm, not cold
> <u>city</u> : Paris – beautiful, clean, not cheap
> <u>place</u> : Eiffel Tower – big, interesting, not new

ACADEMIC WRITING SKILLS

5 🔊 4.28 👤 Write: *Paris is beautiful. Paris is expensive.* on the board. Focus on the second example in Exercise 5. Look at the board, then look at the example again. Ask: *What's different?* Elicit: *It*. Focus on the board. Cross out *Paris* and write: *It* above it. Write: a *1* above *Paris* and a *2* above *It*. Underline the full stop between the sentences. Circle the capital letters. Focus on the last sentence about the Eiffel Tower. Ask a student to read it aloud. Point at the word *It* in the second sentence and say: *What is 'It'?* Elicit: *the Eiffel Tower*. Focus on the sentences about Dubai. Students work in pairs and complete the sentences. Monitor and check students are using *It* correctly and that they are using capital letters. Play the audio for students to check their answers. Go through answers as a class. Ask: *What is 'It'?* about each pronoun.

> **Answers**
> It is big and new. <u>It</u> is not cheap.
> It is big. <u>It</u> is beautiful and new.

CRITICAL THINKING: CREATE

6 👤 Focus on the blank frame for the students' fact files. Read the headings aloud. Demonstrate writing the name of your country on the first line. Students work individually and read and prepare the fact file. Monitor and help if necessary.

7 👤👥 Focus on the gapped sentences and point out the phrase *is a country*. Elicit what is missing from the first gap (country name). Point out the use of *It is* and *It is not …* in the next sentences. Elicit some possible ways to complete the two sentences, e.g. *It is big. It is not small.* Focus on the students' own fact files in Exercise 6 and ask them to complete the sentences. Students work individually and complete the gapped sentences with information from their fact files. Monitor and check grammar, spelling, and the use of capital letters.

UNL**O**CK BASIC SKILLS TEACHER'S BOOK

8 **Students swap books and check each other's writing.**

> **Model answer**
> England is a country. It is beautiful. It is not big.
> Cambridge is a city in England. It is old and small. It is not cheap.
> Cambridge University is in Cambridge. It is old and beautiful. It is not small.

> **Objectives review**
>
> See Introduction on p. 7 for ideas about using the Objectives review with your students.
>
> **WORDLIST AND GLOSSARY**
>
> See Introduction on p. 7 for ideas about using the Wordlist at the end of each unit and the Glossary at the end of the book with your students.
>
> **REVIEW TEST**
>
> Go to esource.cambridge.org to print out the Review test and ideas about how and when to administer the Review test.

RESEARCH PROJECT

> **Create a fact file on a different country**
>
> Show the class some websites which have facts about different countries. As your students are beginners, these websites should be in the students' native language if possible. If not, choose websites with a lot of pictures so students can see how they can use the language they know to describe these places. Divide the class into groups and tell them each group needs to choose one country to research. Students could choose a country which is known to them or one which they would like to visit. If needed, provide students with an English name of the country they choose.
>
> Tell students that each group will design a fact file including a description of the country, photographs of famous places and people, and a map of the country they find online. They should find out about the size of the country, the climate, the capital city and one famous place. Students could use the fact files in Unit 4 as a model.
>
> Allow students class time for the research or encourage them to do this for homework. Give students class time during the next lesson to create their fact files.
>
> Display the fact files in the classroom. Encourage students to ask questions about each other's fact files.

5 WORK

UNLOCK YOUR KNOWLEDGE

👥 Focus on the photograph and point out the sentences and options. Ask a student to read each sentence aloud. Students work in groups and choose options. Focus on sentences 1 and 2. Monitor and help as necessary. Take a class vote on each of the adjectives and write the results on the board, e.g. *interesting* (ten students), *boring* (five students), etc. Focus on the questions in 3. Students work in pairs and answer the questions. Go through answers as a class.

> **Answers**
> 1 doctors 2 and 3 Answers will vary.

LISTENING AND READING 1

Learning objectives

- Name six common jobs – *police officer, pilot, photographer, dentist, bank manager, nurse*
- Understand conversations about other people's jobs
- Ask and answer questions about jobs – *Is he a police officer? Yes he is.*
- Learn three common spellings of /f/ – *father, photographer, coffee*

See p. 6 for suggestions on how to use these Learning objectives with your students.

Lead-in

Write the table below on the board. Focus on the heading *Job*. Say: *Doctor is a job, teacher is a job.* Elicit more jobs students know and write them in the left column.

Job	What is it like?	When do they work?
doctor		
teacher		

Focus on the word *doctor* and the heading of the second column. Use the results of the class vote in UNLOCK YOUR KNOWLEDGE and write two adjectives in the middle column. Focus on the word *teacher* and ask: *What is it like?* Take another class vote and complete the column.

Focus on the third column. Read out the question *When do they work?* And say: *Morning, afternoon, evening, night?* Say: *I work* (times of day you work). Elicit answers (e.g. morning, afternoon, etc.) for *doctor* and *teacher*. Elicit the days (e.g. Sunday, Monday, etc.) on which doctors and teachers usually work. Write these in the column using the initial capital letters (SMTWTFS).

Students work in pairs and discuss the other jobs in the first column (if there are any). Take feedback as a class and complete the table.

VOCABULARY: JOBS

1 🔊 5.1 👥 Focus on the photographs. Play the audio for students to listen and read. Encourage them to follow the audio by pointing at each word as they hear it. Drill the job titles. See p. 9 for advice on drilling. Check understanding of the words. See p. 7 for advice on concept checking.

Demonstrate the next part of the exercise with a student. Point to a photograph and encourage a student to say the job title. Then encourage the student to point at a photograph, and say the job title yourself. Students work in pairs. Monitor and correct any errors.

PRONUNCIATION FOR SPEAKING

2 🔊 5.2 👤 Write two stress patterns and job titles on the board with bubbles above the vowels (Oo *dentist*, Ooo *manager*). Sound out the stress patterns using neutral sounds, e.g. DUH-duh for Oo and DUH-duh-duh for Ooo. Clap your hands on the stressed syllables. Face the students and say: *dentist*, clearly emphasizing the stressed syllable and clapping. Repeat for *manager*. Encourage students to join you saying the words and clapping on the stressed syllables.

Focus on the stress patterns and words in the book. Play the audio while students listen and look. Play again for students to repeat.

Elicit the pronunciation of *police* and *nurse*. Write these words on the board and cross out the silent letters: *police*, *nurse*

Write these words on the board: *teacher, manager, photographer, officer*. Ask: *Which two letters are in all of the words?* (er). Elicit the sound that *er* makes /ə/.

> **Optional activity**
>
> Extend the work with the table in the Lead-in. Add all the new jobs from Exercise 1. Students work in small groups and discuss the jobs. Take feedback as a class.

READING FOR KEY INFORMATION

3 🔊 5.3 👤 Focus on the photograph of Sena. Ask: *What is Sena's job?* Read the first question in the book aloud. Say: *Yes or no?* in a questioning tone. Say: *Yes, she is. / No, she isn't.* (No, she isn't.) Demonstrate looking at the photograph and circling the correct option. Students work individually. Play the audio for students to check their answers. Go through answers as a class. Ask the questions and elicit the full short answers. Drill the questions and short answers, focusing on sentence stress. (Is <u>he</u> a po<u>lice</u> officer? <u>Yes</u>, he <u>is</u>.) See p. 9 for advice on drilling.

> **Answers**
>
> 2 Yes, he is. 3 No, he isn't. 4 Yes, she is.

LISTENING FOR DETAIL

4 🔊 5.3 👤 Focus on names on the left. Encourage students to read out the names one by one. Focus on the words on the right. Say: *Listen and match.* Demonstrate the exercise using the completed example. Play the audio for students to listen and match. Go through answers as a class. Encourage students to recall the line they heard (This is my sister Sena. He's a police officer in Ankara. He's a friend from the USA. Is she a bank manager? Yes, she is.).

> **Answers**
>
> 2 Atilla   police officer in Ankara
> 3 Joel   friend from the USA
> 4 Kate   bank manager

SPEAKING

5 👥 Focus on the speech bubbles. Drill the questions and short answers, focusing on sentence stress. (Is <u>she</u> a <u>dentist</u>? <u>Yes</u>, she <u>is</u>.) See p. 9 for advice on drilling.

Demonstrate the exercise with a student. Point to a photograph from Exercise 1 and ask: *Is he a bank manager?* Elicit the correct answer: *Yes, he is.* or *No, he isn't.* Students work in pairs and ask and answer questions about the people in the photographs in Exercise 1. Monitor and check.

ACADEMIC WRITING SKILLS

6 👤 Write: *Is she a nurse? Yes she is.* on the board. Circle the question mark and the full stop. Write and circle these punctuation marks at the top of the board. Delete the punctuation from the two sentences. Point at the two punctuation marks and elicit the correct one for each gap.

Focus on the sentences in the book and point out the completed example. Students work individually and complete the gaps by writing the missing punctuation marks. Go through answers as a class. Write the correct sentences on the board and circle the punctuation marks.

> **Answers**
>
> 2 Is he a dentist<u>?</u> 3 Yes, he is<u>.</u> 4 Yes, she is<u>.</u>
> 5 Is he a pilot<u>?</u>

SOUND AND SPELLING: *ph, f, ff*

7 🔊 5.4 👥 Focus on the two examples in the book and elicit the pronunciation of each word. Point out the highlighted letters and say: *Listen. Can you hear* /f/? (yes). Say each word. Ask: *What sound does 'f' make?* (/f/), *What sound does 'ph' make?* /f/. Then say: *'f'* /f/ *father, 'ph'* /f/ *phone*. Drill the sound and each word.

Point out the gapped letters in words 3–5. Say: *Listen and write.* Play the audio. Students work individually. Students check their answers in pairs. Go through the spellings as a class and then drill the words. See p. 9 for advice on drilling. In stronger classes, elicit more words with *ph* and *f*, e.g. *funny, fast, family, farmer, food, football, photograph, elephant, pharmacy*.

> **Answers**
>
> 3 co<u>ff</u>ee 4 <u>ph</u>otogra<u>ph</u>er 5 <u>f</u>riend

WRITING

8 👤 Choose two students in the class. Focus on the jobs in Exercise 1. Pretend to think and say: *Malek is a police officer.* Write: *Name: Malek, Job: police officer* on the board. Repeat with the second student, but this time encouraging other students to suggest a job from Exercise 1.

Students work individually and complete the boxes about other students in the class. Monitor and check for correct use of capital letters.

72 UNL**O**CK BASIC SKILLS TEACHER'S BOOK

WORK UNIT 5

SPEAKING

9 Point out the REMEMBER box and read through the phrases as a class. Elicit variations to complete each phrase. Check understanding by asking the questions and eliciting the correct responses. Demonstrate the exercise with a student. Think of a job from Exercise 1, but don't tell students. Write another student's name on the board and three tally marks. Encourage the students to ask questions, e.g. *Is he a pilot?* If you didn't chose the job *pilot* for the student in Exercise 8, cross one of the tally marks out. Students have three chances to guess the job you've chosen for the student. Students work in small groups and talk about the people they wrote about in Exercise 8.

LISTENING AND READING 2

Learning objectives

- Talk about daily routine – *start work/classes, finish work/classes, go to work, go to university, go to the library, go home, meet friends*
- Understand people describing their routines
- Use capital letters for the names of institutions – *Cambridge University*
- Complete a personal schedule
- Learn three common sounds of the letter *o* – (*officer, go, work*)
- Describe your own routine – *I start classes at 9:00.*

See p. 6 for suggestions on how to use these Learning objectives with your students.

Lead-in

You will need enough sets of printable Flashcards 3.2 for each pair of students. Go to esource.cambridge.org to print the flashcards.

Shuffle each set of cards. Divide the class into pairs and give each a set of cards. Ask students to arrange the flashcards in the correct order on their desks. Monitor and help as necessary. Quickly go through the answers as a class by asking students to hold up the cards one at a time as you say the days of the week. Point out any errors. Collect the cards.

Write the days of the week on the board with missing capital letters: _unday, _onday, etc. Ask students to write the complete words in their notebooks.

VOCABULARY: MY DAY

1 (5.5) Focus on the photographs. Play the audio for students to listen and read. Encourage them to follow the audio by pointing at each word as they hear it. Drill the verb phrases. See p. 9 for advice on drilling. Check understanding of the words. Say: *Do I go to work on Thursday? Saturday? Do I go to work in the evening?*

Write the following on the board: *go _work, go _ university, go _ the library, go _ home.* Focus on the verb phrases in Exercise 1. Point at the gaps on the board and elicit that *to* is missing from all except *go home.* Underline *the* in *go to the library.* Elicit that this is the only phrase which includes *the.* Remove everything except the places from the board. Encourage students to recall the phrases without checking their books.

Demonstrate the next part of the exercise with a student. Point to a photograph and encourage a student to say the verb phrase. Then encourage the student to point at a photograph and say the verb phrase yourself. Students work in pairs. Monitor and correct any errors.

Common student errors

Missing words: Arabic and Turkish L1 students frequently omit the preposition *to* after *go.*

These are some typical errors: *I go the university by car. You can go the market. We go coffee shops, malls, and restaurants.*

See p. 148 for tips on how to help students with **Missing words** errors.

Optional activity

You will need printable Flashcards 5.2. Go to esource.cambridge.org to print the flashcards. You will also need something to cover the cards with, such as a large folder.

Hold up the first card behind the folder so students cannot see it. Slowly pull the card out to your right, so students can see a bit of the picture. Encourage students to guess the verb phrase on the card. Slowly reveal more and more of the card until a correct answer is given. Award the card to the student who guessed correctly and repeat for all cards in the set.

LISTENING FOR KEY INFORMATION

2 (5.6) Focus on the sentences and the photograph. Ask students to read the sentences. Read the first sentence aloud. Say: *Yes or no?* in a questioning tone. Play the audio. Students work individually and circle *Yes* or *No.* Play again if necessary.

UNLOCK BASIC SKILLS TEACHER'S BOOK 73

Students work in pairs and check their answers. Go through answers as a class. Read the script aloud. Students follow in their books and identify the relevant parts of the text. For the *No* answers, elicit the correct information.

> **Answers**
> 1 Yes 2 Yes 3 No (She is a student.)

READING FOR KEY INFORMATION

3 (5.6) Focus on the diary. Read the information and times for Tuesday. Point out the completed example (university) and the words in the box. Say: *Read and write*. Students work individually and complete the diary. Students check their answers in pairs. Go through answers as a class.

> **Answers**
>
> **Tuesday**
> 7:30 go to university
> 8:00 start classes
> 3:00 finish classes
> 3:30 meet friends
>
> **Wednesday**
> 8:30 start work
> 4:30 finish work
> 5:00 go to the library

ACADEMIC WRITING SKILLS

4 Write the name of your university/college/school on the board. Circle the capital letters and explain that we write names of universities/colleges/schools with initial capital letters. Remove the words from the board. Write: *i study english at cambridge university*. Ask: *What's wrong?* Move your pen slowly across the sentences, encouraging students to shout *Stop!* when you get to the mistakes. Elicit the corrections: *I study English at Cambridge University*. (four capitals).

Focus on the sentences in the book. Demonstrate the exercise by adding the capital letter to the first sentence. Students work individually. Go through answers on the board.

> **Answers**
> 1 I study Maths at Cambridge University.
> 2 I study Business at Riyadh University.

> **NOTICE**
>
> Write this sentence on the board: *I study English __ Cambridge University*. Focus on the NOTICE box. Point out the highlighted preposition and elicit *at* from students to complete the sentence on the board. Focus on the sentence in the NOTICE box again. Ask: *Where does he study?* and elicit: *at Cambridge University*. Ask: *Where do you study?* and elicit the correct sentence from them.

GRAMMAR: PRESENT SIMPLE AFFIRMATIVE

5 (5.7) Write this jumbled sentence on the board: *I / Business / study*. Focus on the table in the book. Play the audio and encourage students to follow the text by pointing at each line as they hear it. Focus on the sentence on the board and use appropriate hand gestures to indicate that students need to reorder the words. Elicit the correct word order: (I study Business.). Repeat with: *friends / we / meet* (We meet friends.).

Play the audio again and drill the sentences. See p. 9 for advice on drilling. Encourage students to create new sentences using the words in the box.

6 (5.8) Write on the board:
work / I / start
_____ at 7:00.

Point at the words above the line and use appropriate hand gestures to indicate that students need to reorder the words. Elicit: *I start work at 7:00*. Point to the completed example sentence. Students work individually. Monitor and help as necessary. Play the audio for students to check. Go through answers as a class.

> **Answers**
> 2 I finish work at 3:30. 3 I go home at 4.00.
> 4 We start classes at 8:30. 5 We finish classes at 3:30.

WRITING

7 Focus on the diary. Read the headings. Point out the completed example (go to university) and the words in the box. Point out the empty times and say: *Write about you*.

WORK — UNIT 5

Demonstrate writing the times and activities you do on the board in the same format as the diary. Students work individually and complete the diary. Monitor and help as necessary. Students compare their diaries in pairs.

> **Answers**
> Answers will vary.

SOUND AND SPELLING: o

8 (5.9) Focus on the words. Ask: *Which letter is in all of the words?* (o). Play the audio. Students listen and repeat. Model the phoneme /ɒ/ and then say the first word: *coffee*. Ask: *Can you hear /ɒ/?* Help students to understand the question by cupping your ear and using culturally appropriate gestures to indicate *Yes* or *No*. Repeat with *officer* (yes). Repeat the procedure and model *go*, *home*, *work*, *word* (all no). Elicit the *o* sound in *go* and *home* /əʊ/ and the *o* sound in *work* and *word* /ɜː/. Play the audio again. Students listen and repeat the words. Correct any errors with the phonemes.

SPEAKING AND WRITING

> **Common student errors**
>
> **Pronouns:** Japanese L1 learners sometimes leave out subject and object pronouns because they are not needed in Japanese with verbs other than *be*. Here is an example of this error:
> *Go to university by car.*

9 Point out the REMEMBER box on p. 206 and demonstrate the exercise by talking about your own daily schedule using the grid in Exercise 7. Ask students to turn to Student's Book p. 97. Then point out the blank grids. Say: *Listen and write.* Encourage a student to tell you about their routine using their table on Student's Book p. 97 Exercise 7. Demonstrate listening and writing down their schedule in the blank grid on Student's Book p. 206. Students work in pairs. The first student describes their daily routine using their notes in Exercise 7. The other student listens and writes. Then students swap roles. Monitor and note any errors. Conduct a feedback stage at the end of the exercise. See p. 8 for advice on conducting feedback on speaking activities.

LISTENING AND READING 3

> **Learning objectives**
>
> - Use verb phrases to talk about what people do in different jobs – *read emails, write emails, help people, meet people, travel to different countries, take photographs*
> - Understand descriptions of other people's working days
> - Use the verb *work* with prepositions to describe where, who, when and what – *work in the city, work at a bank/university, work with people, work at night / in the morning/evening/afternoon, work on a computer*
> - Complete a description of what another person does in their job
> - Talk about what other people do – *He starts work at 9.00. She works at a bank. He writes emails.*
>
> See p. 6 for suggestions on how to use these Learning objectives in your lessons.

> **Lead-in**
>
> Write these words on the board, one at a time, letter by letter:
> *people*
> *photograph*
> *email*
> *country*
> Stop after each letter and encourage students to guess the word. If a student gives you the correct word, ask the rest of the class to spell out the remaining letters. Say: *How do you spell that?*
>
> Focus on *people*. Say: *How many? One? More?* Use your hand to push higher to support the meaning of *more*. Then focus on *email* and repeat (one). Elicit how to form the plural by writing *five* in front of *email*. Elicit the *s*. Continue with *photograph* and *country*. Students may not yet know how to form the plural *-y* becomes *-ies*. Ask them to open their books on p. 98 and find the answer in Exercise 1.

> **Common student errors**
>
> The biggest spelling problems for Arabic L1 students are with vowels. Within this, double vowels or clusters of vowels, such as in the following words, are likely to cause problems:
> *friend, people, country, emails, January, February*

UNLOCK BASIC SKILLS TEACHER'S BOOK

VOCABULARY: WORK

1 🔊 5.10 👥 Focus on the photographs. Play the audio for students to listen and read. Encourage them to follow the audio by pointing at each word as they hear it. Point out *to* in *travel to different countries* and ask students to underline it. Focus on the phrases and elicit that the noun in each phrase is plural except *city*. Drill the verb phrases. See p. 9 for advice on drilling. Check understanding of the words. See p. 7 for advice on concept checking.

Demonstrate the next part of the exercise with a student. Point to a photograph and encourage a student to say the verb phrase. Then encourage the student to point at a photograph, and say the verb phrase yourself. Students work in pairs. Monitor and correct any errors.

SOUND AND SPELLING: VOWELS WITH TWO LETTERS

2 🔊 5.11 👥 Write the vowels on the board: a, e, i, o, u. Point out the completed example in Exercise 1. Ask: *What word is this?* (read). Repeat with the second word (email). Point at the gaps in the second word and elicit the missing letters (a,i). Students complete the words with the missing vowels. Play the audio for students to check their answers. Write the answers on the board for weaker students. Drill the vocabulary as a class and focus on the correct pronunciation of the vowel sound /iː/.

> **Answers**
> 2 em*ai*l 3 m*ee*t 4 p*eo*ple 5 countr*ie*s

READING FOR MAIN IDEAS

3 🔊 5.12 👥 Focus on the photographs and ask: *What's her job? What's his job?* Elicit the job titles (A a doctor, B a photographer, C a bank manager). Point out the letters on each photograph and the boxes top left of each photo. Say: *Read, listen and match.* Demonstrate writing a letter in a box. Play the audio. Go through answers as a class.

> **Answers**
> 1 A 2 C 3 B

LISTENING FOR KEY INFORMATION

4 🔊 5.12 👥 Focus on the texts in Exercise 3. Point out the options in Kate's text (8:00/9:00; students/people). Demonstrate circling the correct options. Play the audio. Students work individually. Play the audio again and go through answers as a class.

> **Answers**
> 1 Kate starts work at <u>8:00</u> in the evening. She works at night. She helps <u>people</u>.
> 2 Aki starts work at 9 o'clock. He works <u>in the city</u>. He reads and writes emails. He meets people. He finishes work at <u>5:30</u>.
> 3 Salim travels to different countries. He takes photographs. He works <u>at night</u> and in the morning. His camera is big and <u>expensive</u>.

> **Optional activity**
> Ask students to cover the texts in Exercise 3 but look at the pictures. Read out the sentences below. Students say who you are describing in each.
> 1 He takes photographs. (Salim)
> 2 He works in the city. (Aki)
> 3 He works at night. (Salim)
> 4 She helps people. (Kate)
> 5 His camera is big. (Salim)
> 6 She works at night. (Kate)

> **NOTICE**
> Write these sentences on the board: Works __ the city. Works __ night. Focus on the NOTICE box. Point out the highlighted prepositions and elicit these from students to complete the phrases on the board. Ask students to find and underline these phrases in the text in Exercise 3. Focus on the phrases in the NOTICE box again. Allow students a minute to read the information there.

5 🔊 5.13 👥 Focus on the words 1–4 on the left. Encourage students to read out the words one by one. Then focus on the phrases on the right. Say: *Read and match.* Demonstrate the exercise using the completed example 1. In weaker classes, students could look at Exercise 3 to check their answers. Play the audio for students to check their answers. Drill the phrases. See p. 9 for advice on drilling.

> **Answers**
> 2 the afternoon 3 at 9:00 4 university

WORK UNIT 5

GRAMMAR: PRESENT SIMPLE AFFIRMATIVE *HE* AND *SHE*

> ◉ **Common student errors**
>
> **Verbs:** Japanese L1 learners frequently fail to add the third person -s to verbs as in Japanese, verbs do not change for person or number. Here is an example of this error:
> *She go to the market.*

6 (◀) 5.14 Focus on the grammar table. Play the audio and encourage students to listen and read. Write this table on the board:

| She | read | emails. |
| He | help | people. |

Point at the central column in the book and then at the central column on the board. Ask: *What's missing?* Elicit: *s*. Play the audio again and drill the sentences in the grammar table. See p. 9 for advice on drilling. Write these sentences on the board:

She works in a bank. ✓✗
I works in a bank. ✓✗
He writes emails. ✓✗
They writes emails. ✓✗

Read each sentence and then focus on the tick and the cross. Elicit that the sentences with *I* and *They* are incorrect. Elicit the correct sentences (I work in a bank. They write emails.) and correct the sentences on the board.

> ◉ **Common student errors**
>
> **Extra words:** Arabic L1 students tend to insert the word *be* before other verbs.
>
> These are some typical errors: *I am go to the university. My friend Samira is studies English too. It is useful because it is helps people.*
>
> See p. 148 for tips on how to help students with **Extra words** errors.

7 (◀) 5.15 Focus on the word under the line in sentence 1. Focus on the photograph. Say: *He or She?* (He). Say: *Start or starts?* Read the correct sentence 1 aloud. Demonstrate writing the corrected verb on the line. Play the audio. Students work individually and complete the sentences. Go through answers as a class. Monitor and check students' use of third person s.

> **Answers**
>
> 2 He <u>reads</u> books.
> 3 He <u>writes</u> emails.
> 4 She <u>starts</u> work at 6:30.
> 5 She <u>helps</u> people.
> 6 She <u>works</u> in the morning.

WRITING AND SPEAKING

8 Ask students to work in small groups. Divide the class into Group As and Group Bs. Tell Group As to go to Student's Book p. 200 and Group Bs to Student's Book p. 203. Focus on the photographs and the gapped sentences below them. Groups work together and write about the photographs. Monitor and help with ideas as necessary. Ask students in each group to swap books and check each other's spelling.

Point out the REMEMBER box on p. 200 / 203 and read through the phrases as a class. Elicit some possible phrases (e.g. *He works at night. Is he a pilot?*). Group As make sentences about their photo and Group Bs ask questions to try and guess the job. Then groups swap.

WATCH AND REMEMBER

> **Learning objectives**
>
> - Understand people talking about different jobs – *Is he a pilot? She's a doctor. I work in Riyadh.*
> - Understand months of the year – *It starts in June. It's in September.*
> - Practise discussing your own working life – *I work in an airport. Are you a dentist?*
>
> See p. 6 for suggestions on how to use these Learning objectives in your lessons.

> **Lead-in**
>
> Students work in small groups. Give them one minute to brainstorm as many different types of jobs as they know in English. The group with the most jobs after one minute wins.

PART 1

In Part 1, three descriptions of jobs are given (pilot, doctor and photographer).

BEFORE YOU WATCH

1 Focus on the photographs and the jobs. Students work individually and match.

UNLOCK BASIC SKILLS TEACHER'S BOOK   77

> **Answers**
> 1 d 2 b 3 a 4 c

2 (🔊 5.16) 👤 Play the audio for students to listen and check their answers in Exercise 1. Go through answers as a class. Students work individually and write the jobs under the photographs. Monitor and check students' handwriting.

> **Answers**
> a a doctor b a nurse c a photographer d a pilot

WATCH

3 ▶️ 👤 Focus on the sentences and the options. Students read the sentences. They watch Part 1 and circle the correct options. Go through answers as a class.

> **Answers**
> 1 pilot 2 doctor 3 a nice

AFTER YOU WATCH

In stronger classes, Exercise 4 should be completed by students after watching Part 1. In weaker classes, students can watch Part 1 again and complete Exercise 4 or use the audio script at the back of the book.

4 (🔊 5.17) 👤👥 Focus on the options in each sentence. Ask students to read the sentences carefully and circle the correct option. Students work in pairs and check their answers. Go through answers as a class. Point out the different word stress in *photographs* and *photographers*.

> **Answers**
> photographs, interesting, nice

PART 2

In Part 2, three people talk about their jobs, referring specifically to months of the year.

BEFORE YOU WATCH

5 (🔊 5.18) 👤👥 Focus on the photographs. Play the audio for students to listen and read. Encourage them to follow the audio by pointing at each word as they hear it. Check understanding of the words. Demonstrate the next part of the exercise with a student. Point to a photograph and encourage a student to say the words. Then encourage the student to point at a photograph and say the words. Students work in pairs. Monitor and correct any errors.

WATCH

6 ▶️ 👤👥 Focus on the sentences and the options. Students read the sentences. They watch Part 2 and circle the correct options. Go through answers as a class.

> **Answers**
> 1 Switzerland 2 Riyadh 3 London

AFTER YOU WATCH

7 👤👥 Focus on the gapped sentence. If necessary, elicit that the first gap should be a job and the second gap a place. Students complete the sentence and then share their answers in small groups. In stronger classes, students could provide more details.

> **Answers**
> Answers will vary.

PART 3

In Part 3, students remember key information from the lesson and extend their vocabulary.

REMEMBER

8 ▶️ 👤👥 Focus on the words in the box and the gapped sentences. Students watch Part 3 and complete the sentences with words in the box. Students work in pairs and check their answers. Go through answers as a class.

> **Answers**
> 1 a pilot 2 a nurse 3 January 4 June

MORE VOCABULARY: JOBS

9 👤 Focus on the photographs and the line under each. Say: *Look at the photographs. Match.* Demonstrate drawing a line between *waiter* and *c*. Students work individually, matching and then writing each job under the correct photograph. Monitor students' spelling.

| Answers
| a an actor b a driver

ASK AND ANSWER

10 In groups, students practise asking and answering the questions. Change groups to give them more opportunities to practise.

> **Optional activity**
>
> Students talk about their holidays. Write: *I go on holiday in …* and *place* and *month* on the board. Say: *I go on holiday in the UK. I go on holiday in June.* Ask students to talk about their holidays and find someone who goes to the same place or in the same month.

⊙ LANGUAGE FOCUS

> **Learning objectives**
>
> - Name the months of the year – *January, February, March, April, May, June, July, August, September, October, November, December*
> - Use capital letters for months of the year – *January, February*
> - Use a set of vocabulary to describe events in the academic year – *the first day of university, the winter holiday, the summer holiday, the (Maths/English) exam*
> - Understand short dialogues about events in the academic year
> - Ask and answer questions about events in the academic year – *When is the winter holiday? In December.*
>
> See p. 6 for suggestions on how to use these Learning objectives in your lessons.

> **Lead-in**
>
> Write these categories: *Days of the week, Subjects* on the board. Divide the class into small groups. Ask them to write one letter and one or two words. Say: *Days beginning with M* (Monday). Write: *M Monday* on the board under *Days of the week*. Now give another category and letter. Only use ideas which have been covered by vocabulary in the course, e.g.
> *A subject beginning with M* (Maths)
> *A day of the week beginning with F* (Friday)
> *A subject beginning with E* (English)
> *Two days of the week beginning with S* (Saturday, Sunday)
> *Two subjects beginning with B* (Business, Biology)
> *Two days of the week beginning with T* (Tuesday, Thursday)
> *A subject beginning with C* (Chemistry)
> Students join with another group and compare lists. Ask them to check their spelling in the book.

VOCABULARY: MONTHS

1 ◀)) 5.19 Focus on the calendar. Play the audio for students to listen and read. Encourage them to follow the audio by pointing at each word as they hear it. Drill the months of the year. See p. 9 for advice on drilling. Check understanding of the words using the calendar. Ask about important events in the students' own country(ies) and culture(s), e.g. *When is Ramadan this year? When is Eid-al-Adha this year? When is National Day? When is your birthday?*

Demonstrate the next part of the exercise with a student. Point to a calendar page and encourage a student to say the month. Then encourage the student to point to another calendar page, and say the month yourself. Students work in pairs. Monitor and correct any errors.

ACADEMIC WRITING SKILLS

2 Focus on the calendar. Point out the capital letters and underline the first capital letter in *January*. Students work individually and underline the capital letters in the months. Write the months of the year on the board: _anuary _ebruary _arch _pril _ay _une _uly _ugust _eptember _ctober _ovember _ecember. Ask students to copy the months and write the missing capital letters in their notebooks, and go through answers as a class.

PREPARING TO LISTEN

3 ◀)) 5.20 Focus on the photographs. Ask: *When is this?* about each photograph. Point out the sentences under the photographs and read the first sentence aloud: *The winter holiday is in December.* Point to December in the first sentence and *December* in the calendar in photograph c. Use the completed example to demonstrate the exercise. Students work individually, reading and matching the sentences to the photographs. Play the audio. Allow students to make any corrections. Go through answers as a class. Check understanding of the new vocabulary (winter holiday, summer holiday, first day, exam). Write the words on the board and ask these questions (your answers will depend on your context):

Winter *Is winter hot, warm or cold in this country? Which months are winter months?* Point at the calendar.

Summer *Is summer hot, warm or cold in this country? Which months are summer months?* Point at the calendar.

Holiday *Is today a holiday?* (no) *Do I work on a holiday?* (no) *Do you go to university on a holiday?* (no) *Which months are holidays?* Point at the calendar.

First day *What's the first day of the week? When's the first day of the year?* Point at the calendar. *When's the first day of university?* Point at the calendar.

Exam Use photograph a in Exercise 3. *Is this an exam?* (yes) *Do you have an exam today? Do you have an English exam today? When do you have an English exam?* Point at the calendar.

> **Answers**
> 2 d 3 a 4 b

LISTENING FOR KEY INFORMATION

4 (5.21) Focus on the questions. Read out the first question and point out the options. Go through the questions as a class and encourage students to guess the answers. Demonstrate the exercise using the completed example. Say: *Listen and circle.* Play the audio. Students work individually, listening and circling the correct option. Go through answers as a class.

> **Answers**
> 2 In September.
> 3 In November.
> 4 In December.
> 5 In January.

> **NOTICE**
> Write this question and response on the board: *When is the English exam? __ May.* Focus on the NOTICE box. Point out the highlighted preposition and elicit *in* from students to complete the sentence on the board. Ask questions about events at your college/university or in your country and elicit answers with *in* + month.

> **Optional activity**
> **Aural gap fill** Follow the procedure on p. 12.
> 1 When <u>is</u> the English exam?
> 2 When is <u>the</u> summer holiday?
> 3 When is the first day <u>of</u> university?
> 4 The maths exam is <u>in</u> May.

ACADEMIC WRITING SKILLS

5 (5.22) Students listen and write the missing letters. Students check their answers in pairs. Then students practise spelling the months aloud. Demonstrate by pointing at the first month in Exercise 1 (January) and saying: *How do you spell* (January)? Elicit the spelling. Students work in pairs and practise asking and answering spelling the months. Monitor and correct errors.

> **Answers**
> 1 April 2 August 3 October 4 February
> 5 September 6 November

READING AND WRITING

6 Focus on the calendar. Point out the gaps for missing months. Tell students to look at Exercise 4 and find the correct months in the questions and answers. Point out the completed example and say: *Which question?* pointing to Exercise 4 (question 2). Point out the month they circled (September). Students work individually and complete the calendar. Monitor and check that students are using capital letters correctly. Students work in pairs and compare answers.

> **Answers**
>
> | December | English exam |
> |---|---|
> | November | Maths exam |
> | January | winter holiday |
> | July | summer holiday |

SPEAKING

7 Divide the students into two groups: Student As and Student Bs. Say: *Student As look at Student's Book p. 201. Student Bs look at Student's Book p. 204.* Focus on the REMEMBER box and elicit variations to complete the question, e.g. *When is the first day of university?*

Focus on the notes. Point out that Student As have half of the information about when these events are and Student Bs have the other half. Demonstrate the exercise by asking: *When is*

WORK UNIT 5

the winter holiday? and eliciting the answer. Demonstrate writing the answer on the line.

Student As speak first and ask: *When is the (first day of university)?* Student Bs answer. Then swap roles. Monitor and note any errors, especially with use of the definite article (*the*) and question forms. Use the notes you made for feedback at the end of the exercise. See p. 8 for advice on conducting feedback on speaking activities.

ACADEMIC LISTENING AND SPEAKING

Learning objectives

- Use images to make predictions about what people do in their jobs
- Understand people describing their work lives
- CT: Understand an ideas map
- CT: Apply background knowledge and create an ideas map
- Use main stress correctly in questions with adjectives – *Is it easy? Is it boring?*
- Give a short presentation about what another person does in their job
- Ask follow-up questions after a presentation

See p. 6 for suggestions on how to use these Learning objectives in your lessons.

Lead-in

Write these sentences on the board completing them with incorrect information about events at your university/school/college.
The English exam is in (month).
The summer holiday is in (month).
The first day of (university/school/college) is in (month).
The winter holiday is in (month).
Say: *Yes or no?* in a questioning tone. Encourage students to read the sentences and tell you what the mistake is. Encourage the whole class to help with spelling. Stronger classes could work in pairs and either write or say incorrect sentences about other events (e.g. cultural or personal) for their partner to correct.

USING VISUALS TO PREDICT CONTENT

1 🔊 5.23 👤 Write these sentences on the board: *I work with students. I work on a computer. I work in the university.* Point out the prepositions (*at, in, with*) and elicit how they are used after work. Remove the sentences from the board. Write: ____ *people* _____ *place* _____ *a computer.* Elicit the prepositions.

Focus on the photographs of Maitha and John and ask: *What are their jobs?* (manager, pilot). Ask students to make predictions about them: *Where are they from? Are their jobs interesting?*

Point out sentence halves 1–6. Then focus on the phrases on the right. Say: *Read and match.* Demonstrate the exercise using the completed example. Students work individually and complete the exercise. Play the audio for students to check. Go through answers as a class.

Answers

2 She works in   the city.
3 She reads and writes   emails.
4 He is   a pilot.
5 He works   at night.
6 He travels to   interesting places.

LISTENING FOR DETAIL

2 🔊 5.23 👤👥 Focus on the sentences. Read the first sentence aloud. Say: *Yes or no?* in a questioning tone. Elicit the correct answer (no). Ask individual students to read the other sentences. Play the audio. Students work individually and circle *Yes* or *No*. Play the audio again if necessary.

Students work in pairs and check their answers. Go through answers as a class. For the No answers, elicit the correct information. Use the audio script on Student's Book p. 221 to show students which line the information was in.

Answers

1 No (She's from Egypt.)
2 Yes
3 No (She meets bank managers.)
4 Yes
5 No (He's from the UK.)
6 Yes

CRITICAL THINKING: REMEMBER

3 🔊 5.23 👤 Focus on the ideas map. Read the central circle aloud. Ask: *Who?* and point to the pictures of Maitha and John (Maitha). Point out the completed examples (reads and writes emails, interesting) to model the task. Students work individually and write the missing words without looking at 1 and 2. Play the audio. Students listen and check their answers. Go through answers as a class. Students could look at 1 and 2 to find the answer in weaker classes.

UNLOCK BASIC SKILLS TEACHER'S BOOK   81

> **Answers**
> in the <u>city</u>
> starts at <u>10:00</u>
> finishes at <u>7:30</u>
> <u>meets</u> bank managers

> **Optional activity**
> Students look at the script for Track 5.23 on Student's Book p. 221 and use it to create an ideas map about John. Students work in pairs or individually. When the map is complete, students compare their map with other students'.

CRITICAL THINKING: ANALYZE

4 Tell students that they are going to give a short presentation about a job. Focus on the photographs and indicate that students should choose one job. Students work individually and circle a job. Ask: *What job are you going to talk about?* Elicit answers from several students. Focus on the question headings: *Where? What? What is it like?* Say: *Read and circle*. Students work individually and circle the words that relate to the job they chose. Monitor and help with ideas as necessary.

> **Answers**
> Answers will vary.

Focus on NOTICE box. Read out examples as a class. Give students a minute to read the information there.

PREPARING TO SPEAK

5 Focus on the ideas map. Point to the central circle. Ask: *What job?* Tell students to write the job they chose in Exercise 4. Point out the question words in the other circles. Students work individually and complete the map with their ideas from Exercise 4.

PRONUNCIATION FOR SPEAKING

6 (5.24) Focus on the questions and point to the underlined words. Play the audio and clap or make an appropriate hand movement to emphasize the stressed words. Drill the main stress as a class. For advice on drilling see p. 9. Encourage students to clap with you.

SPEAKING TASK

7 You will need to give a short presentation about a job. Try to choose ideas that students are unlikely to choose. Model the speaking exercise by giving a short presentation. Use the Model answer below as a guide. When you have finished, focus on the speech bubbles and elicit ideas from the students. Tell students to practise their presentations in pairs. Ask for a volunteer from the class to give their presentation first. Stand nearby as each student speaks and encourage them to look at their notes, if needed. Encourage the other students to ask questions at the end of each presentation.

> **Model answer**
> A: A photographer works in different countries. She works with a camera and meets interesting people. She starts at 7 o'clock in the morning and finishes at 4 o'clock in the afternoon.
> B: Is it interesting?
> A: Yes, it is.
> B: Is it easy?
> A: No, it's not.

ACADEMIC READING AND WRITING

> **Learning objectives**
> - Use headings to preview a text
> - Understand an advertisement for a course
> - Spell vocabulary learned in Unit 5 accurately
> - CT: Understand notes in relation to a model text
> - CT: Create a set of notes
> - Use *and* to link verb phrases in writing
> - Complete a description of university life
>
> See p. 6 for suggestions on how to use these Learning objectives in your lessons.

> **Lead-in**
> Write: *computers* in a circle at the centre of the board. Draw lines coming out from the circle. Now add *the internet* in a circle connected to one of the lines. Elicit words students associate with this, e.g. *shopping*, *email*, *Wi-Fi*, etc. Write these at the ends of the lines. Continue with *Microsoft®*, *Apple®* and *laptop*.

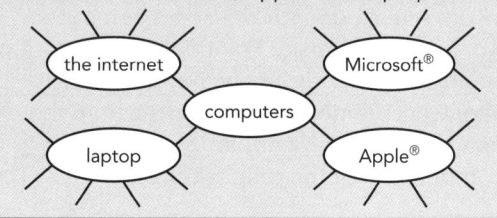

WORK UNIT 5

PREPARING TO READ

1 Focus on the numbered words and the pictures for matching. Point out the completed example. Students match and write the letters in the boxes. Go through answers as a class. If possible, use a laptop to show students each thing in real life.

> **Answers**
> 2 a 3 b 4 d

READING FOR MAIN IDEAS

2 Focus on the heading in the text in Exercise 2. Focus on the sentence in Exercise 2. Say: *Read and circle*. Students circle the correct option.

> **Answers**
> classes

READING FOR DETAIL

3 (5.25) Focus on the text. Play the audio and encourage students to point at each word as they hear it. Focus on the sentences and the *Yes/No* answers. Read the first sentence aloud and say: *Yes or no?* in an enquiring tone. Students work individually and choose the correct options. Monitor and check that students are reading carefully. Students work in pairs and check their answers. Go through answers as a class. Encourage students to correct the *No* answers.

> **Answers**
> 2 Yes 3 No (6:30) 4 No (Room 23) 5 Yes
> 6 No (January)

4 Focus on the words and phrases and point out the completed example (Microsoft Word™). Students work individually and tick ✓ the ideas mentioned in the flyer in Exercise 3. Go through answers as a class.

> **Answers**
> computers PowerPoint® emails

ACADEMIC WRITING SKILLS

5 (5.26) Write the vowels on the board: *a, e, i, o, u*. Point out the completed example in the book. Ask: *What word is this?* (finish). Repeat with the second word (start). Point at the space for a missing vowel in the second word and elicit the missing letter (a). Students complete the words with the missing vowels. Play the audio for students to check their answers. Write the answers on the board.

> **Answers**
> 2 st<u>a</u>rt 3 st<u>u</u>dy 4 w<u>o</u>rk 5 st<u>u</u>d<u>e</u>nt

PREPARING TO WRITE

6 Focus on the photograph. Elicit what the student studies (IT). Write: *Ganesh wants to be an IT teacher.* on the board. Write the sentence on the left of the board. Ask: *Is Ganesh an IT teacher today?* (no). Draw a timeline on the board and write a future year. Write: *Ganesh is an IT teacher.* beside it. Return to *today*. Say: *Ganesh wants to be an IT teacher.* Drill the sentence. Underline *wants to be*.

Ask students, if appropriate, *What do you want to be?* Elicit the complete sentence: *I want to be a (teacher, manager, etc.)*. Students complete the table with their own situations.

> **Answers**
> Answers will vary.

CRITICAL THINKING: UNDERSTAND

7 Focus on the student notes and the gapped realia. Point out the completed gap. Say: *Where is Tesla University?* and point to the text above. Elicit: *Mumbai*. Demonstrate the exercise by writing *Mumbai* on the next line. Students work individually and complete the gaps with the words from the notes above. Go through answers as a class.

> **Answers**
>
> - study at <u>Tesla University</u> in <u>Mumbai</u> studies <u>IT</u>, Maths (and) <u>English</u>.
> - classes start in <u>September</u>
> - classes finish in <u>June</u>
> - IT student
> - in the afternoon go to <u>the library</u> meet <u>friends</u>
> - in the evening go <u>home</u> read <u>books</u>

UNL⚙CK BASIC SKILLS TEACHER'S BOOK 83

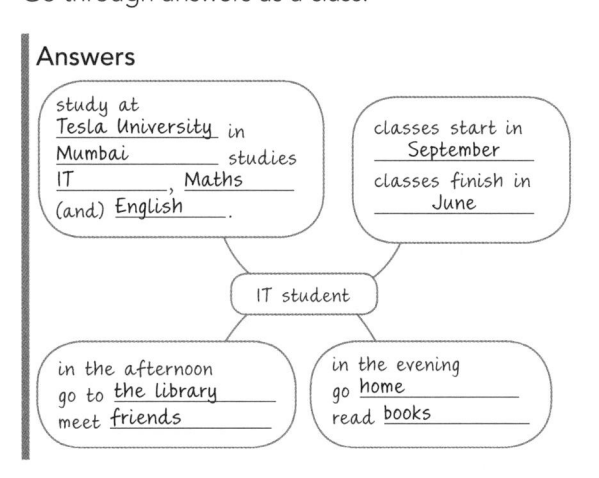

CRITICAL THINKING: CREATE

8 Focus on the gapped student notes. Point out the first gap. Say: *What is your university? Where is it?* Elicit the name of your university and city. Students work individually and complete the notes with their own ideas. Monitor and help with ideas as necessary.

> **Answers**
> Answers will vary.

ACADEMIC WRITING SKILLS

9 Write: *I go to the library. I meet friends.* on the board. Underline the full stop and the second *I*. Focus on the two sentences in the example in the book. Point out the highlighted word *and*. Focus on the board. Elicit how to change the two sentences into one. Students work individually to complete the sentences. Go through the answers as a class.

> **Answers**
> I go home and read books.
> My classes start in September and finish in June.

> **Optional activity**
> Write these sentences in two columns on the board:
>
> | | |
> |---|---|
> | We start classes at 9:00. | She takes photographs. |
> | She travels to different countries. | I read books. |
> | I go to the library. | We finish classes at 10:00. |
>
> Point from the left to the right. Encourage students to match the sentences with *and* (e.g. We start classes at 9:00 and finish classes at 10:00.). Focus on the fact that the subjects are the same by circling each pair of subjects in a different colour.
> Repeat the exercise with these, more challenging, sentences:
>
> | | |
> |---|---|
> | I take photographs. | She writes emails. |
> | He goes to work. | I read books. |
> | She takes photographs. | He goes home. |

WRITING TASK

10 Focus on the notes in Exercise 8 and the gapped sentences in Exercise 10. Read the first gapped sentence aloud. Demonstrate the exercise by miming writing a job in the first gap in the book. Students work individually and complete the gaps with the information from their notes. Monitor and help with handwriting and spelling. If students have problems with the gapped sentences with *and*, refer them to the examples in Exercise 9.

11 Students swap books and check each other's writing.

> **Model answer**
> I am a student.
> I study at university in Turkey. I study Biology and English.
> My classes start in September and finish in May.
> In the afternoon, I go home and study.
> In the evening, I meet friends and read books.

> **Objectives review**
> See Introduction on p. 7 for ideas about using the Objectives review with your students.
>
> **WORDLIST AND GLOSSARY**
> See Introduction on p. 7 for ideas about using the Wordlist at the end of each unit and the Glossary at the end of the book with your students.
>
> **REVIEW TEST**
> See esource.cambridge.org for the Review test and ideas about how and when to administer the Review test.

RESEARCH PROJECT

> **Create a flyer for an English course.**
>
> Show the class some websites for English language courses. Because your students are beginners, these websites should be in the students' native language if possible. Divide the class into groups and tell each group to create an English course they want to do.
>
> Tell students that each group will design a flyer including a description of what they will learn, what exams they will do, and the course information, such as times, dates, location, teachers' names, etc. This information can be real, from websites or students can write about your place of study. Tell students to use the Academic Reading text on p. 106 as a model.
>
> Allow students class time for the research or encourage them to do this for homework. Give students class time during the next lesson to create their flyers.
>
> Display the flyers in the classroom. Encourage students to read each other's flyers and choose the course they would like to do.

6 FOOD AND HEALTH

UNLOCK YOUR KNOWLEDGE

Focus on the photograph and pre-teach the word *food*. Write: *food* on the board. Try to elicit what food is shown in the photograph (fruit and vegetables).

Focus on the questions. The first question, (Look. Where is it?) is about a country. Ask a student to read each question aloud. Students work in groups and answer the questions. Monitor and help as necessary. Take a class vote on question 3 and write the results on the board, e.g. *cheap* (ten students), *expensive* (five students), etc. Elicit examples of places where students think food is cheap or expensive (e.g. names of shops and restaurants).

> **Answers**
> 1 Australia
> 2 and 3 Answers will vary.

LISTENING AND READING 1

> **Learning objectives**
> - Name a variety of foods and drinks – *coffee, tea, water, juice, bread, cheese, rice, fish, salad, vegetables, fruit, meat*
> - Use the verbs *eat* and *drink* – *eat meat, drink tea*
> - Understand descriptions of other people's diets
> - Write about and talk about your own diet – *I drink tea and coffee. I don't drink juice.*
> - Spell consonant clusters *dr, fr* and *br* – (*drink, fruit, bread*)
>
> See p. 6 for suggestions on how to use these Learning objectives in your lessons.

> **Lead-in**
> You will need printable Flashcards 6.1, photographs only. Go to esource.cambridge.org to print the flashcards.
>
> Explore your students' knowledge of food and drink. Focus on the flashcards and try to elicit the words *food and drink* or *eat and drink*. Write these on the board.
>
> Write the times of day below on the board. Then pretend to be thinking and write: *coffee* next to *morning*. Point at *morning* and ask: *What food? What drink?* Mime eating and drinking if necessary. Try to elicit food and drink items for each time of day. It is fine to repeat food items at different times of day, e.g. rice in every meal.

> *morning afternoon evening*
> Encourage students to guess what you usually eat and drink at these times. Indicate yourself and say: *I eat … I drink …* and point to *morning*. Use gestures to elicit guesses. Students work in pairs and guess the food and drink that the other eats and drinks at different times of day.

VOCABULARY: FOOD

1 🔊 6.1 Focus on the photographs. Play the audio for students to listen and read. Encourage them to follow the audio by pointing at each word in the book as they hear it. Drill the verbs and types of food and drink. See p. 9 for advice on drilling. Check understanding of the words. See p. 7 for advice on concept checking.

Demonstrate the next part of the exercise with a student. Point to a photograph (to drink / to eat) and then a type of food and drink. Encourage a student to say the verb and type of food and drink. Then encourage the student to point at a photograph, and say the verb and type of food and drink yourself. Students work in pairs. Monitor and correct any errors.

> **Optional activity**
> **Chain sentences:** Follow the procedure on p. 11. With stronger classes, do not use the flashcards and allow students to extend the exercise by talking about food and drink that has not been taught in this lesson.
> 1 cheese and fish
> 2 I eat cheese and fish
> 3 I eat cheese and fish. I drink coffee and tea.

LISTENING FOR DETAIL

2 🔊 6.2 Focus on the photographs of food and drink. Ask: *What's this?* about each kind of food or drink. Then focus on the people. Ask: *What's her/his name?* (Naomi/Vinood), *Where is she/he from?* (France/India). Say: *Listen and match.* Point out the tick boxes and the letters A and B for matching. Play the audio. Students work individually and match the food and drink to the people. Go through answers as a class.

> **Answers**
> B Naomi A Vinood

READING FOR DETAIL

3 🔊 6.2 👤 Focus on the names. Ask: *Who's this?* to ensure students recognize the people from Exercise 2. Demonstrate the exercise by pointing out the completed example. Students work individually and circle the correct information. Play the audio for students to listen and check their ideas. Go through answers as a class.

> **Answers**
>
> **Naomi**: I eat bread and cheese. I eat potatoes and meat. I don't eat rice.
> I drink coffee and water. I don't drink juice.
> **Vinood**: I eat rice and fish. I eat bread and vegetables. I don't eat meat.
> I drink tea and water. I don't drink juice.

> **NOTICE**
>
> Write: *I don't eat rice.* on the board. Circle and say: *don't*. Then write: *I do not eat rice.* underneath. Point at *I don't* and encourage students to say the words. Then point at *I do not*. Say: *Say I don't. Write I do not.* Focus on the NOTICE box. Allow students a minute to read the information there.

> **Optional activity**
>
> **Aural dictation (contractions):** Follow the procedure on p. 11.
> 1 I don't drink coffee. (I do not drink coffee.)
> 2 We don't drink tea. (We do not drink tea.)
> 3 They don't go to university. (They do not go to university.)
> 4 I don't read emails. (I do not read emails.)

SPEAKING

4 👥 Focus on the speech bubbles. Drill the sentences. Vary the food and drink items you use in the drill. See p. 9 for advice on drilling. Demonstrate the exercise with a student. Point at the photographs in Exercise 1. Say: *I eat* (foods you eat). *I don't eat* (foods you don't eat). Encourage the student to respond with the foods they eat and don't eat. Repeat for *drink*. Students work in pairs.

ACADEMIC WRITING SKILLS

5 🔊 6.3 👤 Point at the first word and then Exercise 1. Ask: *What word is this?* (drink). Repeat with the second word (fruit). Point at the first space for a missing letter in the second word and elicit the missing letter (f). Students complete the words with the missing letters. Play the audio for students to check their answers. With weaker classes, write the answers on the board.

> **Answers**
>
> 2 fruit 3 bread

> ⦿ **Common student errors**
>
> **Sound and spelling:** Arabic, Turkish and Japanese L1 students have problems with consonant clusters. Speakers tend to insert short vowel sounds to split the clusters, for example:
>
> *drink* /dɪrɪnk/ *fruit* /fʊruːt/ *bread* /bʌred/
>
> This is heard in speaking and seen in the spelling of Arabic and Turkish L1 students (*dirink, furuit/firuit, biread/buread*). Therefore raising your students' awareness of consonant clusters is important. Students need to be aware of the correct spelling of the cluster for their writing to be intelligible.
>
> However, spelling accurately is much more important than speaking accurately. Research shows that there are fewer breakdowns in communication if students add short vowel sounds between consonants, e.g. *split* /sɪpɪlɪt/ than if they delete consonants, e.g. *split* /slɪt/ /spɪt/.

WRITING

6 👤👥 Focus on the gapped sentences and then Exercise 1. Say: *Write about you.* Students work individually and complete the sentences with information about themselves. Students swap books and check each other's writing for correct spelling.

SPEAKING AND WRITING

7 👥 Tell students to turn to Student's Book p. 207. Focus on the REMEMBER box. Demonstrate the exercise with a student. Point to the space for a name and the two columns with *Yes* and a tick ✓ and *No* and a cross ✗ underneath. Draw a table on the board. Complete it about yourself and use the form in the REMEMBER box to describe the food and drink you do and don't eat. Students work in pairs and complete one table each. Then change the pairs. Continue until students have spoken to two other students. Monitor and correct any errors. Students swap books and check each other's writing.

FOOD AND HEALTH UNIT 6

LISTENING AND READING 2

Learning objectives

- Use verb phrases to talk about daily routine – *get up, go to bed, have breakfast, have lunch, have dinner, drive to work, walk to university*
- Learn two common sounds of the letters *ea* – *breakfast, eat*
- Understand another person describing personal and family routines
- Complete diaries with details of a daily routine
- Describe other people's daily routines – *They do not get up at 9:30. He does not go to bed at 9:30.*
- Use sentence stress accurately to describe your own routine – *I get up at seven o'clock.*

See p. 6 for suggestions on how to use these Learning objectives in your lessons.

Lead-in

You will need printable Flashcards 6.2, words and pictures separate. Go to esource.cambridge.org to print the flashcards.
Team pelmanism: Review the verb phrases using the flashcards. Then follow the procedure on p. 10.

VOCABULARY: DAILY ROUTINE

1 (6.4) Focus on the photographs. Play the audio for students to listen and read. Encourage them to follow the audio by pointing at each word in the book as they hear it. Drill the verb phrases. See p. 9 for advice on drilling. Check understanding of the new words by using concept checking questions: *Do I get up at night?* (no), *When do I get up?* (morning), etc. See p. 7 for advice on concept checking.

Write the following on the board: *go _ bed, walk _ university, drive _ work*. Focus on the photographs and words in Exercise 1. Point at the gaps in the words on the board and elicit that *to* is missing from each. Complete the verb phrases on the board. Erase everything except the places from the board. Encourage students to recall the phrases without looking at their books.

Demonstrate the next part of the exercise with a student. Point to a photograph and encourage the student to say the verb phrase. Then encourage the student to point at a photograph and say the verb phrase yourself. Students work in pairs. Monitor and correct any errors.

SOUND AND SPELLING: *ea*

2 (6.5) Focus on the words. Ask: *Which letters are in all of the words?* (ea). Go through all the words as a class and elicit the correct pronunciation for each one. Focus on words 1–3 on the left. Focus on the words on the right. Say: *Listen and match the sounds.* (Indicate you are talking about sounds by cupping your ear.) Demonstrate the exercise using the completed example 1. Play the audio for students to listen and match. Go through the answers as a class and drill each word.

Answers

2 /iː/ tea, meat 3 /e/ bread, breakfast

Optional activity

To reinforce a common sound of *ea* /iː/ give a short test of some of the words taught in this course so far. Read out these words:

1 read 2 teacher 3 jeans 4 easy 5 cheap 6 clean 7 please

With stronger classes, you could add: 8 bread 9 breakfast 10 year

Students listen and write the words in their notebooks. Students swap notebooks. Then write the answers on the board. Students check each other's writing for correct spelling.

LISTENING FOR DETAIL

3 (6.6) Focus on the photograph. Ask: *What are their names?* (Mia and Lena), *Are they sisters or friends?* (Do not confirm yet.). Read out the sentences and point out the options. Play the audio. Students work individually, listening and circling the correct option. Refer to the texts in Exercise 4 (Paragraph 2 Sentences 3 and 4) and check the answer. Ask students if Mia and Lena are sisters or friends to confirm the answer (sisters).

Answer

lunch

READING FOR DETAIL

4 (6.6) Focus on the text and say: *Listen and read.* Play the audio again. Encourag students to follow the text by pointing to each line in the book as they hear it. Focus on times 1–7 on the left. Encourage students to say the times there one by one. Then focus on the sentences on the right. Say: *Read and match.*

UNL*CK BASIC SKILLS TEACHER'S BOOK   87

Demonstrate the exercise using the completed example. Find the time 6:30 in the text and circle it. Read the preceding part of the sentence (We get up at 6:30.). Students work individually, reading and matching the times to the sentences. Go through answers as a class. Encourage students to show you the place in the text where they found the answer and read it aloud.

> **Answers**
>
> 2 7:00   They have breakfast.
> 3 12:30 Mia has lunch with friends.
> 4 4:00   They finish classes.
> 5 7:30   They have dinner.
> 6 10:00 Lena goes to bed.
> 7 11:00 Mia goes to bed.

> **NOTICE**
>
> Focus on the NOTICE box. Allow students a minute to read the information there. Write these sentences on the board:
>
> She go to work. ✓✗
>
> I go to work. ✓✗
>
> He have breakfast at 9:00. ✓✗
>
> They have breakfast at 9:00. ✓✗
>
> Read each sentence and then focus on the tick ✓ and the cross ✗. Elicit that the sentence with *He* and *She* are incorrect. Rub out the ticks next to those sentences. Elicit the correct sentences (She goes to work. He has breakfast.). Elicit the correct spelling for *goes* and *has* and correct the sentences on the board. Drill the sentences. See p. 9 for advice on drilling.

GRAMMAR: *DON'T* AND *DOESN'T*

5 🔊 6.7 Focus on the grammar table. Play the audio for students to listen and read. Write the table below on the board:

	do not	drink coffee.
	does not	drive to work.
		walk to university.

Point at the left-hand column in the book and then at the left-hand column on the board. Ask: *What's missing?* Elicit the missing pronouns (I, You, We, They / He, She). Focus on the auxiliary verbs *do* and *does*. Say: *I*. Elicit: *do not*. Say: *She*. Elicit: *does not*. Drill the sentences. Vary the pronouns you use. See p. 9 for advice on drilling. Use the table in the book to elicit as many different correct sentences as possible from the class.

6 🔊 6.8 Focus on the options under the line in the first sentence (does not / do not). Focus on the first photograph. Say: *They or He?* (They). Say: *Listen* and read the completed example aloud. Demonstrate circling the correct option under the line (do not). Point at the next sentence *They _____ drive to university.* and the options under the line. Students work individually and circle the correct options. Play the audio for students to check. Go through answers as a class. Then ask students to write the correct answers in the gaps. Monitor and check students' spelling.

> **Answers**
>
> 2 do not 3 does not 4 does not

WRITING AND SPEAKING

7 👥 Write: *I get up at eight o'clock.* on the board. Underline *up* and *eight*. Say the sentence aloud for students to repeat, emphasizing the stressed words.

Focus on the speech bubble in Exercise 7. Demonstrate the exercise with a student. Point to the space for a name and the verb phrases in the 3rd person underneath. Point out the 3rd person verb forms. Talk about yourself and use the form in the speech bubbles to describe your routine. Be sure to include all the verb phrases on the list. Say: *Listen and write*. Students work in pairs and take turns to talk about their routines and complete the notes with their partner's routine. Monitor and correct any errors.

SPEAKING

8 👥 Focus on the REMEMBER box and the notes in Exercise 7. Demonstrate the exercise by talking about Mia in Exercises 3 and 4 (Mia gets up at 6:30. She has breakfast at 7:00.). Students work in new pairs and talk about the people they made notes about in Exercise 7.

FOOD AND HEALTH — UNIT 6

LISTENING AND READING 3

Learning objectives

- Use verb phrases to describe healthy and unhealthy activities – *get up early, go to bed late, drink green tea, eat fruit and vegetables, eat red meat, drink coffee with milk and sugar*
- Describe your own lifestyle – *I don't eat red meat. I go to bed early.*
- Understand descriptions of healthy and unhealthy lifestyles in other countries
- Use quantifiers to describe typical lifestyles – *A lot of people eat fish. Not a lot of people drink coffee. They eat a lot of red meat. They drink some green tea.*
- Describe the lifestyle in your own country – *A lot of people eat red meat. Some people eat fish.*

See p. 6 for suggestions on how to use these Learning objectives in your lessons.

Lead-in

You will need printable Flashcards 6.3, photographs only. Go to esource.cambridge.org to print the flashcards.

Write the words *have* and *go* on the board. Circle each word and draw lines from the circle (see below). Tell students to copy what you have drawn into their notebooks.

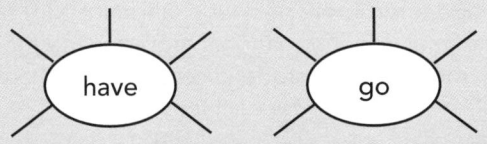

(have)   (go)

Shuffle the flashcards and show them one by one. Students work in pairs and write the second part of the verb phrase (the object or complement, e.g. *home, to work*, etc.) at the end of the lines. Students swap notebooks with another pair. Go through answers as a class on the board.

Use the words to review times of day. Say: *I go to work at 9:00.* Invite a student to continue: *I go to university at (8:30).* Students work in pairs and talk about their daily routines.

VOCABULARY: HEALTH

1 🔊 6.9 👥 Focus on the photographs. Play the audio for students to listen and read. Encourage them to follow the audio by pointing at each word in the book as they hear it. Drill the verb phrases. See p. 9 for advice on drilling. Check understanding of the new words. Say: *Do I get up at 10:00?* (no), *What time do I get up?* (e.g. 6:30, 7:00), *Do I go to bed at 8:00?* (no), *What time do I go to bed?* (e.g. 1:00, 2:00), *What kind of tea do I drink?* (green), *What kind of meat do I eat?* (red), *What do I have in my coffee?* (milk and sugar). Elicit which is milk and which is sugar in the photograph. Elicit examples of fruit and vegetables (lemon, carrots).

Demonstrate the next part of the exercise with a student. Point to a photograph and encourage the student to say the verb phrase. Then encourage the student to point at a photograph and say the verb phrase yourself. Students work in pairs. Monitor and correct any errors.

SPEAKING

2 👥 Focus on the dialogue in speech bubbles. Drill the sentences. Vary the verb phrases you use in the drill. See p. 9 for advice on drilling.

Demonstrate the exercise with a student. Point at the photographs in Exercise 1. Say: *I (things you do). I don't (things you don't do).* Encourage the student to respond with things they do and don't do. Students work in pairs and talk about the vocabulary in Exercise 1. Take feedback on any differences they found, e.g. *I eat red meat. Akihiro doesn't eat red meat.*

SCANNING FOR KEY INFORMATION

3 👤👥 Focus on the sentences. Ask a student to read both sentences. Ask students to quickly find the information in the text (under the headings *go to bed / get up*). Students work individually and circle *Japan* or *Canada* in the sentences. Students compare their answers in pairs. Go through answers with the class, asking students to show you where in the text they found the information for each answer.

Answers
1 Japan 2 Canada

LISTENING FOR KEY INFORMATION

4 🔊 6.10 👤 Focus on the text and point out the options. Say: *Listen, read and circle.* Students work individually and circle the correct options. Play the audio again and go through answers as a class.

UNLOCK BASIC SKILLS TEACHER'S BOOK   89

> **Answers**
>
> A lot of people in Japan go to bed late and get up early. They eat a lot of <u>fish</u>. Some people eat red meat. They eat a lot of fruit and vegetables. Not a lot of people drink <u>coffee</u> with milk and sugar.
> People in Canada go to bed early and get up early. A lot of people eat red meat and <u>potatoes</u>. They eat a lot of bread. Not a lot of people eat rice. Some people drink <u>green tea</u>.

GRAMMAR: *A LOT OF, SOME, NOT A LOT OF*

5 🔊 6.11 Focus on the photographs and play the audio. Encourage students to point at each photograph as they hear the sentence. Play the audio again and focus on the table. Drill the sentences. See p. 9 for advice on drilling. Encourage students to make new, grammatically-correct sentences with the language in the table.

> **NOTICE**
>
> Write: *I eat _____ fish.* on the board. Focus on the NOTICE box. Students read the sentences one by one. Elicit the missing words (a lot of) to complete the sentence on the board. Write these words on the board: *sugar, red meat, coffee*. Elicit sentences with *a lot of* and the different food and drinks. Drill the sentence on the board with different food and drink and vary the subject (*I, you, we, they, he, she*). See p. 9 for advice on drilling. Use the diagrams on the board to elicit new grammatically correct sentences with the quantifiers.

> 👁 **Common student errors**
>
> **Missing words:** Arabic L1 students tend to omit the proposition *of* in the phrase *a lot of*.
>
> These are some typical errors: *I have a lot food and drink. Yesterday, I bought a lot clothes. We eat a lot rice.*
>
> See p. 148 for advice on how to help students with **Missing words** errors.

READING FOR DETAIL

6 Focus on the headings: *Japan* and *Canada*. Focus on the options under the line in the first sentence. Focus on the second sentence in the text in Exercise 4. Say: *Read again and circle.* Demonstrate circling the correct option under the line in Exercise 6. Students work individually and circle the correct options.

Go through answers as a class. Ask students to show you the place in the text in Exercise 4 where they found the answer. Then ask students to write the answers in the gaps. Monitor and check students' spelling.

> **Answers**
>
> **Japan**
> <u>Some</u> people eat red meat.
> <u>Not a lot of</u> drink coffee with milk and sugar.
> **Canada**
> <u>A lot of</u> people eat red meat and potatoes.
> People eat <u>a lot of</u> bread.
> <u>Some</u> people drink green tea.

> **Optional activity**
>
> **Running dictation:** Follow the procedure on p. 12.
>
> Divide the class into Team As and Team Bs. Use two different texts from Exercise 6. Team As – Japan. Team Bs – Canada.

WRITING

7 Write the name of your students' country on the board. Ask: *What do a lot of people eat in (your country's name)?* Write: *A lot of people eat …* on the board. Accept all answers, not only the ideas in this lesson. Write the words on the board, eliciting the spelling if possible. Repeat for *Some people …* and *Not a lot of people …* In international groups, write the names of all the students' countries and only elicit three ideas for each country.

Focus on the table and read the headings aloud. Students work individually and write their ideas in the table. Students swap books and check each other's spelling.

SPEAKING

8 Focus on the REMEMBER box and read through the phrases as a class. Use the table in Exercise 5 to elicit variations to complete the phrases, e.g. *A lot of people eat fish. Some people eat fish. Not a lot of people eat rice.*

Demonstrate the exercise using the table in Exercise 7. Students work in new pairs. Monitor and help as necessary. Note any errors and any correct use of language which has not been covered in the course so far as you monitor. Use the notes you made for feedback at the end of the exercise. See p. 8 for advice on conducting feedback on speaking activities.

FOOD AND HEALTH — **UNIT 6**

WATCH AND REMEMBER

Learning objectives

- Understand sentences about food and drink – *I drink coffee. He eats lots of fish.*
- Understand questions about different types of meals – *What do you have for breakfast/lunch?*
- Practise talking about what people in different countries like to eat – *They drink tea.*
- Practise talking about what you eat and drink – *I drink … I eat a lot of …*

See p. 6 for suggestions on how to use these Learning objectives in your lessons.

Lead-in

Write the times below on the board:
08:00
12:00
15:00
20:00
Say: *bread* and point at the times. Elicit what time students eat bread. Accept all answers. Ask students what time they eat *fruit, vegetables, meat, rice, cheese*. Ask students what time they drink *tea* and *coffee*.

PART 1

In Part 1, two people talk about the food and drink which is common in Turkey and Dubai.

BEFORE YOU WATCH

1　Students match the pictures and write the words from the box. Monitor and check students' writing.

2　(6.12)　Play the audio. Students listen and check their answers in Exercise 1.

> **Answers**
> a breakfast　b lunch　c dinner

WATCH

3　Students watch the video and predict the answers. Clarify any unknown words when going through the answers (e.g. *cheap, expensive, noodles, libraries*). Students watch Part 1 and check their predictions. Go through answers as a class.

> **Answers**
> 2 coffee　3 cheap　4 noodles　5 early　6 markets　7 fish

AFTER YOU WATCH

In stronger classes, Exercise 4 should be completed by students after watching Part 1. In weaker classes, students can watch Part 1 again and complete Exercise 4 or use the audio script at the back of the book.

4　Tell students to try and remember the information from the video. Focus on the words in the box. Students work individually, read the sentences and complete the gaps. Students work in pairs and check their answers. Go through answers as a class.

> **Answers**
> 1 dinner　2 Some, expensive　3 eat, cheap

PART 2

In Part 2, a young woman from England discusses what her family eats and drinks.

BEFORE YOU WATCH

5　Focus on the photographs and the words. Say: *Match*. Students work individually and match the photographs.

6　(6.13)　Play the audio. Students listen and check their answers in Exercise 5. Students write the words on the lines. Monitor and check students' writing.

> **Answers**
> 1 b　2 c　3 a

WATCH

7　Focus on the letter A for Amy and G for grandfather and point at the completed example in the book. Students watch Part 2 and match the people with the food and drink. Go through answers as a class.

> **Answers**
> Amy: fruit, green tea
> Grandfather: bread, cheese, sugar

UNL*O*CK BASIC SKILLS TEACHER'S BOOK　**91**

PART 3

In Part 3, students remember key information from the lesson and extend their vocabulary.

REMEMBER

8 ▶ 👥 Students watch Part 3 and complete the gapped sentences. Students work in pairs and check their answers. Go through answers as a class.

> **Answers**
> 2 cheese 3 vegetables (and) fruit 4 market

MORE VOCABULARY: FOOD

9 👤 Students work individually and match the words to the photographs, then write the food under the correct photograph. Go through answers as a class.

> **Answers**
> a noodles b olives c dates

ASK AND ANSWER

10 👥 In groups students practise asking and answering the questions. Change groups to give them more opportunities to practise.

👁 LANGUAGE FOCUS

> **Learning objectives**
> - Describe feelings – I'm fine. I'm not bad. I'm not well. I'm tired. I'm great. I'm hungry. I'm busy.
> - Understand short conversations about feelings
> - Ask and answer questions about feelings – How are you? I'm not bad.
>
> See p. 6 for suggestions on how to use these Learning objectives in your lessons.

> **Lead-in**
> **Classroom messages**: Follow the procedure on p. 12.
> 1 <u>Hi</u>! How are <u>you</u>?
> 2 I'm <u>hot</u>.
> 3 I'm <u>not</u> hot. I'm <u>cold</u>.
> Underline the stressed words and drill the sentences. Demonstrate sentences 1–3 as a dialogue with a student. Students work in pairs and practise the dialogue.

VOCABULARY: FEELINGS

1 🔊 6.14 👥 Focus on the photographs and the words to describe feelings. Play the audio for students to listen and read. Encourage students to follow the audio by pointing at each word or phrase in the book as they hear it. Drill the words to describe feelings. See p. 9 for advice on drilling. Check understanding using these sentences:

When I go to bed late, I am … (tired)
When I eat old meat, I am … (not well)
When I don't eat breakfast, I am … (hungry)
When I work on Monday, Tuesday, Wednesday, Thursday, Friday and Saturday, I am … (busy).

Demonstrate next part of the exercise with a student. Point to a photograph and encourage the student to say the correct word or phrase. (One picture has a word and a phrase.) Then encourage the student to point at a photograph and say the correct word yourself. Students work in pairs. Monitor and correct any mistakes.

> 👁 **Common student errors**
>
> **Wrong word:** Arabic L1 students often replace *be* with *have* or *do* before adjectives which describe physical feelings and health.
>
> These are some typical errors: *She doesn't well at the moment. Here are some flowers because you have sick. This diet doesn't healthy.*
>
> See p. 148 for tips on how to help students with **Wrong word** errors.

2 🔊 6.15 👤 Focus on the options under the line in the first sentence. Focus on the photograph. Say: *Fine or not well?* (not well). Say: *Listen* and read the completed example aloud. Demonstrate circling the correct option under the line.

Students work individually and circle the correct options. Play the audio for students to check. Go through answers as a class. Then ask students to write the correct answers in the gaps. Monitor and check students' spelling and use of capital letters.

> **Answers**
> 2 great 3 not bad 4 busy 5 hungry 6 tired

USING VISUALS TO PREDICT CONTENT

3 👤 Focus students' attention on the photographs. Focus on dialogues 1–4. Point out the options in each dialogue. Students read and circle the phrases they think are correct.

92 UNLOCK BASIC SKILLS TEACHER'S BOOK

FOOD AND HEALTH   **UNIT 6**

LISTENING FOR KEY INFORMATION

4 🔊 **6.16** Play the audio for students to check their answers. Go through answers as a class. Drill each dialogue. Focus on the speech bubble above the photograph in dialogue 2. Drill this first. Then focus on each conversation one by one, returning to the speech bubble each time.

> **Answers**
> 1 B: I'm <u>fine</u>. And you?
>   A: I'm <u>great</u>. Thank you.
> 2 B: I'm <u>not well</u>.
>   A: <u>I'm sorry.</u>
> 3 B: I'm <u>hungry</u>.
>   A: <u>Me too.</u> Let's have lunch.
> 4 B: I'm <u>busy</u>. I have a lot of classes.
>   A: Me too. I'm <u>tired</u>.

PRONUNCIATION FOR SPEAKING

5 🔊 **6.17** 👥 Focus on the sentences and point out the highlighted words. Point out that there is more than one highlighted word in two sentences. Play the audio and clap or make an appropriate hand movement to emphasize the stressed syllable. Drill the sentence stress as a class. See p. 9 for advice on drilling. Encourage students to clap with you.

> **Optional activity**
>
> Write: *Hello. How are you?* on the board.
>
> Encourage students to stand up and walk around the classroom. Knock on your desk. Students stop. Say: *Hello. How are you?* to another student. The other student replies and then asks: *How are you?* The first student replies. When you knock on the desk again, they say goodbye and walk around again. Knock on the desk again, and they stop and speak to a new student. Demonstrate this type of mingling exercise the first time you use it.
>
> **Alternative to mingling:** If mingling activities are not appropriate for your context, ask students to sit in groups in a circle and speak to the person next to them. Then speak to the person on the other side. Then swap seats with someone else in the circle.

SPEAKING

6 👥 Focus on the REMEMBER box and read through the phrase as a class. Drill all the phrases. Elicit appropriate uses of the phrases in the REMEMBER box. (See p. 6 for advice on communicating with beginners.)

Say: *I'm sick.* (I'm sorry.) *I'm hungry.* (Me too.) (Let's have lunch.) *How are you?* (I'm fine. Thank you. And you?)

Divide the class into Student As and Student Bs. Point out the different role play cards and icons. Say: *I'm Student A.* Say to a Student B: *Hello! How are you?* Encourage them to respond using the first icon (☺) on Student B's card: *I'm great. Thank you. And you?* Reply: *I'm hungry.* Then encourage Student B to ask a Student A: *How are you?* Student A responds by looking at the third icon (☹) on Student A's card. (I'm not well.) Encourage Student B to continue the dialogue. (I'm sorry.)

Students work in pairs and do six short dialogues. Monitor and help as necessary. Note any errors and any correct use of language which has not been covered in the course so far. When most of the pairs have finished, Student As and Student Bs swap role cards. Use the notes you made for feedback at the end of the exercise. See p. 8 for advice on conducting feedback on speaking activities.

ACADEMIC LISTENING AND SPEAKING

> **Learning objectives**
> - Use images to make predictions about a survey
> - Understand another person describing their diet
> - CT: Understand a survey
> - CT: Apply knowledge to complete a survey
> - Use sentence stress correctly in positive and negative sentences with quantifiers – *I eat a lot of sugar.*
> - Give a short presentation about your own diet
>
> See p. 6 for suggestions on how to use these Learning objectives in your lessons.

> **Lead-in**
>
> You will need printable Flashcards 6.1. Go to esource.cambridge.org to print the flashcards. You need the sides with pictures only and some sticky tack.
>
> Review the names of the food and drink taught in Unit 6. Stick the flashcards with the pictures only to the board and number them 1–13. Divide the class into two teams. Tell students they need to name the food or drink and spell the word accurately to get the card. Ask Team A to choose a card (1–13) and name and spell the food or drink. If they make a mistake, stop them and offer the other team the opportunity to name the food or drink and spell the word. If the team is successful, take the card from the board and give it to them. The exercise is finished when all the cards have been awarded.

UNLOCK BASIC SKILLS TEACHER'S BOOK

PREPARING TO LISTEN

1   Focus on the photographs and ask: *What's this?* about each one. Encourage all answers, but do not confirm anything yet. Ask students to read and match the sentences with the photographs. Go through answers as a class.

> **Answers**
> 1 b   2 c   3 a

CRITICAL THINKING: UNDERSTAND

2   (6.18)   Focus on the survey and the photograph of Mark. Point out the types of food and drink in the left hand column. Focus on the first tick ✓ and encourage students to read the headings (a lot of, coffee). Focus on the sentences under the survey and ask students to read the survey and circle the correct options. Students work in pairs. Play the audio. Students listen and check their answers. Go through answers as a class.

> **Answers**
> 1 coffee   2 tea   3 fish

CRITICAL THINKING: APPLY

3   Focus on the survey in Exercise 2 and the speech bubbles in Exercise 3. Read the first speech bubble aloud. Say: *Who says this?* (Mark). Point at the survey and encourage students to tick the correct box. Say: *Read and tick*. Students work in pairs and complete the survey using the sentences in the speech bubbles.

> **Answers**
>
> | | a lot of | some | not a lot of |
> |---|---|---|---|
> | coffee | ✓ | | |
> | water | | | ✓ |
> | tea | | ✓ | |
> | juice | | | ✓ |
> | sugar | ✓ | | |
> | fruit and vegetables | | ✓ | |
> | fish | | | ✓ |
> | red meat | ✓ | | |

LISTENING FOR DETAIL

4   (6.18)   Focus on the sentences. Ask students to read the sentences. Read the first sentence aloud. Say: *Yes or no?* in a questioning tone. Elicit the correct answer (no). Ask individual students at random to read the other sentences. Play the audio. Students work individually and circle *Yes* or *No* for each sentence. Play again if necessary.

Students work in pairs and check their answers. Then go through answers as a class. For the No answers, elicit the correct information from students. You could use the audio script on Student's Book p. 222 to show students which line the information was in. Read the script aloud. Students follow in their books and identify the relevant parts of the text.

> **Answers**
> 2 Yes
> 3 Yes   4 No (I eat some fruit and vegetables.)
> 5 No (I eat a lot of red meat.)

CRITICAL THINKING: APPLY

5   Focus on the blank survey. Point out the blank space for a name. Say: *Write your name. Then read and tick*. Students work individually and complete the survey about themselves. Monitor and help as necessary. You may wish to complete the survey yourself in preparation for Exercise 7.

PRONUNCIATION FOR SPEAKING

6   (6.19)   Focus on the sentences and point out the highlighted syllables and words. Point out that there is more than one highlighted syllable and word in each sentence. Play the audio and clap or make an appropriate hand movement to emphasize the stressed syllable. Drill the sentence stress as a class. For advice on drilling see p. 9. Encourage students to clap with you.

> **Optional activity**
>
> **Aural dictation**: Follow the procedure on p. 11.
> I <u>eat</u> a <u>lot</u> of red m<u>eat</u>.
> I drink a <u>lot</u> of c<u>o</u>ffee.
> I eat br<u>ea</u>d for br<u>ea</u>kfast.
> She eats fish for d<u>i</u>nner.
> I drink some fr<u>ui</u>t j<u>ui</u>ce.
>
> Ask students to say each sentence and find two vowel sounds that are the same in each sentence. Do one together as an example.

FOOD AND HEALTH — UNIT 6

SPEAKING TASK

7 Focus on the REMEMBER box and read through the phrases as a class. Use the survey in Exercise 5 to elicit variations to complete the phrases, e.g. *I eat a lot of fish. I don't eat a lot of red meat. I drink some tea.*

Demonstrate the exercise using the survey in Exercise 5. You will need to give a short presentation about food and drink (similar to Mark in Exercise 3). Tell students to practise their presentations in pairs. Ask for a volunteer from the class to give their presentation first. Stand nearby as each student speaks and help as necessary by encouraging them to look at their notes, if they are finding the exercise difficult.

Note any errors and any correct use of language which has not been covered in the course so far as you monitor. Use the notes you made for feedback at the end of the exercise. See p. 8 for advice on conducting feedback on speaking activities.

> **Model answer**
>
> My name is Adrian. I drink a lot of coffee. I drink coffee in the morning. I drink some water and tea. I don't drink a lot of juice.
> I don't eat a lot of sugar. I eat some fruit and vegetables. I eat a lot of fish and red meat.

ACADEMIC READING AND WRITING

> **Learning objectives**
>
> - Use charts to preview a text
> - Understand descriptions of healthy and unhealthy lifestyles in other countries
> - Spell vocabulary learned in Unit 6 accurately
> - CT: Understand a food pyramid
> - CT: Create a personal food pyramid
> - Complete a description of your own diet
>
> See p. 6 for suggestions on how to use these Learning objectives in your lessons.

> **Lead-in**
>
> **Alphabet categories:** Follow the procedure on p. 11.
> Categories: Countries, Food and drink
> B (Brazil, Bahrain, bread)
> C (Canada, coffee, cheese)
> F (France, fish, fruit)
> J (Japan, juice)
> M (Mexico, meat)
> S (Saudi Arabia, Singapore, salad)
> T (Turkey, tea)
> When you have worked through all the letters, elicit sentences with the pairs of words on the board, e.g. *They eat a lot of bread in Brazil. They don't eat a lot of cheese in Canada.* (It doesn't matter if the sentences are true or not.)

PREPARING TO READ

1 🔊 6.20 Pre-teach the word *healthy*. Write: *healthy* and *not healthy* on the board.

Say: *I'm great. I eat a lot of fruit and vegetables. I go to bed early. I am healthy.* (Point to *healthy*.)

I'm not well. I don't eat a lot of fruit and vegetables. I eat a lot of sugar. I drink a lot of coffee. I am not healthy. (Point to *not healthy*.)

Drill the pronunciation of *healthy*. Point out that *ea* makes the /e/ sound as it does in *bread* and *breakfast*.

Focus on the photographs and the letters A and B. Point out the two sentences and the boxes to write a letter. Say: *Read and match*. Students work individually, reading the sentences and matching them to the photographs. Students then listen to check their answers.

> **Answers**
>
> 1 A 2 B

> **NOTICE**
>
> Write: *for breakfast* and *for lunch and dinner* on the board. Then write: *I eat _____ for breakfast.* Elicit possible words to fill the gap. Repeat *I eat _____ for lunch and dinner.* Drill the sentences.
> Focus on the NOTICE box. Allow students a minute to read the information there.

USING VISUALS TO PREDICT CONTENT

2 👤 Focus on the headings (South Korea and USA) and the pie charts in the text. Read the sentences in Exercise 2 aloud. Students work individually, looking and circling the correct options. Go through answers as a class, using the pie charts to explain the answers.

> **Answers**
> 1 A lot of 2 Some

READING FOR DETAIL

3 (🔊 6.21) 👥 Focus on the sentences under the text. Read the first sentence aloud. Say: *Yes or no?* in a questioning tone. Elicit the correct answer (no). Encourage students to read all of the sentences, then ask them to read the text and find the information. Students work individually, reading the text and circling *Yes* or *No* for each sentence.

Students work in pairs and check their answers. Then go through answers as a class. Read out each sentence. Students say *Yes* or *No* and show you where they found the information in the text. For the No answers, elicit the correct information from students.

Focus on these phrases in the text: *good for you* and *not good for you*. Students find and underline these phrases in the text. Say: *Which words means 'healthy?* (good for you). *Which words means not healthy?* (not good for you).

> **Answers**
> 2 No (For breakfast, they eat a lot of fruit and vegetables.)
> 3 Yes 4 Yes 5 No (They eat red meat for lunch and dinner.) 6 Yes

4 (🔊 6.22) 👤 Focus on the text in Exercise 3. Focus on the words in the box, the sentences and the gaps in Exercise 4. Complete the first gap as a class. Read the sentence aloud. Say: *For breakfast they eat (what?) and vegetables.* Encourage students to find the information in the text in Exercise 3 and use the words in the box to fill in the gaps. Students work individually and complete the sentences with the correct information. Monitor and check that students are reading carefully. Play the audio for students to check their answers. Go through answers as a class. Explain the answers using the text.

> **Answers**
>
> South Korea
> For lunch and dinner, they eat ___fish___.
> They get up ___early___.
> the USA
> For breakfast, they eat sugar and ___bread___.
> For lunch and dinner, they eat ___red meat___.
> They get up ___late___.

> **Optional activity**
>
> Write on the board:
> South Korea 1 2 3
> The USA 1 2 3
> Read the sentences below aloud. Do not say the part in brackets (). Ask students to write one word only for each number.
> South Korea
> 1 People in South Korea do not eat a lot of (sugar).
> 2 People in South Korea eat a lot of (fish/fruit/vegetables).
> 3 A lot of people in South Korea are (healthy/tired).
> The USA
> 1 People in the USA eat a lot of (sugar/bread/meat).
> 2 They go to bed (early).
> 3 A lot of people in the USA are (busy).
> Students work in pairs and compare their ideas. Take feedback on any differences of opinion. Students check their ideas and spelling in the text in Exercise 3.

ACADEMIC WRITING SKILLS

5 (🔊 6.23) 👤 Write the vowels on the board: *a, e, i, o, u*. Point out the completed example in the book. Ask: *What word is this?* (cheese). Point at the spaces for missing vowels in the second word and elicit the missing letters (ui). Students complete the words with the missing vowels. Play the audio for students to check their answers. Write the answers on the board.

> **Answers**
> 2 fr<u>ui</u>t 3 v<u>e</u>g<u>e</u>tabl<u>e</u>s 4 m<u>ea</u>t 5 f<u>i</u>sh 6 s<u>u</u>gar
> 7 br<u>ea</u>d 8 r<u>i</u>ce

CRITICAL THINKING: APPLY

6 👥 Focus on the food pyramid and check understanding of the diagram by pointing at the key and eliciting that the top section represents cheese. Ask: *Is this a lot of cheese?* (no). Demonstrate the exercise by pointing at the bottom segment of the pyramid and eliciting what this represents (a lot of rice and bread). Focus on the first sentence and point out the example. Students work in pairs and complete the notes with the information shown in the pyramid. Go through answers as a class.

> **Answers**
> I eat a lot of fruit and <u>vegetables</u>.
> I eat some <u>red meat</u>.
> I do not eat a lot of <u>fish</u>.
> I do not eat a lot of <u>cheese</u>.

CRITICAL THINKING: CREATE

7 Focus on the next pyramid. Say: *This is your pyramid.* Point out the blank key. Say: *Write your food here.* Point out the words in the box. Ask: *What do you eat?* to a student. Elicit words that are not in the box. Elicit food and drink words that your class are likely to want to know for the exercise and write them on the board. Demonstrate looking at sections of the triangle. Say: *I eat a lot of* (bread). and label the key for the lowest section of the pyramid. Students work individually and complete the food pyramid key. Monitor and help as necessary. You may wish to complete the pyramid yourself in preparation for Exercise 8.

WRITING TASK

8 Focus on the food pyramid in Exercise 7 and the gapped sentences in the book. Read the first gapped sentence in the book: *I eat a lot of _____.* Focus on the pyramid and elicit which section the sentence is about. Demonstrate the exercise by writing your own answer in the first gap. Students work individually and complete the gaps with the information from their food pyramid. Monitor and help with handwriting and spelling. If students have problems with the fourth gapped sentence with *do*, refer them to the model text on p. 125.

9 Students swap books and check each other's writing. Remind students to check the use of capital letters.

FOOD AND HEALTH — UNIT 6

> **Model answer**
> I eat a lot of fruit and vegetables.
> I eat a lot of fish.
> I eat some cheese.
> I do not eat a lot of bread.
> I do not eat a lot of meat.

> **Objectives review**
>
> See Introduction on p. 7 for ideas about using the Objectives review with your students.
>
> **WORDLIST AND GLOSSARY**
>
> See Introduction on p. 7 for ideas about using the Wordlist at the end of each unit and the Glossary at the end of the book with your students.
>
> **REVIEW TEST**
>
> Go to esource.cambridge.org to print the Review test and for ideas about how and when to administer the Review test.

RESEARCH PROJECT

> **Create a healthy eating pyramid and present the results.**
>
> Show the class websites where they can find out about a healthy diet. Divide the class into groups and tell them each group needs to create a food pyramid about what a healthy diet includes. They should find examples of the kinds of food in each section that are common in their country and use photographs and the names of the foods as they are written in English.
>
> Tell students that each group will give a presentation about their pyramid. Let students know how long their presentation should be (2–3 minutes).
>
> Allow students class time to research food names and images or they could do this for homework. Give students class time during the next lesson to create their displays and plan their presentations. You could help them with ideas for how to present their results:
>
> *Healthy people eat a lot of vegetables. In our country people eat a lot of* (vegetable names in English, e.g. *carrots, peas, cabbage*).
>
> *Healthy people eat some meat. In our country people eat chicken and lamb.* etc.
>
> Students should give their presentations in the next lesson. Encourage them to write down new vocabulary from other groups' presentations in their vocabulary notebooks.

7 PLACES

UNLOCK YOUR KNOWLEDGE

👤 👥 Focus on the photograph. Ask: *What is this? Where is this place? What is this place like?* Elicit ideas from the class.

Focus on the questions. Students work individually, reading and circling their ideas. Students compare their answers in small groups. Go through answers as a class.

> **Answers**
> 1 Students' own answers. 2 Turkey

LISTENING AND READING 1

> **Learning objectives**
> - Name places in a city – *a park, a hospital, a beach, a train station, a shopping centre, an airport, an office building*
> - Understand people describing areas – *I live near an office building and a hospital.*
> - Use *a* and *an* correctly – *an office building, an airport*
> - Describe your area – *I live near a beach and an airport. I don't live near a park.*
> - Pronounce words with *r* /r/ and silent *r* – *park, airport*
>
> See p. 6 for suggestions on how to use these Learning objectives in your lessons.

> **Lead-in**
> Write: *Places* as a heading on the board. Then write these words on the board, one word at a time, letter by letter: *university, bank, library, Japan, Dubai.* Stop after each letter you write and encourage students to guess the word. If a student gives you the correct word, ask the rest of the class to spell out the remaining letters.
>
> Concept check the word *places.* Ask yes/no questions: *Is Dubai a place?* (yes), *Is a bank a place?* (yes), *Is a pencil a place?* (no), *Is a country a place?* (yes), *Is July a place?* (no). Tell students they are going to learn about places in a city. Remove Japan and Dubai from the board. Check students' current knowledge of the vocabulary area by asking them to name more places in a city.

VOCABULARY: PLACES IN A CITY 1

1 🔊 7.1 👥 Focus on the photographs. Play the audio for students to listen and point to the places that they hear. Check understanding and drill the vocabulary. See pp. 7 and 9 for advice on concept checking and drilling.

Demonstrate the exercise with a student. Point to a photograph and encourage the student to say the correct word or phrase. Then encourage the student to point at a photograph and say the correct word or phrase yourself. Students work in pairs. Monitor and correct any mistakes with vocabulary or pronunciation.

SOUND AND SPELLING: *r*

2 🔊 7.2 👥 Focus on the words. Ask: *Which letter is in all of the words?* (*r*). Play the audio for students to listen and repeat. Model the phoneme /r/ and then say the first word *train.* Ask: *Can you hear /r/?* Help students to understand the question by cupping your ear and using culturally appropriate gestures to indicate *Yes or No.* Repeat with each of the words: *train* (yes), *room* (yes), *three* (yes), *centre* (no), *park* (no), *airport* (no). Play the audio again. Students listen and repeat the words. Correct any errors with the phonemes /r/, /ɑː/ or /ɔː/.

LISTENING FOR KEY INFORMATION

3 🔊 7.3 👤 Focus on the photographs of the places and the numbers. Play the audio and ask students to match the numbers to the photographs. Go through answers as a class.

> **Answers**
> a 2   b 1   c 3

4 🔊 7.3 👤 Focus on the texts. Point out the options in each text. Play the audio again for students to listen and circle the correct words. Go through answers as a class.

> **Answers**
> **Asma:** a shopping centre
> **Taito:** an office building
> **Steve:** a hospital

PLACES   UNIT 7

> **NOTICE**
>
> Focus on the NOTICE box. Write the vowels *a, e, i, o, u* on the board. Ask: *What is the first letter in train?* (t). Point at the vowels on the board. Ask: *Is the letter t here?* (no). Point at the word *train*. Then point at the article *a* before *train*. Say: *a train*. Ask: *What is the first letter in office?* (o). Point at the vowels on the board. Ask: *Is the letter o here?* (yes). Point at the article *an* before *office*. Say: *an office*. Repeat the procedure with *airport*. Drill the pronunciation of all of the sentences in the NOTICE box.
>
> Write: *university* on the board and underline the first letter *u*. Say: *a university*. Exaggerate the /j/ sound. Indicate, by cupping your ear, that it is the sound that is important. Write: *a university and a yacht* on the board and model the articles and pronunciation again.

SPEAKING

5 👥 Focus on the top two photographs and the speech bubbles. Drill the sentences in the speech bubbles with the whole class.

Focus on the first photograph. Ask: *What's this?* (a train station). Focus on the tick ✓ on the photograph. Ask: *Do I live near a train station?* (yes). Say: *I live near a train station.* Repeat for the second photograph of an airport.

Students work in pairs and take turns to say sentences for the second row of photographs. Monitor and correct any mistakes. Go through answers as a class.

> **Answers**
>
> 3 I live near a train station. 4 I live near a beach.
> 5 I live near an office building. 6 I don't live near an airport. 7 I don't live near a hospital. 8 I don't live near a shopping centre.

> **Optional activity**
>
> Elicit the written form of *don't* (*do not*) and write it on the board. Ask students to write the negative sentences for the photographs of the beach and the office building in Exercise 5. Students swap notebooks and check each other's writing.

READING FOR DETAIL

6 👥👥 Focus on the map. Point to each building and ask: *What's this?* Point to: '*I live here.*' on the map. Focus on sentences 1–7. Read the first sentence aloud: *I live near a park.* Say: *Yes or no?* in a questioning tone. Elicit the correct answer (yes). Students work individually, looking at the map and circling *Yes* or *No* for each sentence.

Students work in pairs and check their answers. Then, go through answers as a class. Point to each place on the map and read the sentence. Students say: *yes* or *no*. For the No answers, elicit the correct information from students.

> **Answers**
>
> 2 Yes
> 3 Yes
> 4 No (I do not live near a beach.)
> 5 No (I live near an office building.)
> 6 Yes
> 7 No (I do not live near a train station.)

WRITING

7 👥👥 Focus on the photographs. Write on the board: *a hospital ___ an airport*. Point at the gap and ask students to read the first sentence and tell you the missing word (and). Elicit the correct second sentence (I live near a park and an office building.). Students work individually and write the sentences. Monitor and check students are using *a* and *an* correctly. Students swap notebooks and check each other's writing.

> **Answers**
>
> 2 I live near a park and an office building. / I live near an office building and a park.
> 3 I live near a shopping centre and a train station. / I live near a train station and a shopping centre.

SPEAKING AND WRITING

8 👥 Focus on the REMEMBER box. Elicit variations with different places in a city. Divide the class into Student As and Student Bs. Tell Student As to go to Student's Book p. 201 and tell Student Bs to go to Student's Book p. 204. Allow students a short time to look at their maps and think about what they are going to say. Focus on the REMEMBER box and the language they need to use. Focus on the gapped sentence. Say: *Student As speak and Student Bs listen and write*. Monitor and correct any pronunciation errors. Encourage Student As to help Student Bs with spelling. Then students swap roles.

UNL*CK BASIC SKILLS TEACHER'S BOOK   99

LISTENING AND READING 2

Learning objectives

- Name places in a city – *a restaurant, a factory, etc.*
- Understand texts describing cities – *There are some beaches. There are a lot of students.*
- Use *There is* and *There are* correctly – *There is an airport. There are a lot of restaurants.*
- Describe a map – *There is a train station and a big shopping centre.*

See p. 6 for suggestions on how to use these Learning objectives in your lessons.

Lead-in

Write: *Country* and *Capital city* on the board in two columns. Say: *London* and write it in the *Capital city* column. Then say: *the UK* and write it in the *Country* column. Then write: *Abu Dhabi* in the *Capital city* column. Elicit the country (the UAE). (You can vary the second capital city you use here. Use a capital city that is well-known to your students.)

Write four more cities in the *Capital city* column, e.g. *Ankara, Tokyo, New Delhi, Cairo*. Students work in pairs and try to name the countries in English (Turkey, Japan, India, Egypt). Give students two minutes only, then go through answers as a class. You could make this a competitive game by awarding a point for each correct country name, and another point if they can spell it correctly.

Point at *the UK* and elicit more UK cities if students know any (Edinburgh, Manchester, Liverpool, Birmingham, Cambridge, Oxford, Brighton, etc.) Tell students they are going to read about a city in the UK.

VOCABULARY: PLACES IN A CITY 2

1 🔊 7.4 Focus students' attention on the photographs.

Play the audio for students to listen and point to the places they hear. Check understanding and drill the vocabulary. See pp. 7 and 9 for advice on concept checking and drilling.

Demonstrate the exercise with a student. Point to a photograph and encourage the student to say the correct word or phrase. Then encourage the student to point at a photograph and say the correct word or phrase yourself. Students work in pairs. Monitor and correct any mistakes with vocabulary or pronunciation.

USING VISUALS TO PREDICT CONTENT

2 Focus on the map and the photographs in Exercise 3. Focus students' attention back on the sentence in Exercise 2. Model the pronunciation of *Brighton* and ask students to repeat it. Point out the options in the second sentence. Students work individually and circle their answer.

Ask students to read the first sentence of the text in Exercise 3 to check their answer.

Answer
a city

LISTENING FOR KEY INFORMATION

3 🔊 7.5 Focus on the map. Elicit the names of the places illustrated on the map. Focus on the text. Point out the options in the text. Tell students they are going to read, listen, and circle the answers. Play the audio once all the way through. Students work individually. Play the audio again and go through answers as a class.

Answers
Brighton is a city in <u>the UK</u>.
A lot of people travel to Brighton in the <u>summer</u>.
There is a train station and a <u>big</u> shopping centre.
There are <u>two</u> universities.

READING FOR DETAIL

4 Focus on the sentences. Ask a student to read the first sentence aloud. Ask students to find the information in the text in Exercise 3 (Sentence 3: There are some beaches and parks.) Students work individually and circle the options in 2–4. Students compare their answers in pairs. Go through answers as a class, asking students to show you the sentence in the text in Exercise 3 in which they found the information for each answer.

Answers
2 restaurants (There are a lot of restaurants and hotels near the beaches.)
3 an airport (And there is an airport.)
4 beautiful (Brighton is really beautiful.)

NOTICE

Focus on the NOTICE box. Write: *a beach* on the board. Underline the final letters which affect the spelling of the plural a *bea<u>ch</u>*. Write on the board: *some beach_ _*.

Ask students to look at the NOTICE box and tell you the spelling of the plural form (beach<u>es</u>). Repeat the procedure for *university*.

PLACES — UNIT 7

GRAMMAR: *THERE IS / THERE ARE*

5 🔊 7.6 👤 Focus on the grammar table. Point out *a/an* on the singular nouns and ask: *How many?* (one). Point out the *s* at the end of the plural nouns and ask: *How many?* (some, five, a lot of). Play the audio for students to listen and read. Check understanding. See p. 7 for advice on concept checking. Play the audio again for students to listen and repeat.

> 👁 **Common student errors**
>
> *There is / There are* is a challenging language area for Arabic L1 students. They often make the following mistakes with *there is / there are* and quantifiers:
>
> **Spelling:** *ther* instead of *there is* in the top 10 spelling errors at this level.
>
> **Wrong word:** *their* instead of *there*
>
> **Verb form:** Failure to make the verb agree: *There is a lot of shops. There are a bank.*
>
> **Noun form:** Failure to make the noun agree after quantifiers *a lot of* and *some*.
>
> *There are a lot of different kind of shop. I get a lot of present.*
>
> See p. 148 for activities which you can use to work on these types of error.

6 👤 Focus on the options in the first sentence. Ask a student to read the sentence aloud. Ask: *How many? One beach or some beaches?* (some beaches). Point at the table in Exercise 5 and say: *There are some hotels.* Students work individually, reading the sentences in Exercise 6 and circling *is* or *are*. Ask students to check their answers in the text in Exercise 3. Go through answers as a class.

> **Answers**
> 2 are 3 is 4 is 5 are 6 is

> **Optional activity**
>
> **Aural gap fill:** Follow the procedure on p. 12.
> 1 There <u>is</u> a teacher in the classroom.
> 2 There <u>are</u> 15 students in the classroom.
> 3 There <u>are</u> four books in my bag.
> 4 There <u>is</u> a computer in my bag.
> 5 There <u>is</u> a hospital near the airport.
> 6 There <u>are</u> a lot of doctors in the hospital.

7 🔊 7.7 👤 Focus on the options in the first sentence. Ask a student to read the sentence aloud. Ask: *There is or There are?* (There is). Ask: *A factory or some factories?* (a factory). Point at the table in Exercise 5 and say: *There is a train station. There is an airport.* Students work individually, reading the sentences and circling the correct options. Play the audio for students to listen and check. Go through answers as a class. Then ask students to write the correct answers in the gaps. Monitor and check students' spelling of the plural forms in particular.

> **Answers**
> 2 two libraries
> 3 some beaches
> 4 a university
> 5 a lot of hotels

WRITING

8 👤👥 Tell students they are going to write about their city. Focus on the first gap and say: *This is …* and indicate the place where you are now. Elicit the name of your city. Tell students to complete the first sentence. Focus on the second sentence. Ask: *How many?* (one). Say: *In* (your city's name), *there is …* Elicit suggestions (a beach, a university, etc.). Students work individually or in pairs to complete the remaining sentences. Monitor and help students with ideas as necessary. Students swap notebooks with another pair and check each other's writing.

SPEAKING

9 👥 Focus on the REMEMBER box. Read through the phrases as a class. Elicit some examples (*There is a beach. There are some factories.*). Students work in new pairs. Demonstrate the exercise with a student. Say: *There is a (university). There are (a lot of shops).* Encourage the student to continue with variations of *There is* and *There are* sentences. Students work in pairs, look at their notes in Exercise 8, and take turns to speak.

LISTENING AND READING 3

Learning objectives

- Name famous places in a city – *an old street, an interesting market, a busy square, a famous stadium, tall buildings*
- Understand texts about two international cities – *There's an old street. There's an interesting market.*
- Use adjectives accurately before nouns – *It's a famous city. There's an old market.*
- Describe a famous place – *Jeddah is a famous city. There is an old market.*

See p. 6 for suggestions on how to use these Learning objectives in your lessons.

Lead-in

You will need printable Flashcards 7.1, photographs only. Go to esource.cambridge.org to print the flashcards.

Team spelling test: Follow the procedure on p. 11.

VOCABULARY: FAMOUS PLACES

1 🔊 7.8 Focus on the photographs. Play the audio. Ask students to listen and point to the places that they hear. Check understanding and drill the vocabulary. See pp. 7 and 9 for advice on concept checking and drilling.

Demonstrate the exercise with a student. Point to a photograph and encourage the student to say the correct phrase. Then encourage the student to point at a photograph and say the correct phrase yourself. Students work in pairs. Monitor and correct any mistakes with vocabulary or pronunciation.

LISTENING FOR KEY INFORMATION

2 🔊 7.9 Focus on the city names in each sentence. Ask: *Where are Rabat and Marrakesh?* (Morocco). Continue with Rio de Janeiro (Brazil) and Salvador (also Brazil). Play the audio for students to listen and match the people with the cities. Go through answers as a class.

Answers

1 Ali is from Marrakesh.
2 Carmen is from Rio de Janeiro.

READING FOR DETAIL

3 🔊 7.9 Focus on the sentences and the words in the box. Ask a student to read the first sentence aloud. Ask students to find the information in the text about Ali (Sentences 2 and 3: I live in Marrakesh. It's a beautiful city.) Ask students to read sentences 2–6, then play the audio again while students read and listen. Students work individually and complete sentences 2–6. Students compare their answers in pairs. Go through answers with the class, asking students to show you the sentences in the text in which they found the information for each answer.

Answers

2 old (Ali: There are a lot of old streets and buildings.)
3 interesting (Ali: There is an interesting market.)
4 big (Carmen: It's a big city.)
5 tall (Carmen: There are a lot of tall buildings and new houses.)
6 famous (Carmen: I live near a famous stadium – the Maracanã Stadium.)

GRAMMAR: ADJECTIVES

4 🔊 7.10 Focus on the grammar table. Point out the articles which come before the adjectives. Write on the board: *a market*. Ask: *What is it like?* Elicit an adjective, e.g. *beautiful/interesting*. Ask: *Where in the sentence?* Point at the words on the board. Elicit the correct place for the adjective (after the article, before the noun). Repeat with another example (e.g. *some houses*). Play the audio for students to listen and read.

⊙ Common student errors

Missing words: Arabic and Turkish L1 students frequently omit *a/an*. This error often occurs when an adjective comes before a noun. These are some typical errors: *It's nice city. It's interesting place. He is good doctor.*

See p. 148 for tips on how to help students with **Missing words** errors.

5 🔊 7.11 Write: *old / city / an* on the board. Elicit the correct order for the words (an old city). Ask students to tell you the name of an old city (e.g. Petra, Rome, London, etc.) Write a sentence on the board, pausing after each word so students can tell you the next word: (Students' idea) *is an old city*. Point out the full stop at the end of the sentence.

102 UNLOCK BASIC SKILLS TEACHER'S BOOK

Focus on the completed example in the book and read it aloud. Students work individually and complete the sentences. Monitor and help as necessary. Check students are using full stops. Play the audio for students to listen and check. Go through answers as a class.

> **Answers**
> 2 a lot of interesting buildings.
> 3 some beautiful streets.
> 4 a famous place.
> 5 a busy square.

SPEAKING

6 Focus on the photograph and ask: *What is this?* (a street), *Where is it?* (in London), *Is it busy?* (yes), *Is it old?* (yes), *Is there a shopping centre?* (yes). Focus on the matching exercise and read the completed example aloud. Students work individually, reading and matching to make as many sentences as they can. Students work in pairs and compare their answers orally. Monitor and note down any mistakes with the target language. Go through any corrections on the board as a class.

> **Answers**
> Answers will vary.

WRITING

7 Students work individually. Ask them to write sentences using words from Exercise 6. Monitor and check they are using correct punctuation. Allow five minutes for the exercise. Students swap books and check each other's writing.

> **Answers**
> Answers will vary.

> **Optional activity**
>
> **Chain sentences:** Follow the procedure on p. 11.
> 1 a market and a beach
> 2 an old market and a beautiful beach
> 3 There is an old market and a beautiful beach.

WATCH AND REMEMBER

> **Learning objectives**
>
> - Understand sentences about interesting places in a city – *There's a big shopping centre. There's an airport.*
> - Understand directions – *Turn right. Turn left. Go straight on.*
> - Practise telling people how to get somewhere – *Turn left. Go straight on.*
>
> See p. 6 for suggestions on how to use these Learning objectives in your lessons.

> **Lead-in**
>
> Ask students to discuss, in pairs or groups, some of the places in their home city which they find interesting.

PART 1

In Part 1, two people talk about some of the interesting places in the UAE and South Korea, including shopping centres, hotels and factories.

BEFORE YOU WATCH

1 Focus on the photographs and the words. Students work individually and match.

2 (◀) 7.12 Play the audio. Students listen and check their answers in Exercise 1. Students write the words under the photographs. Monitor and check students' writing.

> **Answers**
> a an office building b a shopping centre c a hotel
> d a car factory

WATCH

3 ▶ Focus on the sentences with options and the completed example. Read it aloud. Students read the sentences and predict the answers. Students watch Part 1 and check their predictions. Go through answers as a class.

> **Answers**
> 2 tall building 3 fish 4 good 5 tall 6 walks 7 beaches

> **NOTICE**
>
> Focus on sentence 3 (*There are a lot of fish in the hotel.*) Ask: *One fish or many?* (many). Point out no *s* for plural. Focus on the NOTICE box. Read the correct example as a class. Point out verb (*are*) for plural.

PLACES   UNIT 7

UNLOCK BASIC SKILLS TEACHER'S BOOK   103

AFTER YOU WATCH

In stronger classes, Exercise 4 should be completed by students after watching Part 1. In weaker classes, students can watch Part 1 again and complete Exercise 4 or use the audio script at the back of the book.

4 Students complete the gapped paragraph with words from the box. Students work in pairs and check their answers. Go through answers as a class. Model the word stress (i.e. ex*pen*sive, *in*teresting, *beau*tiful).

> **Answers**
> tall, big, interesting, beautiful, expensive

PART 2

In Part 2, a man gives directions to another man.

BEFORE YOU WATCH

5 (7.13) Focus on the photographs. Play the audio. Ask students to listen and point to the directions that they hear. Check understanding and drill the vocabulary. See pp. 7 and 9 for advice on concept checking and drilling.

WATCH

6 Students watch the video and choose the correct map. Students work in pairs and check their answer. Check the answer as a class.

> **Answer**
> a

AFTER YOU WATCH

7 Students watch Part 2 again and complete the gap. In weaker classes, tell students to write down *parks* and to tick ✓ it every time they hear it. Check the answer as a class.

> **Answers**
> 2 three

PART 3

In Part 3, students remember key information from the lesson and extend their vocabulary.

REMEMBER

8 Focus on the gapped sentences. Say: *Watch Part 3 and say.* Students watch Part 3 and answer the questions. Students complete the gapped sentences. Students work in pairs and check their answers. Go through answers as a class. Ask students which of the words they have written is an adjective (sentence 4).

> **Answers**
> 1 building 2 the shopping centre, the hotel 3 cars
> 4 interesting

MORE VOCABULARY: PLACES

9 Focus on the photographs and the words. Students work individually and match. Go through answers as a class. Students write the words under the photographs. Monitor students' writing.

> **Answers**
> a boats b station c bridge

ASK AND ANSWER

10 Students ask and answer the question in pairs. Students repeat the dialogue with a new partner, talking about different places.

⦿ LANGUAGE FOCUS

> **Learning objectives**
>
> - Describe the locations of buildings – *on Green Street, on the right, on the left, next to the restaurant, between the hospital and the shop, near the park*
> - Understand dialogues about the locations of buildings – *My house is on Green Street.*
> - Write sentences about the locations of buildings – *The market is between the shopping centre and the bank.*
> - Understand dialogues about directions – *Where is the bank? It's near the stadium. Turn right.*
> - Ask for, clarify, and give simple directions – *Turn right. I'm sorry. Could you say that again please?*
>
> See p. 6 for suggestions on how to use these Learning objectives in your lessons.

> **Lead-in**
>
> **Classroom messages:** Follow the procedure on p. 12.
> 1 I live near a park and a bank.
> 2 The library is a beautiful building.
> 3 There is an interesting market near the shopping centre.

PLACES   UNIT 7

VOCABULARY: LOCATION

1 🔊 7.14 👥 Focus on the pictures. Ask: *Where is this?* about each different place in the pictures. Encourage guesses, but don't confirm anything yet. Play the audio for students to listen and point to the pictures one by one as they hear the words. Check understanding and drill the vocabulary. See pp. 7 and 9 for advice on concept checking and drilling.

Demonstrate the exercise with a student. Point to any picture and encourage the student to say the correct phrase. Then encourage the student to point at a different picture and say the correct phrase yourself. Students work in pairs. Monitor and correct any mistakes with vocabulary or pronunciation.

2 👤👥 Focus on the map. Ask: *Where are you?* Students point to the location *You are here!*. Point to each building and street name and ask: *What's this?* Read the first sentence aloud. Say: *Yes or no?* in a questioning tone. Elicit the correct answer (yes). Students work individually, looking at the map and circling *Yes* or *No* for each sentence. Students work in pairs and compare their answers. Go through answers as a class. Use the map to explain the incorrect answers. For the No answers, elicit the correct information from students.

> **Answers**
> 2 Yes
> 3 No (The bank is on the left.)
> 4 No (The park is next to the stadium.)
> 5 Yes
> 6 Yes

> **Optional activity**
> You will need printable Flashcards 7.1 and 7.2 which can be printed at esource.cambridge.org and some sticky tack.
> Use some sticky tack to stick the cards to the board. Use these combinations of flashcards:
> *park, office building, shopping centre* (in a row, close together)
> Say: *This is a street.* Elicit as many possible sentences as you can about the buildings and their locations. (The park is next to the office building. The office building is between the park and the shopping centre., etc.)
> Now add another row of cards, opposite the other cards.
> *train station, restaurant, hospital*

Say: *This is the other side of the street.* Use gestures to help communicate your meaning. Split the class into teams of three or four. This time, students knock on the desk when they have thought of a sentence. Award a point to the team for each grammatically correct sentence a student says. Subtract a point for repetition or long pauses. Keep score on the board. The first team to get five points is the winner.

READING AND WRITING

3 🔊 7.15 👤 Focus on the options in the first sentence. Ask: *On Old Street or between Old Street?* (on Old Street). Ask a student to read the sentence aloud. Point at the pictures in Exercise 1 and say: *on Green Street.* Students work individually, reading the sentences and the options and circling the correct answers. Play the audio for students to listen, and check. Go through answers as a class. Then ask students to write the correct answers in the gaps. Monitor and check students have copied the phrases without missing any small words.

> **Answers**
> 2 next to 3 near 4 on the right 5 between

> 👁 **Common student errors**
>
> Arabic L1 students frequently omit *be*. This error often occurs before a prepositional phrase. These are some typical errors:
> *My house ^ next to the bus station. My home ^ in Station Road. The house ^ in Dubai Street behind the hospital.*
> See p. 148 for tips on how to help students with **Missing words** errors.

LISTENING FOR KEY INFORMATION

4 🔊 7.16 👤 Focus on the first photograph. Ask: *Who is asking questions? Who is answering questions?* (the man on the left is asking questions). Repeat with the second photograph (the woman on the left is asking questions). Focus on the speech bubbles. Point out the options in the speech bubbles. Play the audio. Ask students to read, listen and circle the correct words. Go through answers as a class.

> **Answers**
> **Male 2:** New Street is on the <u>left</u>.
> **Female 1:** <u>Excuse me.</u> Where's the bank?
> **Female 2:** … near <u>the square</u>. It's <u>between</u> two restaurants.

UNL*O*CK BASIC SKILLS TEACHER'S BOOK   **105**

> **NOTICE**
>
> Focus on the NOTICE box. Focus on the map in Exercise 2. Point to the library and New Street. Say: *It's on New Street.* Say the sentence and ask students to repeat after you. Ask: *Where's the bank?* and encourage students to direct you from *You are here!* on the map to the bank.

PRONUNCIATION FOR LISTENING

5 🔊 7.17 👥 Focus on the four sentences. Point out the highlighted words and syllables. Say the sentences aloud, exaggerating the sentence stress. Say the highlighted words very loudly and clearly and the other words quietly. Play the audio for students to repeat. Drill the sentences. See p. 9 for advice on drilling.

Focus on the first dialogue in the speech bubbles in Exercise 4 again. Students work in pairs and practise the short dialogues. Monitor and correct any pronunciation errors. See p. 9 for advice on teaching stress.

SPEAKING

6 👥 Divide the class into Student As and Student Bs. Tell Student As to look at Student's Book p. 201 and Student Bs to look at Student's Book p. 204. Focus on the maps. Ask: *Where are you?* Students point to the location *You are here!* Focus on the REMEMBER box and the questions they need to ask. Say: *Student As ask questions and Student Bs answer.* Ask a pair of students to start first taking on the roles of both A and B. Students practise the dialogues in pairs. Students swap roles after each dialogue. Continue the exercise until students have practised all the dialogues.

ACADEMIC LISTENING AND SPEAKING

> **Learning objectives**
>
> - Understand short descriptions of an interesting place in a city
> - CT: Remember notes on an ideas map from a short presentation
> - CT: Apply existing knowledge to an ideas map for an oral presentation
> - Give a short presentation about an interesting place in a city
>
> See p. 6 for suggestions on how to use these Learning objectives in your lessons.

> **Lead-in**
>
> Write name poems about a city or a country with your class. Write the name of the city/country vertically down the left-hand side of the board and horizontally as shown in bold. Elicit words beginning with each letter that the students associate with the place, e.g.
>
> **D**ubai
> **U**niversities
> **B**usy
> **A**irport
> **I**nteresting
>
> Encourage students to think about food, places, people, adjectives, activities and things, e.g. *What is it like? What places are there? What do you eat in* (Dubai)? etc. Allow them to flick through their books to look for words. You may wish to prepare some ideas before the lesson for the place you choose, so that you can anticipate any possibly difficult letters to find a word for.

USING VISUALS TO PREDICT THE CONTENT

1 👥 Focus on the photographs. Point at the photographs of the two people and ask: *What is his/her name?* (Advik, Rachel), *Where is he/she from?* (India, Singapore). Point at the photographs of the places. Ask: *What's this?* (a market, a street). Read the sentences about Chandi Chowk aloud. Focus on the options. Students work in pairs and circle the adjectives which describe the market in the photographs. Then repeat for Orchard Road. Do not confirm students' guesses yet.

LISTENING FOR DETAIL

2 🔊 7.18 👤 Play the audio once all the way through. Students work individually and check their ideas in Exercise 1. Play the audio again and check the answers with the class as you hear them.

> **Answers**
>
> Chandni Chowk: busy, old
> Orchard Road: new, clean, interesting

3 🔊 7.18 👥 Focus on the sentences. Ask students to read all of the sentences. If they can remember the answers, allow them to circle them, but do not confirm if they are correct at this time. Read the first sentence aloud. Say: *Yes or no?* in a questioning tone. Elicit the correct answer (yes). Play the audio. Students work individually and circle *Yes* or *No* for each sentence. Students work in pairs and

106 UNLOCK BASIC SKILLS TEACHER'S BOOK

PLACES   UNIT 7

compare their answers. Go over answers as a class. For the No answers, elicit the correct information from students.

> Answers
> 2 No (There are a lot of small shops …)
> 3 Yes 4 No (It isn't very old.) 5 Yes 6 Yes

CRITICAL THINKING: REMEMBER

4 🔊 7.19 Focus on the ideas map. Read the central circle aloud. Ask: *Who?* and point to the photographs of Advik and Rachel on p. 140 (Rachel). Point to each circle and ask different students to read the words there. Then focus on the gaps and the words in the box. Point out the completed example (famous street) to model the task. Students work individually and write the missing words in the circles. Play the audio for students to listen and check their answers. Go through answers with the class. In weaker classes, students could use the audio script (Track 7.18) on Student's Book p. 222 to find the answers.

> Answers
> 2 shopping centre 3 buildings 4 new

CRITICAL THINKING: APPLY

5 Focus on the blank ideas map. Tell students that they will give a short presentation about an interesting place in their city and they will first prepare some ideas. Elicit some ideas about places to write about. Students work individually and write the name of the interesting place in the centre of their ideas map. Tell students they can use the nouns and adjectives in the box or any other words to complete the ideas map. Monitor and help with ideas. If, when the time is up, any students cannot think of enough ideas, use the whole class as a source of ideas.

PRONUNCIATION FOR SPEAKING

6 🔊 7.20 This exercise focuses on the pronunciation of *There's* and *There are*. Model the pronunciation of each expression with slightly exaggerated mouth movements. Encourage students to repeat after you. Play the audio for students to repeat.

Students work in pairs and practise saying the sentences. Monitor and correct any pronunciation errors. Make sure students are not over-stressing the target words. These should be weak forms.

SPEAKING TASK

7 You will need to prepare a short presentation about an interesting place from your own city (similar to the speakers in Exercises 2 and 3) before the lesson. Try to choose an unusual place that students are unlikely to choose. Model the speaking exercise by giving this short presentation. Focus on the REMEMBER box. Tell students to practise their presentations in pairs. Ask for a volunteer from the class to give their presentation first. Stand nearby as each student speaks and help as necessary by encouraging them to look at their notes, if they are finding the exercise difficult.

> Model answer
> I live near King's Cross train station in London.
> There is a beautiful square near the train station.
> There are famous hotels and expensive restaurants.
> There are tall buildings and a lot of small shops.
> King's Cross train station is an interesting place in my city.

> **Optional activity**
>
> **Role play:** Role plays are excellent fluency activities, but may not be appropriate or possible in every teaching context.
>
> Students role play bus tours to the place they talked about in Exercise 7. Demonstrate the exercise with a volunteer. Put two chairs at the front of the class. Ask the student to sit next to you. Say: *We're on the bus.* Look around as if you are on a bus. *This is King's Cross train station.* Gesture indicating the outside of the building. Say: *There is an expensive hotel.* Gesture towards a different place. Encourage the student to respond, e.g. *It's beautiful!* You can whisper the suggested response to them to help them get the idea. Continue in this way, using the ideas from your presentation.
>
> Divide the class into Student As and Student Bs. Student As are guides. Student Bs are companions. Monitor and note down any good examples of language the students use and any typical mistakes. Allow a few minutes for the exercise. Then students swap roles.
>
> Use the notes you made for class feedback at the end of the lesson. See p. 8 for ideas for giving feedback after speaking activities.

UNLOCK BASIC SKILLS TEACHER'S BOOK

ACADEMIC READING AND WRITING

> **Learning objectives**
>
> - Understand a text about places in and around a university
> - CT: Understand a student's notes about a map
> - CT: Evaluate places on a map and describe them
> - Complete a text describing details of places in and around a university
>
> See p. 6 for suggestions on how to use these Learning objectives in your lessons.

> **Lead-in**
>
> Write the name of your university or college at the top of the board. Then write: *Places*.
>
> Give students oral clues to the places in your university, e.g. *It is new. There are a lot of books. There are some computers.* (library)
>
> *It is busy. There is a lot of food and drink.* (restaurant)
>
> *There are pencils and pens. There are notebooks. It is cheap.* (shop)
>
> *There are a lot of teachers. There are no students.* (teachers' room)
>
> *There are a lot of computers. There is Wi-Fi.* (student lounge / computer room)
>
> Make the sentences true about your university or college. Encourage students to guess. Write correct answers on the board. Then students work in pairs or small groups and take turns to give each other clues to the places in the university/college.

PREPARING TO READ

1 Focus on the photographs in Exercise 1 and Exercise 2. Ask: *What's this?* (a university, a student house, a library). Read the sentence and options aloud. Students work in pairs and circle the places which they expect to find at a university. Go through answers as a class.

> **Answers**
>
> a library, classrooms, student houses, office buildings

SCANNING FOR KEY INFORMATION

2 Write: *the city, student houses, library* on the board. Ask students to find and underline these words in the text, but not to read the text yet. Allow 20 seconds for this exercise.

3 Ask students to read sentences 1–3. Students find the answers by looking at the words they underlined. Allow 40 seconds for this exercise. When the time is up, go through answers as a class.

> **Answers**
>
> 1 Yes 2 No 3 Yes

4 🔊 7.21 Focus on the text in Exercise 2. Play the audio for students to listen and read. Focus on gapped sentences 1–5. Ask a student to read the first sentence aloud. Ask students to quickly find the information in the text (Sentence 1 Our university is near the city centre on Volkan Street.). Ask students to read sentences 2–5 and quickly find the information. Students compare their answers in pairs. Go through answers with the class, asking students to show you the sentences in the text in which they found the information for each answer.

> **Answers**
>
> 2 Street 3 2,000 4 expensive 5 library

READING FOR DETAIL

5 Focus on the map. Ask: *Where is Volkan Street? Where is the library?*, etc. Point out the numbered gaps for labels and the words in the box. Ask students to read the text on Student's Book p. 142 again and label the map using the words from the box. Students work individually and then check their answers in pairs. Go through answers as a class, asking students to show you the sentences in the text in which they found the information for each answer.

> **Answers**
>
> 1 train station 2 restaurant 3 office buildings

CRITICAL THINKING: ANALYZE

6 Focus on the maps and the letters *a* and *b*. Read the first sentence aloud (The university is near a beautiful beach.). Point at the sentence and ask: *Places?* Point at the words *university* and *beach* in the sentence. Demonstrate underlining them in the book. Repeat the procedure for the next sentence. Ask students to read all the sentences, underline the places, and match them to map *a* or *b*. Students work individually and then check their answer in pairs. Go through answers as a class, asking students to show you the details on the map which show the information for each answer.

> **Answer**
>
> All match map b.

PLACES — UNIT 7

ACADEMIC WRITING SKILLS

7 🔊 7.22 👤 Write the vowels on the board: *a, e, i, o, u*. Point out the completed example. Ask: *What word is this?* (restaurant). Repeat with the second word (classrooms). Elicit the missing vowels (a, oo). Students complete the words with the missing vowels. Play the audio for students to listen and check their answers. Monitor and check that weaker students are keeping up with the audio and checking their answers correctly. With weaker classes, write the answers on the board.

> **Answers**
> 2 cl*a*ssr*oo*ms 3 l*i*brary 4 tr*ai*n st*a*tion 5 h*ou*se
> 6 *o*ffice b*ui*lding 7 p*a*rk

> **⊙ Common student errors**
>
> In this unit, *there, restaurant* and *interesting* are all in the top 10 misspelled words by Arabic L1 students. These are typical errors: *ther, resturant, intersting*
> To focus on these words, write on the board:
> there ther _ the _ _ th _ _ _
> restaurant rest _ _ rant rest _ _ _ ant res _ _ _ _ ant
> interesting int _ _ esting inter _ _ ting int _ _ _ _ ting
> Focus on the first word (there). Ask students to spell it aloud. Then remove the complete word from the board. Ask them to spell the word out again and complete the first word's gap with an *e* if they are successful. Then remove the completed word. Continue like this with all of the words.

CRITICAL THINKING: EVALUATE

8 👤👥 Focus on the places 1–5. Ask students to find these places in map *a* in Exercise 6. Ask: *What is the train station like?* Tell students to choose an adjective from the list in Exercise 8. Tell students that they will have different answers, there are no right answers, but note that *good* is not likely to be matched with *train station, office building* or *park*. Students compare their ideas in small groups.

> **Answers**
> Answers will vary.

WRITING TASK

9 👤 Focus on the handwritten notes. Tell students they are going to write about map *a* in Exercise 6. Read the first sentence and elicit *station*. Read the second sentence and ask students to look at the map and the words they wrote in Exercise 8 and give you ideas. Accept all possible answers. Students work individually to complete the sentences about map *a*. Monitor and help with ideas as necessary.

10 👥 Students swap books and check the other student's spelling and punctuation. Ask them to find one thing that was the same and one thing that was different in their texts. Take class feedback. Ask the students to correct each other's texts. Students can write a second draft in their notebooks as homework or in class.

> **Model answer**
>
> The university is near the train station.
> There is an old library next to the classrooms.
> There are student houses near a good restaurant.
> There is a park next to the train station.
> There is an office building between the restaurant and the park.

> **Objectives review**
>
> See Introduction on p. 7 for ideas about using the Objectives review with your students.
>
> **WORDLIST AND GLOSSARY**
>
> See Introduction on p. 7 for ideas about using the Wordlist at the end of each unit and the Glossary at the end of the book with your students.
>
> **REVIEW TEST**
>
> Go to esource.cambridge.org to print the Review test and for ideas about how and when to administer the Review test.

RESEARCH PROJECT

> **Give a presentation on a city in a different country**
>
> Show the class some websites advertising different cities as travel destinations, preferably in the students' L1 or with a lot of photographs. Divide the class into groups and tell them each group needs to choose a city which is known to them or which they would like to visit. If necessary, provide students with an English name of the city.
>
> Tell students that each group will give a 2–3 minute presentation using photographs and maps of the places they find online.
>
> Allow students class time for the research or encourage them to do this for homework. Give students class time during the next lesson to plan their presentations. Encourage students to make idea maps and to divide up the speaking between different group members.
>
> After students have given the presentations, encourage other students to ask questions.

UNLOCK BASIC SKILLS TEACHER'S BOOK

8 SPENDING

UNLOCK YOUR KNOWLEDGE

👥 Focus on the photograph. Point out the questions. Ask a student to read each question aloud. Students work in groups and answer the questions. Monitor and help as necessary. Take feedback as a class. Ask: *What is this food? Where is this shop? What is this shop like?* Elicit ideas from the class.

> **Answers**
> 1 b 2 b 3 Students' own answers.

LISTENING AND READING 1

Learning objectives

- Name consumer items – *smartphone, video game, newspaper, bank card, laptop, watch, T-shirt, tablet*
- Understand conversations about consumer items
- Describe possessions using noun phrases with articles and adjectives – *a beautiful bag, an old T-shirt*
- Ask and answer questions about possessions – *How many smartphones do you have? I have two smartphones.*

See p. 6 for suggestions on how to use these Learning objectives in your lessons.

Lead-in

You will need printable Flashcards 8.1. Go to esource.cambridge.org to print the flashcards. You will also need something like a large folder or blank piece of card to cover the cards with.

Hold up the first card behind the folder so that students cannot see it. Slowly pull the card out to your right, so that students can see a little bit of the photograph. Encourage students to guess the object on the card. Slowly reveal more and more of the card. Award the card to the student who guessed correctly and repeat for all the cards in the set.

Collect the cards and hold them up one at a time. Elicit full sentences about each card. This time award the card to a student who makes a grammatically correct sentence including the word on the card, e.g. *I have two televisions. / How many mobile phones do you have? / There is a radio in the car.* Encourage a variety of sentence structures.

VOCABULARY: THINGS WE BUY

1 🔊 8.1 👥 Focus on the photographs of objects. Play the audio for students to listen and read. Encourage students to follow the audio by pointing at each object as they hear it. Drill the names of the objects. See p. 9 for advice on drilling. Check understanding using printable Flashcards 8.1. Go to esource.cambridge.org to print the flashcards.

Demonstrate the next part of the exercise with a student. Point to an object and encourage a student to say the correct word. Then encourage the student to point at an object and say the correct word yourself. Students work in pairs. Monitor and correct any errors.

SOUND AND SPELLING: *a*

2 🔊 8.2 👥 Focus on the words. Ask: *Which letter is in all of the words?* (a). Play the audio for students to listen and repeat. Model the phoneme /ɑː/ and then say the first word: *car*. Ask: *Can you hear /ɑː/?* Help students to understand the question by cupping your ear and using culturally appropriate gestures to indicate *yes* or *no*. Repeat with *card* (yes) *what* (no) *watch* (no). Elicit the sound in *what* and *watch* (/ɒ/). Elicit the sounds in *take, game* /eɪ/, *bad, bag* /æ/. Play the audio again. Students listen and repeat the words. Correct any errors with the phonemes /ɑː/ /ɒ/ /eɪ/ /æ/.

3 🔊 8.3 👥 Focus on words 1–4 on the left. Encourage students to read out the words one by one with the correct sound of *a*. Then focus on the two lists on the right. Say: *Say and match*. Demonstrate the exercise using the completed example. Students work in pairs, reading out and matching the sounds. Play the audio for students to check. Go through answers as a class. Drill each set of words. For advice on drilling, see p. 9.

> **Answers**
>
> | 2 card | smartphone | market |
> |---|---|---|
> | 3 game | newspaper | name |
> | 4 what | wasp | watch |

110 UNLOCK BASIC SKILLS TEACHER'S BOOK

SPENDING UNIT 8

> **Optional activity**
>
> To reinforce three common sounds of a /ɑː/ /eɪ/ /æ/, give a short test of some of the words taught in this course so far. Read out these words:
>
> 1 late 2 maths 3 start 4 stadium 5 taxi 6 factory 7 manager
>
> With strong classes you could add: 8 tall /ɔː/ 9 small /ɔː/ 10 day /eɪ/
>
> Students listen and write in their notebooks. Students swap notebooks. Then write the answers on the board. Students check each other's writing for correct spelling.

LISTENING FOR GENERAL UNDERSTANDING

4 ◀) 8.4 Focus on the photographs of Tao and Jun. Ask: *What are their names?* Focus on the sentence. Students work in pairs, looking at the photograph and circling the option they think is correct. Say: *Listen and check.* Play the audio. Go through answers as a class.

> **Answer**
>
> a

READING FOR GENERAL UNDERSTANDING

5 ◀) 8.4 Focus on the conversation and point out the options. Say: *Read and circle.* Students work individually and circle the correct options. Play the audio again and go through answers as a class. Point out the plural form of the noun used in *How many…?* Ask students to circle the *s* in each plural noun.

> **Answers**
>
> Tao: How many <u>watches</u> do you have?
> Tao: I look at the time on my smartphones and my <u>laptop</u>.
> Jun: How many <u>smartphones</u> do you have?
> Jun: It's <u>old</u>. I have a lot of <u>T-shirts</u>.

ACADEMIC WRITING SKILLS

6 ◀) 8.5 Focus on the table. Check understanding of the sentences. See p. 7 for advice on concept checking. Point out that articles come before adjectives. Write on the board: *a watch.* Ask: *What is it like?* Elicit an adjective, e.g. *beautiful/expensive.* Ask: *Where?* Point at the words on the board.

Elicit the correct position for the adjective. Focus on the table again. Play the audio for students to listen and read. Drill the sentences in the table, focusing on the weak articles and the stressed adjectives. See p. 9 for advice on drilling. Elicit variations on the sentences in the table.

7 ◀) 8.6 Focus on the first photograph. Say: *What is this?* (a watch). Focus on the options under the line in the first sentence. Point at the words under the line and use appropriate hand gestures to indicate that students need to reorder the words. Say: *Listen* and read the first sentence aloud. Demonstrate reordering the sentence and writing it on the line. Students work individually and write the correct answers on the lines. Monitor and check students' spelling and use of full stops. Play the audio for students to listen and check. Go through answers as a class.

> **Answers**
>
> 2 an expensive smartphone
> 3 an old T-shirt
> 4 an interesting newspaper

SPEAKING AND WRITING

8 Focus on the first two speech bubbles and the table. Demonstrate the exercise with a student. Point to the space for a number in the table and the heading *How many?* Ask: *How many smartphones do you have?* Elicit a full sentence using the speech bubbles, e.g. *I have one smartphone.* Demonstrate writing the answer in the table in the book. Encourage students to ask you a question and respond to this yourself. Monitor and correct errors with question forms, plurals, vocabulary or pronunciation. Ensure students are responding with full sentences. Students work in pairs and talk about the objects in the table, noting the answers in the table.

Focus on the third speech bubble. Students work in new pairs and describe their previous partner to their new partner.

> **Answers**
>
> Answers will vary.

UNLOCK BASIC SKILLS TEACHER'S BOOK 111

LISTENING AND READING 2

Learning objectives

- Name calendar times – *a day, a week, a month, a year*
- Use expressions of frequency – *once a day, twice a year, every month*
- Understand people describing their shopping habits
- Describe how often you buy different things – *I buy a coffee twice a day.*

See p. 6 for suggestions on how to use these Learning objectives in your lessons.

Lead-in

You will need printable Flashcards 8.2, words and pictures separate. Go to esource.cambridge.org to print the flashcards.

Team pelmanism: Review the objects using the flashcards. Then follow the procedure on p. 10.

VOCABULARY: CALENDAR TIME

1 ◀) 8.7 Focus on the pictures. Ask students to listen and follow the audio by pointing at each word or phrase as they hear it. Play the audio. Check understanding by writing on the board: *a day, a week, a month, a year*. Ask about each time period: *How many days (1, 7, 28–31, 365)?* Write the numbers above the words. Drill the words. See p. 9 for advice on drilling.

Write: *once a day, once a week, once a month, once a year* in a horizontal line on the board. Say: *I buy coffee once a day. How many coffees in a year (365)? I buy coffee once a week. How many coffees in a year (52)? I buy coffee once a month. How many coffees in a year (12)? I buy coffee once a year. How many coffees in a year (1)?*

Draw a horizontal arrow under the expressions. Write *more* on the left, under *once a day* and *less* on the right under *once a year*.

Say: *I drink coffee twice a day. How many coffees in a year? (730)*. Write: *twice a day* on the right of the arrow to show it's the most frequent.

Students work individually and copy the arrow and time phrases in their notebooks.

USING BACKGROUND KNOWLEDGE TO PREDICT CONTENT

2 ◀) 8.8 Focus on the photographs in Exercise 2. Point at the photographs of the two people and ask: *What is his/her name?* (Enrique, Namareq), *What's his/her job?* (a bank manager / a student). Focus on the sentences. Read the sentences about the bank manager aloud. Focus on the objects. Students work in pairs and circle the objects they think Enrique buys. Then repeat for Namareq. Play the audio for students to check. Go through answers as a class.

Answers

1 Enrique buys coffee, a smartphone and a laptop.
2 Namareq buys English books, tablets and video games.

READING FOR DETAIL

3 ◀) 8.8 Demonstrate the exercise using the completed example. Say: *Read and listen*. Play the audio and encourage students to follow the text by pointing at the words as they are said. Students work in pairs and match the sentence halves under the text. Go through answers as a class. Encourage students to show you the sentences in which they found the answers.

Answers

1 He buys a newspaper He buys a new smartphone	once a week. twice a year.
2 Namareq buys a new book She buys a new game She buys a new tablet	once a week. twice a month. once a year.

Optional activity

Running dictation: Follow the procedure on p. 12.
Divide the class into Team As and Team Bs. Use two different texts from Exercise 4. Team As – Enrique. Team Bs – Namareq.

GRAMMAR: FREQUENCY EXPRESSIONS 2

4 ◀) 8.9 Write these jumbled sentences on the board: *1 I / twice / buy a book / a month, 2 day / walk to university / we / every*. Focus on the table. Play the audio and encourage students to follow the text by pointing at each line in the book as they hear it. Focus on the sentences on the board. Point at the words and use appropriate hand gestures to indicate that students need to reorder the words. Elicit the correct sentences (1 I buy a book twice a month. 2 We walk to university every day.).

Play the audio again and drill the sentences in the table. Encourage students to create new sentences using the words in the table.

WRITING

5 (◄) 8.10 Focus on the options under the line in the first sentence. Point at the words under the line and use appropriate hand gestures to indicate that students need to reorder the words. Say: *Listen* and read the completed example aloud. Demonstrate reordering the sentence and writing it on the line. Students work individually and write the sentences in the correct order. Monitor and check students' spelling and use of full stops. Play the audio for students to check. Go through answers as a class.

> **Answers**
> 2 She buys a smartphone once a year.
> 3 He buys coffee twice a day.
> 4 They buy video games once a month.
> 5 I buy a newspaper once a week.

SPEAKING

6 Focus on the speech bubbles. Drill the question and answer. Focus on the photographs and the words in the box. Demonstrate the exercise with a student. Point at the first photograph and ask: *How often do you buy a newspaper?* Point at the words in the box and elicit an answer from the student, e.g. *I buy a newspaper every week.*

Students work in pairs and talk about their shopping habits. Monitor and help as necessary. Note any errors and any correct use of language which has not been covered in the course so far as you monitor. Use the notes you made for feedback at the end of the exercise. See p. 8 for advice on conducting feedback on speaking activities.

Take feedback on any differences they found, e.g. *I buy a laptop once a year. Bader buys a laptop twice a year.*

SPENDING   UNIT 8

LISTENING AND READING 3

> **Learning objectives**
> - Use verb phrases to talk about shopping – *go shopping, buy clothes, buy shoes, buy things on the internet, spend money, pay with cash, pay by card*
> - Understand conversations about shopping habits
> - Ask and answer questions about shopping habits – *How often do you go shopping? Where do you buy your clothes? Do you buy things on the internet?*
> - Write questions about shopping habits
> - Learn common spellings of /w/ and /θ/ – *once, twice, where, watch, things, month*
>
> See p. 6 for suggestions on how to use these Learning objectives in your lessons.

> **Lead-in**
> Write these sentences on the board. Make sure that some of the sentences are true about you and some are not true.
>
> 1 I _____ to university every day.
> 2 I _____ a new laptop once a year.
> 3 I _____ lunch in a restaurant twice a month.
> 4 I _____ friends twice a week.
> 5 I _____ to a different country every year.
>
> Elicit the correct verbs and their spellings to complete each sentence from the class (1 drive 2 buy 3 have 4 meet 5 travel). With weaker classes, write the verbs in a box at random.
>
> Students work in pairs. Focus on the first sentence and indicate yourself. Say: *Yes or no?* in a questioning tone. Encourage students to read the sentence and guess if it is true or not. Take a class vote (with hands raised) and then tell them who is right. Tell them the truth e.g. *I drive to university once a week.* Continue with each sentence.

VOCABULARY: SHOPPING

1 (◄) 8.11 Focus on the photographs. Play the audio for students to listen and read. Encourage students to follow the audio by pointing at each verb phrase as they hear it. Drill the verb phrases. See p. 9 for advice on drilling. Check understanding of the new words. Use concept questions. Say: *Do I go shopping in the university?* (no). *Where do I go shopping?* (in the shopping centre / in the city), etc. Pay particular attention to the difference between *pay* and *spend*. See p. 7 for advice on concept checking.

UNLOCK BASIC SKILLS TEACHER'S BOOK   **113**

Write the following on the board: *buy things _ the internet, pay _ cash, pay _ card*. Focus on the photographs and words in Exercise 1. Point at the gaps in the phrases on the board and elicit that *on* is missing from the first gap. Elicit the other missing preposition (*by*). Complete the verb phrases on the board. Remove everything except the nouns from the board. Encourage students to recall the phrases without looking at their books.

Demonstrate the next part of the exercise with a student. Point to a photograph and encourage a student to say the correct verb phrase. Then encourage the student to point at a photograph and say the correct verb phrase yourself. Students work in pairs. Monitor and correct any mistakes.

> ### ⊙ Common student errors
>
> **Extra word:** Arabic and Turkish L1 students often add an unnecessary preposition after *go* in go verb +ing, e.g. *go for/to shopping*.
>
> *I often go for shopping to buy some clothes. I love to go to shopping.*
>
> **Wrong word:** Arabic L1 students often replace *go* with *do* before activities with verb + *ing*, e.g. *go shopping*.
>
> These are some typical errors:
>
> *I do shopping twice a week. It's interesting because you can do swimming and fishing.*
>
> See p. 148 for tips on how to help students with **Extra word and Wrong word** errors.

READING FOR DETAIL

2 🔊 8.12 👤 Focus on the photograph and ask: *What is his name?* (Rob). Focus on *Rob buys things* and the a–c options. Read each possible sentence aloud. Say: *Listen and circle two places*. Play the audio. Students work individually, reading the text and circling two places. Go through answers as a class.

Point out the prepositions used with each of the places. Write these phrases on the board: ___ *the internet*, ___ *the shopping centre*, ___ *the market*. Elicit the correct prepositions from the students (*on, in, at*).

> ### Answers
> a and c

LISTENING FOR KEY INFORMATION

3 🔊 8.12 👤👥 Focus on the text and point out the options. Say: *Listen, read and circle*. Students work individually and circle the correct options in the text. Students work in pairs. Play the audio again and go through answers as a class. Strong classes could practise the dialogues in pairs.

> ### Answers
> **Salim:** How often do you buy new clothes?
> **Rob:** I buy new clothes <u>twice a year</u>.
> **Salim:** Where do you buy your clothes?
> **Rob:** I buy jeans and T-shirts <u>on the internet</u>.
> **Salim:** Do you buy shoes on the internet?
> **Rob:** <u>No, I don't</u>.
> **Salim:** How often do you go shopping?
> **Rob:** <u>Once a week</u>. I spend a lot of money in this shopping centre.
> **Salim:** Do you pay by bank card or by cash?
> **Rob:** I pay <u>by card</u>. It's easy.

> ### Optional activity
>
> You will need one copy of the dialogue for each group of three students. Photocopy the audio script on Student's Book p. 152 and cut the text into the turns taken by each speaker. Shuffle each set of dialogue and fasten it with a paper clip before the lesson.
>
> In class, give out one set of dialogue to each group. Use appropriate hand gestures to indicate that students need to read and reorder the dialogue. Play the audio for Exercise 3 for students to check their answers.

> ### NOTICE
>
> Focus on the NOTICE box. Allow students a minute to read the information there. Ask students to look at the text in Exercise 3 and underline the words *buy, pay* and *spend*. Focus on the prepositions used with these verbs. Ask a student to read the sentences with underlined verbs aloud.

WRITING

4 👤👥 Focus on the words in the box. Point at the first sentence and say: *How often?* Elicit the answer (every week). Say: *Write about you*. Students work individually and write full sentences. Monitor and check students are forming frequency expressions correctly. Students swap books and check each other's writing. Remind students to check the spelling and punctuation. Ask for volunteers to read their sentences to the class.

> ### Answers
> Answers will vary.

SPENDING UNIT 8

GRAMMAR: PRESENT SIMPLE QUESTIONS

5 (8.13) Focus on the table. Play the audio and encourage students to follow the text by pointing at each line as it is said. Write these gapped questions on the board: *1 How often ___ ___ go shopping? 2 Where ___ ___ buy clothes? 3 ___ ___ buy things on the internet?* Focus on the questions on the board. Elicit the correct words for each gap (do you). Elicit possible answers to each question. Play the audio again and drill the questions. See p. 9 for advice on drilling.

6 (8.14) Focus on the word under the line in the first question. Read the question aloud. Demonstrate writing the question form on the line. Students work individually and write the question form on the line. Play the audio for students to listen and check. Monitor and check students' spelling. Go through answers as a class.

> **Answers**
> 2 do you go 3 do you buy 4 do you go
> 5 Do you spend 6 Do you buy

> **NOTICE**
> Focus on the NOTICE box. Allow students a minute to read the information there. Ask students to underline a sentence in Exercise 6 that has the phrase *spend on* (5).

SOUND AND SPELLING: th, w, o

> **◉ Common student errors**
> The consonant sound /θ/ (thing) does not occur in Japanese. Students find it difficult to produce this sound and this leads to spelling errors. This is a typical error: *shin* (thin).

7 (8.15) Focus on the words. Draw attention to the highlighted letters. Play the audio. Students listen and repeat. Model the phonemes /θ/ and /w/ and drill each line of words. Correct any errors with /θ/ and /w/.

SPEAKING

8 Tell students to go to Student's Book p. 207. Focus on the survey. Point at the options under each question. Students work individually, reading and circling their answers. Complete the survey yourself. Put the students in groups of four or five. Demonstrate the speaking exercise. Describe your own survey results. Students work in small groups and individually describe their results. Monitor and check that students are using statement word order. Take class feedback on any interesting answers.

WATCH AND REMEMBER

> **Learning objectives**
> - Understand sentences about what and how often people buy things – *I buy bread twice a week.*
> - Understand sentences about the cost of things and the way people buy them – *A bag of fruit is six lira. I pay by card.*
> - Practise talking about gadgets, and how often you buy them – *How often do you buy ... ? I buy ... once a week / twice a year.*
>
> See p. 6 for suggestions on how to use these Learning objectives in your lessons.

> **Lead-in**
> Students work in pairs and talk about five things they buy every week or month. Take feedback as a class.

PART 1

In Part 1, three people from different countries talk about the products they regularly buy.

BEFORE YOU WATCH

1 (8.16) Focus on the photographs. Play the audio for students to listen and read. Encourage students to follow the audio by pointing at each currency as they hear it. Check understanding of the new words. Demonstrate the next part of the exercise with a student. Point to a photograph and encourage a student to say the correct currency. Then encourage the student to point at a photograph and say the correct currency yourself. Students work in pairs. Monitor and correct any errors.

WATCH

2 Focus on the sentences and the options. Students read the sentences and predict their answers. Students watch Part 1 and check their predictions. Go through answers as a class. Check students understand the word *banana*.

> **Answers**
> 2 pound 3 week 4 three 5 once 6 dollars

AFTER YOU WATCH

In stronger classes, Exercise 3 should be completed by students after watching Part 1. In weaker classes, students can watch Part 1 again and complete Exercise 3 or use the audio script at the back of the book.

3 Focus on the dialogue with gaps and the words in the box. Point at the completed example and read it aloud. Students complete the dialogue with words in the box. Students work in pairs and check their answers. Go through answers as a class. Check students understand the word *cash*.

> **Answers**
> pound, pay, cash

PART 2

In Part 2, four people talk about what they like to buy, talking in particular about gadgets (electronic devices).

BEFORE YOU WATCH

4 Focus on the photographs and the words in the box. Students work individually and match the words to the photographs. Then students write the words. Monitor students' writing. Go through answers as a class. Ask students which of the gadgets they have.

> **Answers**
> a tablet b laptop c video game d bank card

WATCH

5 Focus on the objects and the options on the right. Ask students to predict their answers. Students watch Part 2 and check their predictions. Go through answers as a class.

> **Answers**
> 1 two thousand dirhams 2 cheap 3 ten dirhams

AFTER YOU WATCH

6 Focus on the gapped sentences. Students work individually and write about their spending habits. Students complete the gapped sentences. If students find this hard, provide clues about what word is needed in each gap (i.e. 1 a gadget / an object, 2 a period of time). Students can repeat this exercise several times, writing about different objects they buy.

> **Answers**
> Answers will vary.

PART 3

In Part 3, students remember key information from the lesson and extend their vocabulary.

REMEMBER

7 Focus on the names in the gapped sentences and the words in the box. Students watch Part 3 and answer the questions. Students complete the sentences with words in the box. Students work in pairs and check their answers. Go through answers as a class.

> **Answers**
> 1 fruit 2 a tablet 3 a coffee

MORE VOCABULARY: FOOD

8 Focus on the photographs and the line under each. Say: *Look at the photographs. Match.* Demonstrate drawing a line. Students work individually, matching and then writing under the correct photograph. Monitor students' spelling. Go through answers as a class. Check students' pronunciation of the vowel sounds in /bənɑːnə/ and /æpᵊl/. Ask students which fruit they prefer.

> **Answers**
> a apple b banana c peach

ASK AND ANSWER

9 Students ask and answer the question in pairs. Students repeat the dialogue with a new partner, talking about different objects.

> **Optional activity**
>
> To further practise the time phrases, students discuss other things they do every day / once a week / once a year, etc. e.g. *I play football once a week. I go on holiday twice a year.* Help with any new vocabulary students may need.

SPENDING   UNIT 8

👁 LANGUAGE FOCUS

Learning objectives

- Name high numbers – *one hundred and fifty, ten thousand, five million*
- Name six currencies – *pounds, riyals, dollars, dirhams, lira, euros*
- Understand high numbers and prices
- Ask and answer questions about prices – *How much is this television? It's ten thousand dirhams.*
- Use sentences stress correctly in questions about prices – *How much is this television?*

See p. 6 for suggestions on how to use these Learning objectives in your lessons.

Lead-in

Write the countries and the currency symbols below on the board (not the answers in brackets). Ask about the currency symbols: *What are these?* (Try to elicit the word *money*.). Ask students to work in pairs and match the countries with the symbols. (Some symbols are used by more than one country.) Give students four minutes only, then go through answers as a class. You could make this a competitive game by awarding a point for each correct country name and another point if they can name the currency correctly.

Brazil, Egypt, France, India, South Korea, Japan, Mexico, Oman, Saudi Arabia, Singapore, Turkey, the UK

1 ﷼ (Oman / Qatar / Saudi Arabia, riyal)
2 ¥ (Japan, yen)
3 £ (Egypt / the UK, pound)
4 € (France, euro)
5 ₺ (Turkey, lira)
6 ₩ (South Korea, won)
7 $ (Mexico, peso; Singapore, dollar)
8 R$ (Brazil, real)
9 ₹ (India, rupee)

VOCABULARY: MONEY

1 🔊 8.17 👤👥 Focus on the photographs of money. Ask students to listen and read. Play the audio. Encourage students to follow the audio by pointing at each picture as they hear it. Drill the high numbers. See p. 9 for advice on drilling. Check understanding. Write on the board:

one hundred   one thousand   one million
1 _____   1 _____   1 _____

Elicit how many zeros to add: (100 two, 1,000 three, 1,000,000 six). Write the zeros and circle the commas. Drill each of these words separately. Now write these words (not the answers in brackets):

fifty (50), five hundred (500), five thousand (5,000), five thousand, five hundred (5,500), five thousand, five hundred and fifty (5,550), fifty thousand (50,000), five hundred thousand (500,000), five million (5,000,000).

Read the words aloud and asks students to work in pairs and write the numerals for each of the numbers.

Play the audio again and focus on the currencies. Drill each word and ask: *Where is this money from?* (Europe, the USA, the UK, Turkey, the UAE, Saudi Arabia). If students are unsure about how to say the country names which are written and said as acronyms, write: *the USA, the UK, the UAE* on the board. Read the countries aloud for students to listen and repeat.

Demonstrate the next part of the exercise with a student. Point to a photograph and encourage a student to say the correct words. Then encourage the student to point at another photograph and say the correct words yourself. Students work in pairs. Monitor and correct any errors.

2 🔊 8.18 👤👥 Focus on the numbers (1–6). Encourage students to read out the numbers one by one. Focus on the words on the right. Say: *Match*. Demonstrate the exercise using the completed example. Students work in pairs and match the numbers to the words. Play the audio for students to check. Go through answers as a class. Students work in pairs and practise saying the prices.

Answers

2 three hundred and fifty-five
3 seven hundred and sixty
4 one thousand five hundred
5 forty thousand
6 seven million

WRITING

NOTICE

Focus on the NOTICE box. Read each number aloud and write the numerals on the board (355, 760). Point at the numbers and say them. Mark the place where *and* sits (before tens e.g. 3|55, 6|60). Drill the numbers. Elicit how we say these numbers: *701* (seven hundred and one) *230* (two hundred and thirty).

3 🔊 8.19 👤 Focus on the numeral under the line in the first sentence and the written numbers in the box. Point out the crossed-out number. Read the correct number aloud (six hundred and thirty). Demonstrate looking at the words in the box and completing the written form of the number under the line. Students work individually and complete the numbers. Monitor and check students' spelling. Play the audio and go through answers as a class. Write the numbers on the board.

> **Answers**
> 2 two thousand 3 five hundred 4 thousand 5 million

LISTENING FOR DETAIL

4 🔊 8.20 👤👥 Focus on the large photograph and the speech bubbles. Ask: *Where's this?* (a book market) *What is he buying?* (a dictionary). Point at the second speech bubble and elicit the price. Focus on items 1–5 and the gaps. Say: *Listen and write*. Play the audio for students to listen and write the prices. Students work individually and complete the prices. Play the audio again in weaker classes. Students work in pairs and check their answers. Go through answers as a class with the audio, writing each price on the board.

> **Answers**
> 2 240,000 3 3,000 4 1,700 5 1,500,000

> 👁 **Common student errors**
>
> **Noun form:** Arabic L1 students tend to pluralize the word *million*.
>
> These are some typical errors: *It costs 5 millions for everything. They spend 99 millions on sports.*
>
> See p. 148 for tips on how to help students with **Noun form** errors.

PRONUNCIATION FOR SPEAKING

5 🔊 8.21 👥 Focus on the questions. Point out the highlighted words and syllables. Say the questions aloud, exaggerating the sentence stress. Say the highlighted syllables very loudly and clearly and the other syllables quietly. Play the audio for students to repeat. Drill the questions. See p. 9 for tips on drilling.

Focus on the first dialogue in the speech bubbles in Exercise 4 again. Students work in pairs and practise the short dialogues in Exercise 4. Monitor and correct any errors.

SPEAKING

6 👥 Divide the students into Students A and Students B. Say: *Student As go to page 201. Student Bs go to page 204.* Focus on the REMEMBER box and elicit variations to the question, e.g. *How much is this bag?*

Focus on the photographs and prices. Point out that Student A has half of the information about prices and Student B has the other half. Demonstrate the exercise by drawing an object, e.g. a camera, on the board and writing a price tag next to it. Ask: *How much is this camera?*

Elicit: *It's (200) pounds.* Demonstrate writing the answer on the line.

Student As speak first and ask: *How much is this computer?* Student Bs answer with the correct price: *It's 820 dollars* Then students swap roles. Monitor and note any errors. Use the notes you made for feedback at the end of the exercise. See p. 8 for advice on conducting feedback on speaking activities.

Students swap books and check each other's spelling and use of capital letters.

> **Optional activity**
>
> Write the list below on the board. Pretend to be thinking and then write a price you would pay in your country for a cheap T-shirt. Say: *A cheap T-shirt is (price) in (your country).* Say: *How much is an expensive T-shirt in (your country)?* Students work in pairs and discuss and write down prices. Monitor and ensure students are saying prices (not just writing them down) and using correct language.
>
> 1 a cheap T-shirt, an expensive T-shirt
> 2 a cheap mobile phone, a smartphone
> 3 a cheap car, an expensive car
> 4 a small house, a big house
> 5 cheap shoes, expensive shoes
>
> When students have finished, put them in groups of four to compare their lists. Ask them to agree a final list. Take feedback from different groups on each object.

SPENDING UNIT 8

ACADEMIC LISTENING AND SPEAKING

> **Learning objectives**
> - Understand conversations about spending habits
> - CT: Understand survey questions
> - CT: Apply grammatical knowledge to form survey questions
> - Use intonation correctly in questions – *How often do you buy shoes? Do you buy coffee every day?*
> - Conduct and respond to a survey about spending habits
>
> See p. 6 for suggestions on how to use these Learning objectives in your lessons.

> **Lead-in**
> **Aural dictation:** Follow the procedure on p. 11. Students should write the numerals not the words:
> 135, 270, 560, 1,300, 250,000, 546,000, 1,000,001, 50,000,000 (50 million).
> Write the answers on the board for students to check. Choose students at random to say the numbers aloud.

PREPARING TO LISTEN

1 👤👥 Focus on questions 1–3 and ask a student to read them aloud. Point out the completed example by tracing the line from *How much money do you spend on books?* to *I think I spend 200 lira on books in a month.* Students work individually and then compare their answers in pairs. Play the audio. Go through answers as a class.

> **Answers**
> 2 How often do you buy food?   I buy food once a day.
> 3 Do you have a bank card?   No, I don't.

Focus on question 1. Write this on the board:
1 How much _____ do you spend on books?
2 How much _____ do you _____ on books?
3 How much _____ do you _____ _____ books?

Elicit the missing word in question 1 (money). Then remove the question from the board. Repeat for question 2. Repeat for question 3, but leave the question on the board. Drill the question.

Now write this on the board:
1 I think I _____ 200 liras on books.
2 I think I _____ 200 liras _____ books.
3 I _____ I _____ 200 liras _____ books.
Repeat the procedure as for the questions above.

LISTENING FOR MAIN IDEAS

2 🔊 8.22 👤 Focus on the photograph and ask: *What are their names?* (Kemal, Mustafa). Focus on the sentence starter and the six possible topics (a–f). Point out the completed example and say: *Listen and circle.* Play the audio. Students work individually and circle the things they hear. Go through answers as a class. Use the survey in Exercise 3 to check the answers with weaker classes.

> **Answers**
> a c d

LISTENING FOR KEY INFORMATION

3 🔊 8.22 👤 Focus on the survey. Point out the options. Demonstrate circling the correct options. Play the audio. Students work individually and circle the correct options. Play the audio again and go through answers as a class.

> **Answers**
> 2 twice   3 300   5 100

CRITICAL THINKING: UNDERSTAND

4 🔊 8.23 👤👥 Focus on the gapped survey questions. Point out the words in the box and the completed example. Say: *Read and write.* In weaker classes, indicate students can look at the survey from Exercise 3. Students work in pairs and check their answers. Play the audio for students to check. If necessary, go through answers as a class.

> **Answers**
> 2 How often <u>do you buy</u> books?
> 3 <u>How much money</u> do you spend on tea and coffee every month?
> 4 <u>How often</u> do you buy food?
> 5 How much money <u>do you spend on</u> clothes and shoes in a month?

UNLOCK BASIC SKILLS TEACHER'S BOOK

CRITICAL THINKING: APPLY

5 👤 Focus on the first question and the options under the line. Point at the words under the line and use appropriate hand gestures to indicate that students need to reorder the words. Say: *Listen* and read the correct question 1 aloud. Demonstrate reordering the question and writing it on the line. Students work individually and write the correct answers in the gaps. Monitor and check students' spelling and use of full stops. Play the audio for students to check. Go through answers as a class.

> **Answers**
>
> 2 How often <u>do you buy</u> a new phone?
> 3 How much <u>money do you spend on</u> coffee in a month?
> 4 How <u>often do you buy</u> coffee?
> 5 How <u>much money do you spend on</u> clothes in a month?
> 6 How <u>often do you buy</u> clothes?

PRONUNCIATION FOR LISTENING

6 🔊 8.24 Focus on the questions and the highlighted words: *do you*. Play the audio and use your hand to indicate the rising tone on *do you*. Drill the questions as a class. For advice on drilling see p. 9. Encourage students to use their hands to indicate the rising tone.

> **Optional activity**
>
> Students write two more questions for the spending survey in Exercise 5. They can use these in the Speaking Task. Monitor and help with vocabulary. Check that students are writing grammatically correct questions.

SPEAKING TASK

7 👥 Tell students to go to p. 207. Focus on the REMEMBER box and read through the phrases as a class. Focus on the survey. Ask students to read the questions. Demonstrate the exercise by approaching a student and saying: *Excuse me. What's your name?* Write down the student's name and then ask them the questions. Students work in pairs and ask and answer the questions, recording their answers as they go. Monitor and help as necessary. Note any errors and any correct use of language which have not been covered in the course so far as you monitor.

Use the notes you made for feedback at the end of the exercise. See p. 8 for advice on conducting feedback on speaking activities.

> **Model answer**
>
> A: How much money do you spend on your phone in a month?
> B: (I think) I spend £30 on my phone in a month.
> A: How often do you buy a new phone?
> B: Once a year.
> A: How much money do you spend on coffee in a month?
> B: (I think) I spend £50 on coffee in a month. I drink a lot of coffee.
> A: How often do you buy coffee?
> B: I buy coffee twice a day!
> A: How much money do you spend on clothes in a month?
> B: (I think) I spend £100 on clothes in a month.
> A: How often do you buy clothes?
> B: Once or twice a month.
> A: Thank you.

ACADEMIC READING AND WRITING

> **Learning objectives**
>
> - Use charts to preview a text
> - Understand a text about how people in different countries spend their income
> - Spell vocabulary learned in Unit 8 accurately
> - CT: Understand a model text in relation to a bar chart
> - CT: Apply your knowledge to create a bar chart
> - Use *and* to link clauses in writing – *I spend one hundred dollars on shoes and two hundred dollars on clothes every month.*
> - Complete a description of your spending habits
>
> See p. 6 for suggestions on how to use these Learning objectives in your lessons.

> **Lead-in**
>
> Write the things below on the board. Ask: *Are these things cheap or expensive in this country?* Students work in pairs and discuss.
>
> *Food and drink*
> *Clothes and shoes*
> *Computers and smartphones*
> *Schools and universities*
> *Houses*
> *Doctors and hospitals*
>
> Take a class vote on whether each thing is cheap or expensive in this country. You may wish to research some information about how expensive these things are in other countries to put the students' ideas into perspective.

SPENDING   UNIT 8

PREPARING TO READ

1 🔊 8.25 👤 Pre-teach the word *health*. Write *healthy* and *health* on the board.

Say: *I eat a lot of fruit and vegetables. I go to bed early. I am healthy.* (Point to *healthy*.) *I spend a lot of money on my health.* (Point to *health*.) *Doctors, healthy food and drink, and hospitals are expensive.*

Drill the pronunciation of *health*. Point out that *ea* makes the /e/ sound.

Focus on the sentences and the words in the box. Point out the gapped sentences. Say: *Read and write.* Students work individually and complete the sentences with the words in the box. Play the audio for students to check.

Concept check *percent*. Draw a circle on the board and colour a wedge of this to represent 10 percent. Say: *10 percent.* Drill the word. Colour different proportions of the circle and elicit approximate percentages. Say: *This is my money.* Point to the circle. Write: *10 per cent of my money.* Underline *of*. Leave this on the board for later.

> **Answers**
> 1 percent 2 money 3 spend

2 👥 Students work in pairs. Focus on the first sentence in Exercise 1 and indicate the class. Say: *Yes or no?* in a questioning tone. Encourage students to read the sentences and decide if they are true or not about their class. When they have discussed the first sentence, take a class vote. Continue with each sentence.

> **NOTICE**
> Write: *Students spend a lot of money ___ computers.* on the board. Elicit missing preposition (*on*). Write: *Students pay a lot ___ computers.* on the board. Elicit missing preposition (*for*). Say: *With spend, use on, with pay, use for.* Focus on NOTICE box. Allow students a minute to read the information there.

PREVIEWING

3 👤 Focus on the heading and the chart in Exercise 4. Read the sentence options in Exercise 3 aloud. Students look and circle the right answers. Go through answers as a class, using the chart to explain the answers. Ask students if they know where Pakistan is. Use the world map on pp. 20–21 if they do not know.

> **Answers**
> b Turkey d Mexico e Pakistan
> c money people spend on things.

READING FOR KEY INFORMATION

4 🔊 8.26 👤 Focus on the gaps in the text. Read the sentences aloud. Ask: *What's missing?* (the countries). Students read the texts, look at the chart, and complete the country names. Play the audio for students to check. Encourage them to follow the text by pointing at the words as they hear them. Go through answers as a class, using the chart to explain the answers.

> **Answers**
> Turkey Mexico Pakistan

5 👥 Focus on the sentences. Read the first one aloud: *People in Turkey spend 32% on food and drink.* Say: *Yes or no?* in a questioning tone. Elicit the correct answer (yes). Encourage students to read all of the sentences, then ask them to read the text in Exercise 4 and find the information. Students work individually, reading the text and circling *Yes* or *No* for each sentence.

Students work in pairs and check their answers. Then go through answers as a class. Read out each sentence. Students say Yes or No and show you where they found the information in the text. For the No answers, elicit the correct information from students.

> **Answers**
> 2 No (5%) 3 No (8%) 4 Yes 5 No (50%) 6 Yes

ACADEMIC WRITING SKILLS

6 🔊 8.27 👤 Write the vowels on the board: *a, e, i, o, u*. Point out the completed example. Ask: *What word is this?* (hundred) Point at the space for a missing vowel and elicit the missing letter (*e*).

Students complete the words with the missing vowels. Play the audio for students to check their answers. With weaker classes, write the answers on the board.

> **Answers**
> 1 h<u>u</u>ndred 2 th<u>ou</u>sand 3 m<u>i</u>llion 4 m<u>o</u>nth 5 sh<u>oe</u>s
> 6 sp<u>e</u>nd 7 p<u>a</u>y 8 <u>i</u>nternet 9 sm<u>a</u>rtphone 10 cl<u>o</u>thes

UNL🔒CK BASIC SKILLS TEACHER'S BOOK   **121**

CRITICAL THINKING: UNDERSTAND

7 Focus on the chart. Point out the key and numbers which give the clues to the gaps in the student notes. Use the completed sentence and the chart to demonstrate the exercise. Students work individually and complete the student notes. Monitor and check students' spelling and use of *and* in high numbers. Students work in pairs and check their answers. Write the answers on the board.

> **Answers**
>
> three hundred, fifty-five, one hundred and seventy, two hundred, one hundred and twenty

CRITICAL THINKING: APPLY

8 Focus on the blank chart in Exercise 8. Say: *This is your chart.* Say: *Draw your chart here.* Students work individually and complete the chart. Monitor and help as necessary. Ask: *How much do you spend on … ?* questions to generate ideas. You may wish to complete a chart yourself in preparation for Exercise 10. Students work in pairs, swap charts and compare their answers.

WRITING

9 Write two sentences on the board:

I buy clothes every month.

I buy shoes every month.

Elicit from students which words are different and which are the same. Cross out the words which are the same in the second sentence. Show students how to connect the sentences with *and*: *I buy clothes <u>and</u> shoes every month.*

Students read the example sentences. Show how the repeated words are not repeated in the sentence with *and*.

Point out the pairs of sentences in 1 and 2. Students work individually and connect the sentences. Monitor and check punctuation and spelling. Go through answers as a class.

> **Answers**
>
> 1 I spend twenty riyals on coffee and eighty riyals on food.
> 2 I spend one hundred lira on books and eighty lira on T-shirts.

WRITING TASK

10 Focus on the chart in Exercise 8 and the gapped sentences in the student notebook. Read the first gapped sentence. Focus on the chart and demonstrate the exercise by writing your own answer in the first gap. Students work individually and complete the gaps with the information from their chart. Monitor and help as necessary. If students have problems with the third gapped sentence with *pay*, refer them to the model text on p. 161.

11 Students swap books and check each other's writing.

> **Model answer**
>
> I spend £300 on food.
> I spend £50 on coffee.
> I pay £45 every month for the internet and my phone.
> I spend £120 on clothes and shoes and £50 on books.

> **Objectives review**
>
> See Introduction on p. 7 for ideas about using the Objectives review with your students.
>
> **WORDLIST AND GLOSSARY**
>
> See Introduction on p. 7 for ideas about using the Wordlist at the end of each unit and the Glossary at the end of the book with your students.
>
> **REVIEW TEST**
>
> Go to esource.cambridge.org to print the Review test and for ideas about how and when to administer the Review test.

RESEARCH PROJECT

> **Compare the cost of living in countries around the world.**
>
> Show the class websites where they can see the prices of common goods and services in a few different countries. Divide the class into groups and tell each group to research the prices of a particular thing in different countries around the world. They can choose the country and the item. They should compare five countries and present the results in your local currency. They should prepare a chart.
>
> Allow students class time to research, or they could do this for homework. Give students class time during the next lesson to create their charts.
>
> Students should put up their charts in the next lesson. Encourage students to look at each other's charts and point out any particularly cheap or expensive places to live.

9 TECHNOLOGY

UNLOCK YOUR KNOWLEDGE

Focus on the photograph. Point out the questions. Ask a student to read each question aloud. Students work in groups and answer the questions. Monitor and help as necessary. Take feedback as a class. Ask: *How much do you think it is in dollars?* Take guesses from the class. Tell them who came the closest.

> **Answers**
> 1 b 2 Answers will vary.

LISTENING AND READING 1

> **Learning objectives**
> - Name technology and devices – *a blog, an app, a website, GPS, a USB drive, a webinar*
> - Use verb phrases to describe what we do with technology – *write a blog, look at a website, use GPS, listen to webinars, need a USB drive, buy apps, play video games, learn English online*
> - Use adverbs of frequency – *never, sometimes, often, usually, always*
> - Understand a conversation about using technology
> - Learn the sounds of the letters *p* and *b* GPS a*p*p, *p*lay, la*p*top, USB, *b*log, ta*b*let, *b*uy
> - Ask and answer questions about how often you do things *How often do you buy apps? Sometimes.*
>
> See p. 6 for suggestions on how to use these Learning objectives in your lessons.

> **Lead-in**
> Write the heading *Technology* on the board.
> Give students clues to various types of technology, e.g.
> *It is new. It is expensive. I drive it to work every day.* (car).
> *I have it every day and every place I go: university, my house, my car, the shopping centre. I look at the time on it.* (watch).
> *I have it in my house. It is expensive. I read books and watch videos on it.* (tablet).
> *I take photographs with it. I speak to my friends and family with it. I watch videos on it.* (smartphone).
> *It is in restaurants, shops, houses, airports, universities and offices. I use it on my smartphone, my laptop and my computer.* (Wi-Fi / the internet).
> *They are interesting. My son plays them on his mobile phone.* (video games).

Encourage students to guess. Write correct answers on the board. Then students work in pairs or small groups and take turns to give each other clues to types of technology.

VOCABULARY: COMPUTERS AND THE INTERNET

1 ◀) 9.1 Focus on the photographs. Play the audio for students to listen and read. Encourage students to follow the audio by pointing at each type of technology as they hear it. Drill the names of the objects. See p. 9 for advice on drilling. Check understanding using concept questions, e.g. *Do we read a blog?* (yes) *Do we eat a blog?* (no) *Do I have an app on my book?* (no) *Do I have an app in my car?* (no) *Do I have an app on my smartphone?* (yes). See p. 7 for advice on concept checking.

Demonstrate the next part of the exercise with a student. Point to a picture and encourage a student to say the correct word. Then encourage the student to point at a picture and say the correct word yourself. Students work in pairs. Monitor and correct any errors.

2 ◀) 9.2 Focus on verbs 1–8 on the left of each column. Encourage students to call out the verbs one by one. Check understanding of use. Then focus on words and phrases on the right in each line. Check understanding of *online*. Say: *Read and match*. Point out the completed examples by tracing the line from *look at* to *websites*. Students work individually to complete the exercise and then compare their answers in pairs. Play the audio for students to check their answers. Play the audio again for students to listen and repeat.

> **Answers**
> 1 play video games 2 learn English online 4 use GPS
> 5 write a blog 8 watch webinars

UNLOCK BASIC SKILLS TEACHER'S BOOK 123

> **Optional activity**
> Write the following words from Exercise 2 in two clouds. Students work in pairs and write as many collocations as they can with the two sets of words.
> play: video games
> read: a blog, English online, websites
> write: a blog, (websites)
> buy: apps, video games, a USB drive, a GPS, (websites)
> learn: English online
> use: apps, English online, video games, websites, a USB drive, a GPS
> watch: webinars

LISTENING FOR MAIN IDEAS

3 9.3 Focus on the names in Exercise 3 (*Samir and Kemal, Yuna and Lucia*). Say: *These are names.* Say: *Listen and match.* Play the audio. Students work individually and match. Go through answers as a class.

> **Answers**
> 1 learning English 2 blogs

READING FOR DETAIL

4 9.3 Focus on the dialogue and the sentences below. Read sentence 1 aloud. Say: *Yes or no?* in a questioning tone. Elicit the correct answer (no). Ask students to find the place in the dialogue where Kemal talks about this (*I usually learn English online.*).

Play the audio. Students work individually, reading and listening to the text and writing *Yes* or *No* for each sentence. Students work in pairs and check their answers. Then go through answers as a class. Read out each sentence. Students say Yes or No and show you where they found the information in the text. For the No answers, elicit the correct information from students.

> **Answers**
> 1 Yes 2 Yes 3 Yes 4 No (I never read blogs.) 5 Yes

GRAMMAR: FREQUENCY ADVERBS

5 9.4 Focus on the scale. Check understanding of the scale using the frequency expressions from Unit 8. Write these sentences on the board:

I buy fish at the market. (100% always)
I don't buy fish at the shopping centre. (0% never)
I eat meat five days a week. (usually)
I eat cheese once a month. (sometimes)

Focus on the words in the box. Say: *Write* and demonstrate writing on the scale. Students work individually to fill in the gaps. Go through answers as a class.

> **Answers**
> never (0%) always (100%)

Play the audio again for students to listen and repeat the words. Check understanding of the new vocabulary, using more sentences like the ones above with frequency expressions from Unit 8.

6 Focus on the words on the scale and the sentences in Exercise 4. Say: *Read and match.* Students work individually and match the frequency adverbs with the sentences in Exercise 4. Go through answers as a class.

> **Answers**
> b 4 c 2 d 5 e 1

> ● **Common student errors**
>
> **Word order:** Arabic L1 students tend to make errors with the position of adverbs of frequency in sentences. These are some typical errors:
>
> *Always I go shopping at the weekend. Usually I buy clothes.*
>
> **Punctuation and Spelling:** Arabic L1 students tend to make errors with the form and spelling of adverbs of frequency *always* and *sometimes*. These are some typical errors:
>
> *allways, al ways, sometime, some time*
>
> See p. 148 for tips on how to help students with these errors.

7 9.5 Focus on the table. Play the audio for students to listen and read the sentences. Play the audio again and drill the sentences in the table. Encourage students to create new sentences using the words in the box.

> **Answers**
> Answers will vary.

TECHNOLOGY UNIT 9

WRITING

8 Focus on the gapped sentences and jumbled words. Point at the completed example. Students work individually and complete the sentences. Students work in pairs and check their answers. Go through answers as a class.

> **Answers**
> 2 We <u>usually buy apps</u>.
> 3 He <u>often needs a USB</u> drive.
> 4 They <u>never write a blog</u>.

SOUND AND SPELLING: *p, b*

9 🔊 9.6 Write *p* and *b* on the board. Elicit the names of the letters and one example of a word for each letter (e.g. *pen, book*). Point at the letters and elicit the sounds: /p/ /b/. Drill the phonemes and the two example words.

The sounds /p/ and /b/ need a lot of attention with Arabic L1 students. These are allophonic (the same sound) in Arabic. Arabic students tend to confuse /b/ with /p/ in spoken English, causing communication breakdowns.

Focus on the words in the book and point out the highlighted letters. Play the audio for students to listen and repeat. Correct any errors with the phonemes /b/ or /p/.

SPEAKING

10 Divide the class into Student As and Student Bs. Tell Student As to look at p. 202 and Student Bs to look at p. 205. Demonstrate the exercise by asking a student questions about things which are not on the role play cards, e.g. *How often do you take photographs? How often do you write emails?* Elicit answers. Students should use frequency expressions from Unit 8 as well as the frequency adverbs in this lesson. Allow students a minute to look at their role play cards and think about what questions they are going to ask. Say: *Student As speak first.* Monitor and correct any pronunciation errors. Students swap roles.

LISTENING AND READING 2

> **Learning objectives**
>
> - Name useful objects – *a chair, glasses, a fridge*
> - Use verbs and verb phrases to describe what objects do – *send messages, cook, go online, watch TV*
> - Understand descriptions of smart objects and what people can do with them
> - Pronounce *can* and *can't*
> - Use *can* and *cannot* to write about ability and possibility – *You cannot send messages on a GPS. It can cook.*
> - Use *can* and *can't* to talk about a smart object – *It can go online. You can't watch TV.*
>
> See p. 6 for suggestions on how to use these Learning objectives in your lessons.

> **Lead-in**
>
> Write the words: *on my smartphone* in a circle at the centre of the board. Draw lines coming out from the circle in a spidergram shape. Now write: *the internet* at the top of one of the lines. Elicit words students associate with smartphones e.g. *apps*. Write these words at the ends of the lines. When students have exhausted their ideas, elicit full sentences about using a smartphone and each idea, e.g. *There are apps on my smartphone. I use the internet on my smartphone. I take photographs on my smartphone.*

VOCABULARY: THINGS WE USE

1 🔊 9.7 Focus on the photographs. Play the audio for students to listen and read. Encourage students to follow the audio by pointing at each word in the book as they hear it. Drill the words and phrases. See p. 9 for advice on drilling. Check understanding using printable Flashcards 9.2 and concept questions. See p. 7 for advice on concept questions. Go to esource.cambridge.org to print the flashcards.

Demonstrate the next part of the exercise with a student. Point to a picture and encourage a student to say the correct word or phrase. Then encourage the student to point at a picture and say the correct word or phrase yourself. Students work in pairs. Monitor and correct any errors.

UNL⌀CK BASIC SKILLS TEACHER'S BOOK   125

LISTENING FOR KEY INFORMATION

2 (9.8) Focus on the two technologies. Read each one aloud. Check understanding of the word *smart* (use the example of a smartphone in the Lead-in above). Say: *Listen and write 1 or 2.* Students listen and write 1 or 2. Go through answers as a class.

> **Answers**
> smart fridge 2 smartwatch 1

READING FOR DETAIL

3 (9.8) Play the audio for students to read and listen to the texts again. Focus on sentences (1–6) below the text. Read the first sentence aloud. Say: *Yes or no?* in a questioning tone. Elicit the correct answer (yes). Ask students to find the place in the text where this is mentioned (It has a camera.). Encourage students to read all of the sentences, then ask them to read the text and find the information. Students work individually, reading the text and circling *Yes* or *No*.

Students work in pairs and check their answers. Then go through answers as a class. Read each sentence aloud. Students say Yes or No and show you where they found the information in the text. For the No answers, elicit the correct information from students.

> **Answers**
> 2 Yes
> 3 Yes
> 4 Yes
> 5 No (It can't take photographs)
> 6 No (It can buy food online, but it can't cook food.)

GRAMMAR: CAN AND CAN'T

4 (9.9) Write these jumbled sentences on the board. *1 I / cook / can; 2 cannot / I / cook.* Focus on the table in the book. Play the audio. Focus on the sentences on the board. Elicit the correct word order for each sentence. Encourage students to create new sentences using the words in the box. Concept check *can* sentences using a smartphone. Read out these sentences and elicit Yes and No.

It can drive a car (no).
It can take photographs (yes).
It can send emails (yes).
It can write emails (no).
It can watch TV (no).
I can watch TV on a smartphone (yes).
It can read books (no).
I can read books on a smartphone (yes).
Correct the *no* sentences using *cannot*. Elicit the correct sentences from the class.

> **NOTICE**
> Write: *I can't drive.* on the board. Circle and say: *can't*. Then write: *I cannot drive.* underneath. Point at: *I can't* and encourage students to say the words. Then point at: *I cannot*. Say: *Say can't. Write cannot.* Focus on the NOTICE box. Allow students a minute to read the information there.

5 (9.10) Focus on the phrase under the line in the first sentence. Point out the ticks ✓ and the crosses ✗. Read the correct first half of the first sentence aloud. Demonstrate writing the verb phrase on the line. Elicit the next verb phrase (cannot buy apps.) Students work individually and write the phrases on the lines. Play the audio for students to check. Monitor and check students' spelling. Go through answers as a class.

> **Answers**
> 1 It can go online, but it <u>can't / cannot buy apps</u>.
> 2 It <u>can play video</u>, but it <u>can't / cannot take photos</u>.
> 3 It <u>can go online</u>, but it <u>can't / cannot send messages</u>.
> 4 It <u>can send messages</u>, but it <u>can't / cannot make calls</u>.

> **◉ Common student errors**
> Modal verbs, e.g. *can*, *will*, *must* and *might*, do not exist and are expressed in different ways in both Arabic and Turkish. Students with these L1s have a number of common problems when getting to grips with *can*.
>
> **Word order:** Arabic L1 students tend to use question word order instead of statement word order with *can*.
>
> *Can you buy a lot of things for your house there. Can we use the internet at my house.*
>
> **Verb form:** Arabic L1 students tend to use *to* infinitive or verb + *-ing* after *can*.
>
> *You can going by car. You can to send me a message. If you can to come, I will be happy.*
>
> **Missing word:** Turkish L1 students frequently omit *can* after personal pronouns.
>
> *I (can/will) meet you there. We (can) use the internet in the library. She (can) help you with your problem.*
>
> See p. 148 for tips on how to help students with **these** types of errors.

TECHNOLOGY UNIT 9

PRONUNCIATION FOR SPEAKING

6 🔊 9.11 Focus on *can* and *can't* and the four sentences. Play the audio for students to repeat. Drill the sentences. Vary the verb phrases and pronouns you use. You could use the ideas in the table in Exercise 4.

WRITING AND SPEAKING

7 Divide the class into Student As and Student Bs. Tell Student As to turn to p. 202 and Student Bs to turn to p. 205. Focus on the REMEMBER box and read through the phrases as a class. Tell students to look at their device and decide what it can and can't do. Point out the words and phrases in the box.

Students then work in pairs and tell each other what their device can and can't do.

> **Answers**
> SmartTV
> It can go online, use Wi-Fi, send messages, play video games. It can't cook, take photographs, use GPS.
> GPS
> It can use GPS. It can't cook, send messages, use Wi-Fi, take photographs, go online, play video games.

> **Optional activity**
> **False information:** Follow the procedure on p. 12.
> Students use the text in Exercise 4 to give three pieces of false information. Books closed. Other students listen and say what the false information is.

LISTENING AND READING 3

VOCABULARY: PEOPLE

1 🔊 9.12 Focus on the photographs. Play the audio for students to listen and read. Encourage them to follow the audio by pointing at each work or phrase in the book as they hear it. Drill the words/phrases. See p. 9 for advice on drilling.

Demonstrate the next part of the exercise with a student. Point to a photograph and encourage the student to say the word or phrase. Then encourage the student to point to a photograph and say the word or phrase yourself. Students work in pairs. Monitor and correct any errors.

PREPARING TO READ

2 🔊 9.13 Focus attention on the numbers on the left (1–5). Say: *Listen and match* and demonstrate by pointing to the example. Play the audio. Students work individually to match the items. Students work in pairs to check their answers. Play the audio again for students to listen and check. Go through answers as a class.

> **Answers**
> 2 7 days, 1 week 3 365 days, 1 year
> 4 1,000,000 1 million 5 1,000,000,000, 1 billion

LISTENING FOR MAIN IDEAS

3 🔊 9.14 Focus on the two countries (China and the USA). Tell students to listen and match the country with the correct item. Students work individually and listen and match. Go through answers as a class.

> **Answers**
> 1 China, smartphones 2 USA video games

SCANNING FOR KEY INFORMATION

4 🔊 9.14 Focus students' attention on the reading text. Play the audio. Students listen and follow the text. Focus on items 1–5. Say: *Match* and demonstrate matching item 1, using the example given. Students work in pairs to find and match the numbers. Go through answers as a class.

> **Answers**
> 2 31 million children use smartphones
> 3 25 billion dollars on video games every year
> 4 74 million men play video games every week
> 5 20 million girls play video games every week

GRAMMAR: FREQUENCY EXPRESSIONS 2

5 🔊 9.15 Write: *I look at my mobile phone every _____.* on the board. Focus on the table in the book. Play the audio. Focus on the sentence on the board. Elicit a guess for the time period that is true about you.

Play the audio again and drill the sentences in the table. Encourage students to create new sentences using the words in the box.

UNLOCK BASIC SKILLS TEACHER'S BOOK 127

WRITING

6 🔊 9.16 👤 Focus on the completed example and the words under the line. Use appropriate hand gestures to indicate that students need to reorder the words. Read the completed example aloud. Demonstrate reordering the sentence and writing it on the line. Students work individually and write the correct answers in the gaps. Monitor and check students' spelling and use of full stops. Play the audio for students to check their answers. Go through answers as a class.

> **Answers**
> 2 Adults buy 58 million USB sticks every month.
> 3 People send 4 million photos every year.
> 4 A lot of children watch 100 minutes of TV every day.
> 5 People write 347 blogs every minute.

SPEAKING

7 👥 Tell students to turn to p. 208. Focus on the REMEMBER box. Read through the phrases as a class. Encourage students to give some other examples (e.g. *I look at my mobile phone every minute.*). Focus on the speech bubbles. Drill the phrases. For advice on drilling see p. 9. Focus on the survey. Tell students to read the questions. Demonstrate the exercise by approaching a student and saying: *Excuse me. What's your name?* Write down the students' name and then proceed to ask them the questions. Students work in pairs and ask and answer the questions, recording each other's answers as they go. Monitor and help as necessary. In stronger classes, students could then work in small groups and report on the spending habits of the student that they interviewed.

WATCH AND REMEMBER

> **Learning objectives**
> - Understand statements about smartphone apps and what they do – *I like this app. It can buy food.*
> - Understand questions and statements about computing equipment and terms – *Do you have a USB drive? It can go online.*
> - Practise talking about the devices you own – *I have a laptop.*
>
> See p. 6 for suggestions on how to use these Learning objectives in your lessons.

> **Lead-in**
> Ask students to discuss, with a partner or in groups, how many apps they have on their smartphones and which ones they use the most.

PART 1

In Part 1, five people from different countries talk about apps which they have on their smartphones.

BEFORE YOU WATCH

1 👤 Students match the photographs with the sentences 1–3.

2 🔊 9.17 👤 Play the audio. Students listen and check their answers in Exercise 1. Then they write the sentences under the photographs.

Monitor and check students' writing. As a follow-up, ask students if they have any apps they use for taking photographs or shopping.

> **Answers**
> 1 b 2 a 3 c

WATCH

3 ▶ 👤 Students read the sentences. They watch the video and circle the correct options. Go through answers as a class.

> **Answers**
> 2 the news 3 take photographs 4 call people
> 5 good

AFTER YOU WATCH

In stronger classes, Exercise 4 should be completed by students after watching Part 1. In weaker classes, students can watch Part 1 again and complete Exercise 4 or use the audio script at the back of the book.

4 👤👥 Students complete the monologue with words from the box. Students work in pairs and check their answers. Check students understand the word *download*.

> **Answers**
> 1 app 2 online 3 download 4 help

128 UNLOCK BASIC SKILLS TEACHER'S BOOK

TECHNOLOGY UNIT 9

PART 2

In Part 2, a person talks to a shop assistant about buying a USB drive.

BEFORE YOU WATCH

5 Students match the photographs and write the words. Go through answers as a class. Ask students which of these they own.

> **Answers**
> a a Wi-Fi router b a USB drive c a GPS

WATCH

6 Students read the sentences and options and predict their answers. Students watch the video and check their predictions.

> **Answers**
> 2 work 3 two

AFTER YOU WATCH

7 Ask students about how the words in the boxes have been categorized (i.e. the words in the first box are nouns; the words in the second box are adjectives). Students complete the gapped sentences. Students can repeat this exercise several times with different partners.

> **Answers**
> Answers will vary.

PART 3

In Part 3, students remember key information from the lesson and extend their vocabulary.

REMEMBER

8 Focus on the 4 sentences. Students complete the sentences with a verb and a noun. If necessary, complete the first sentence as a class. Students work in pairs and check their answers. Go through answers as a class.

> **Answers**
> 1 buy food 2 take photographs 3 call people
> 4 emails

MORE VOCABULARY: TECHNOLOGY

9 Students look at the photographs (a–c). Students work individually and match the action with the correct photograph. They then write the action on the line under each photograph. Students check their answers in pairs. Go through answers as a class.

> **Answers**
> 1 b download 2 c save 3 a call

ASK AND ANSWER

10 Focus on the speech bubble. Elicit possible words and phrases to complete the sentences (e.g. *The app I use a lot is a dictionary. It can help you learn new words.*). Drill the phrases. For advice on drilling, see p. 9. Students ask and answer the questions in pairs. Students can swap pairs for additional practice.

> **Optional activity**
> Conduct a quick class survey to see which app is the most popular.

LANGUAGE FOCUS

> **Learning objectives**
> - Use phrases for asking and answering questions about opinions – *What do you think of my new smartphone? I think it's beautiful.*
> - Use phrases for agreeing and disagreeing – *I agree. I think so. I don't think so. I disagree.*
> - Understand conversations in which people give opinions on technology
> - Use main stress correctly when expressing opinions – *I think so too. I disagree.*
>
> See p. 6 for suggestions on how to use these Learning objectives in your lessons.

> **Lead-in**
> **Aural dictation:** Follow the procedure on p. 12.
> *I think red meat is healthy.*
> *I think Japan is beautiful.*
> *I think shopping is interesting.*
> *I think smartphones are cheap in this country.*
> Underline: *I think* in each sentence. Cover the part saying: *I think*. Ask: *Is this true?* Uncover *I think* and indicate yourself and that *I think* means this is your opinion.
> Take a class vote on each sentence. Change these sentences to reflect the vote results, e.g. *We don't think red meat is healthy. We think Japan is beautiful.* Drill the new sentences. See p. 9 for advice on drilling.

UNLOCK BASIC SKILLS TEACHER'S BOOK 129

LISTENING FOR MAIN IDEAS

1 🔊 9.18 Focus on the photographs and the tick boxes. Play the audio for students to listen and write 1, 2 or 3 in each tick box. Play the audio again if necessary. Go through answers as a class.

> **Answers**
> 3 2 1

LISTENING FOR DETAIL

2 🔊 9.18 Focus on the three dialogues. Play the audio for students to read and listen to the texts again. Focus on the sentences below the text. Read the first sentence aloud. Say: *Yes or no?* in a questioning tone. Elicit the correct answer (Yes). Students work individually, reading the text and circling *Yes* or *No*.

Students work in pairs and check their answers. Then go through answers as a class. Read each sentence aloud. Students say Yes or No and show you where they found the information in the text. For the No answers, elicit the correct information from students.

> **Answers**
> 1 Yes
> 2 No (Juan doesn't like smart watches. Carlos does.)
> 3 No (Ercan thinks English apps are cheap. Osman thinks they are expensive.)

> **NOTICE**
> Write: *I need a new app ___ study English.* on the board. Elicit the missing preposition (*to*). If students can't remember, point out Osman's first sentence. Focus on the NOTICE box. Point out the highlighted words. Give students a minute to read the information there.

VOCABULARY: ASKING FOR AND GIVING OPINIONS

3 🔊 9.19 Focus on the questions and possible answers in the table. Play the audio for students to listen to the questions and answers. Encourage students to follow the audio by pointing at each word in the book as they hear it. Drill the questions and answers. See p. 9 for advice on drilling.

> **NOTICE**
> Write: *I think ___ too.* and *I don't think ___.* on the board. If possible, elicit the missing word from each sentence by indicating the table in Exercise 3 (so, so). Focus on the NOTICE box. Allow students a minute to read the information there.

ACADEMIC WRITING SKILLS

4 🔊 9.20 Focus on the words under the line and use appropriate hand gestures to indicate that students need to reorder the words. Read the completed example aloud. Demonstrate reordering the sentence and writing it on the line. Students work individually and write the correct answers on the lines. Monitor and check students' spelling and use of full stops. Play the audio for students to check their answers. Go through answers as a class.

> **Answers**
> 2 I think so too. 3 What do you think?
> 4 I don't think so. 5 What do you think of smart fridges?

PRONUNCIATION FOR SPEAKING

5 🔊 9.21 Focus on the questions and answers. Point out the highlighted words. Say the sentences aloud, exaggerating the sentence stress. Play the audio for students to repeat. Drill the sentences. See p. 9 for advice on drilling.

Focus on the dialogues in Exercise 2 again. Students work in pairs and practise the dialogues. Monitor and correct any pronunciation errors.

SPEAKING

6 Divide the class into Student As and Student Bs. Tell As to turn to p. 202 and Bs to turn to p. 205. Focus on the REMEMBER box. Read through the phrases as a class. Demonstrate the exercise with a student. Point to the sentences and say: *English grammar is easy. What do you think?* Elicit a response from the student, e.g. *Yes, you're right. / I don't think so.* Students work in pairs and ask and answer questions about the four opinions on each role play card. Monitor and correct any errors. Take a class vote at the end of the lesson.

> **Optional activity**
> **Classroom messages:** Follow the procedure on p. 12.
> 1 I think History is boring.
> 2 I don't think sugar is good for you.
> 3 What do you think of the food and drink here?
> Ask the last student to get the message to write it on the board. Elicit corrections from the class. Students work in pairs and discuss the statements and question.

TECHNOLOGY   UNIT 9

ACADEMIC LISTENING AND SPEAKING

Learning objectives

- Use phrases about learning English online – *I play vocabulary games. I read English newspapers online.*
- CT: Understand a discussion about learning English online
- CT: Analyze statements about learning English online
- Use sentence stress correctly in statements – *Students can go to the library.*
- Discuss learning English online and give opinions – *You don't need the internet to study English. Do you agree? I agree. You can play word games in your notebook.*

See p. 6 for suggestions on how to use these Learning objectives in your lessons.

Lead-in

Write the numbers 1–5 in a column down the left-hand side of the board. Ask students to write the numbers on a piece of paper or in their notebooks. Say: *1 Do you learn English online?* Demonstrate writing: *Yes/No* on the board. Encourage students to write. Continue with these questions.

2 What do you think of online English websites?
3 Do you have an English dictionary?
4 Do you use an online dictionary?
5 What do you think of online dictionaries?

Students work in pairs. Ask students to look at their answers together. Can they remember what questions you asked? Go through the questions with the class. Elicit the full question you asked for each.

PREPARING TO LISTEN

1 You will need to be able to explain the options in the survey to students. If you do not know the students' L1, then you could find some websites which are relevant examples of the different online content. Take some screenshots to bring to class (or show students the sites using the technology in your classroom).

Focus on the short survey in the book and check students' understanding of each item. Indicate the tick boxes and read the questions aloud. Students work individually and tick ✓ or cross ✗ each item. Students work in small groups and compare their answers. Take feedback on any differences of study habits.

LISTENING FOR MAIN IDEAS

2 🔊 9.22 Focus on the statements and check understanding. Point at the photographs in Exercise 3. Ask: *What's her name?* about each picture (Amalia, Pilar). Point out the options in Exercise 2. Play the audio. Students work individually and circle the correct option for each person. Play the audio again if necessary. Students work in pairs and check their answers. Then go through answers as a class.

> **Answers**
>
> 1 Amalia <u>agrees</u>. 2 Pilar <u>doesn't agree</u>.

LISTENING FOR KEY INFORMATION

3 🔊 9.23 Focus on the speech bubbles. Point out the options in Amalia's text. Demonstrate circling the correct option. Play the audio. Students work individually and circle the correct options. Play the audio again and go through answers as a class.

> **Answers**
>
> **Amalia:** I buy English <u>books</u> and read English newspapers.
> **Pilar:** English books are very <u>expensive</u> and we don't have a lot of English newspapers in the shops.
> **Amalia:** OK, but there are a lot of English newspapers in <u>the library</u>.
> **Pilar:** On the internet, I buy English <u>apps</u>.

CRITICAL THINKING: UNDERSTAND

4 🔊 9.23 Focus on sentences 1–6. Indicate the boxes and say: *Write A for Amalia and P for Pilar.* Read the first sentence aloud. Say: *Amalia or Pilar?* in a questioning tone. Elicit the correct answer (Amalia). Ask students to find the place in the text where this is mentioned (… there are a lot of English newspapers in the library.). Encourage students to read the sentences, then ask them to read the text and find the information. Students work individually and look at the speech bubbles in Exercise 3. Students work in small groups and compare their answers. Go through answers as a class. Ask students to show you the place in the speech bubbles where they found the answer.

> **Answers**
>
> 3 P 4 A 5 P 6 A

UNLOCK BASIC SKILLS TEACHER'S BOOK   131

CRITICAL THINKING: ANALYZE

5 Focus on the survey and check students' understanding of each item. Indicate the tick boxes. Say: *Do you agree?* Demonstrate by reading the first statement in the left-hand column aloud. Take a class vote on who agrees and who doesn't agree. Demonstrate writing a tick ✓ or a cross ✗ in the box. Students work individually and tick or cross each item. With weaker classes, work through the questionnaire as a class. Students work in small groups and compare their answers.

> **Answers**
> Answers will vary.

PRONUNCIATION FOR LISTENING

6 🔊 9.24 Focus on the four sentences. Point out the highlighted words and syllables. Say the sentences aloud. Exaggerate the sentence stress by saying the highlighted syllables very loudly and clearly and the other syllables quietly. Play the audio for students to repeat. Drill the sentences. See p. 9 for advice on drilling.

> **Optional activity**
> Write these questions on the board. Elicit a possible answer to each one (*You're right. I don't think so.* etc.).
> 1 English is difficult. Do you agree?
> 2 English books are very expensive. Do you agree?
> 3 English newspapers are boring. Do you agree?
> 4 Smartphones aren't interesting. Do you agree?
> Give each student in the class a number 1, 2, 3 or 4. Focus on the questions on the board. Say: *This is your question.* and point to the numbered questions. Check understanding by asking individual students to tell you their question.
> **Mingle**: Follow the procedure on p. 12 (if appropriate to your context).
> **Alternative to mingling**: Follow the procedure on p. 12.

SPEAKING TASK

7 Divide the class into groups of four students. Focus on the REMEMBER box and read through the phrases as a class. Focus on the statement *Some people think the internet doesn't help you learn English.* Students work in groups and give their opinion, with reasons why, using the sentences in Exercise 5. Say: *You don't need the internet to study English. Do you agree?* and elicit a response and a reason why from a student. Other students who disagree say so and give a reason why using the sentences in Exercise 5. Monitor and note any errors and any correct use of language which has not been covered in the course so far. Use the notes you made for feedback at the end of the exercise. See p. 8 for advice on conducting feedback on speaking activities.

> **Model answer**
> A: The internet doesn't help you to learn to study English. Do you agree?
> B: I don't agree. I think it's easy to study on the internet. You can play word games online.
> A: OK, but you can play word games in your notebook. You don't need the internet or a smartphone for this.
> B: Yes, you're right, but it's easy on your smartphone. You can also read English websites.
> A: That's right, but you can go to the library and talk to your teacher in the classroom. You don't need the internet for this.
> B: I don't think so.
> A: You can also buy a paper dictionary. You don't need the internet to study English.

ACADEMIC READING AND WRITING

> **Learning objectives**
> - Scan for numbers in a text
> - Understand a text about technology use in different countries
> - Spell vocabulary learned in Unit 9 accurately
> - CT: Analyze a survey in relation to a model text
> - Use *and* and *but* to link clauses in writing – *I can play games on my tablet and I can watch TV on my smartphone. I can read English websites, but I cannot write a blog.*
> - CT: Understand a survey
> - Complete a description of the results of a survey
>
> See p. 6 for suggestions on how to use these Learning objectives in your lessons.

> **Lead-in**
> Write these sentences on the board:
> *Smartphones are good for children. Do you agree?*
> *Smartphones are good for students. Do you agree?*
> Students work in pairs and give their opinions. Monitor and note any errors with language from the unit. Use the notes you made to give feedback. See p. 8 for advice on conducting feedback on speaking activities.

TECHNOLOGY UNIT 9

PREPARING TO READ

1 👤 Focus on the picture and ask: *What can you see?* (people, the internet). Read the first sentence. Say: *Yes or No?* in a questioning tone. Elicit the answer (students' own answers). Encourage students to read the sentences and think about their opinions. Students work individually, reading the sentences and circling *Yes* or *No* for each one.

READING FOR MAIN IDEAS

2 👤 Do the exercise together as a whole class. Read sentences a–c aloud. Play the audio for students to read and listen to the text in Exercise 3. Students work individually and circle a, b or c. Check the answer as a class.

> **Answer**
> b

SCANNING FOR KEY INFORMATION

3 🔊 9.25 👤 Focus on the first gap. Ask students if they can remember the answer. Point out the second and third gaps and focus on the chart. Play the audio for students to read and listen to the text again. Say: *Read and write*. Students find the countries and the correct data and complete the text. Go through answers as a class.

> **Answers**
> 40% 95% 88%

READING FOR DETAIL

4 👤👥 Focus on the sentences. Read the first sentence aloud. Say: *Yes or No?* in a questioning tone. Elicit the correct answer (yes). Encourage students to read all of the sentences, then ask them to read the text again and find the information. Students work individually, reading the text and circling *Yes* or *No* for each sentence.

Students work in pairs and check their answers. Then, go through answers as a class. Read each sentence aloud. Students say *Yes* or *No* and show you where they found the information in the text or chart. For the No answers, elicit the correct information from students.

If students come from one of the countries mentioned in the chart in Exercise 3, focus on the chart and discuss it as a class; ask students whether they agree or disagree with the numbers in the chart.

> **Answers**
> 2 No (See chart: 73%)
> 3 Yes
> 4 No (See chart: 95% of people use the internet)
> 5 No (See chart: 88%)

ACADEMIC WRITING SKILLS

5 🔊 9.26 👤 Write the vowels on the board: *a, e, i, o, u*. Point out the semi-completed example. Ask: *What word is this?* (websites). Point at the spaces for two missing vowels and elicit the missing letters *i* and *e*. Students complete the words with the missing vowels. Play the audio for students to check their answers. Monitor and check that weaker students are keeping up with the audio and checking their answers correctly. With weaker classes, write the answers on the board.

> **Answers**
> 1 webs<u>i</u>t<u>e</u>s 2 bl<u>o</u>g 3 web<u>i</u>nars 4 <u>o</u>nl<u>i</u>ne
> 5 USB dr<u>i</u>ve 6 p<u>eo</u>ple 7 <u>a</u>dults 8 childr<u>e</u>n

CRITICAL THINKING: ANALYZE

6 👤👥 Focus on the photograph of Li Wei and point out the *Student name*. Focus on the short survey and Li Wei's text below. Indicate the tick and cross and the completed examples. Say: *Read and tick or cross*. Students work individually and tick or cross each item. Students work in pairs and compare their answers. Go through answers as a class.

> **Answers**
> I …
> use a mobile phone every <u>day</u>.
> <u>usually</u> use a mobile phone to learn English.
> read English websites. ✓
> write a blog in English. ✗
> watch webinars. ✓
> learn English online. ✓
> use Microsoft Word®. ✓
> use PowerPoint®. ✗
> read English eBooks. ✓
> watch English TV. ✓

> **NOTICE**
>
> Write these sentences on the board:
> I can drive a car_ but I cannot drive a bus_
> I play video games _ but I don't watch TV_
> Write a comma and a full stop at the top of the board. Circle them to make them stand out.
> Focus on the NOTICE box and point out the highlighted word *but*. Elicit the missing punctuation from the sentences on the board. (, .)

ACADEMIC WRITING SKILLS

7 Write this example sentence on the board: *I learn English at university and I read English websites online.*

Show students that *and* means we add another equal idea. Elicit more ideas to add to the sentence, e.g. *… and I listen to webinars.*

Now write this sentence on the board: *I have a smartphone, but I don't have a laptop.*

Point at and underline: *I have, I don't have.* Show that *but* means we add opposite or contrasting ideas. Highlight the comma before *but* by circling it. Elicit more ideas, e.g. *… but I don't have a computer.*

Focus students on the completed example in Exercise 7. Go through the first sentence together. Read the two sentences aloud and say: *and or but?* (and). Students work individually and join sentences 2–4. Go through answers as a class. Ask individual students to read the sentences aloud.

> **Answers**
> All of the sentences are linked with *but*.

> **Optional activity**
>
> Write five sentence starters with *but* on the board, e.g. *I drink coffee, but … .* Ask students to work individually and complete the sentences. Monitor and check students are using contrasting ideas and correct spelling. Students work in pairs and compare their ideas.

CRITICAL THINKING: UNDERSTAND

8 Students should now be familiar with all the ideas in the survey and the format. Indicate the tick and cross. Students work individually and tick or cross each item.

> **Answers**
> Students' own answers.

WRITING TASK

9 Focus on the survey in Exercise 8 and the gapped sentences in the student notebook. Read the first gapped sentence. Focus on the survey and ask: *How often?* Demonstrate by writing your own answers in the first gap.

Students work individually and complete the gaps with the information from their survey. Monitor and help with spelling and punctuation. If students' answers do not exactly fit the frame, then encourage them to modify it.

10 Students swap books and check each other's writing. Remind students to check the spelling.

> **Model answer**
>
> I use a mobile phone every day. I sometimes use a mobile phone to learn English. I read emails in English and I write emails in English. I read English websites, but I don't write a blog in English. I learn English online and I use Microsoft Word® in English.

> **Objectives review**
>
> See Introduction on p. 7 for ideas about using the Objectives review with your students.
>
> **WORDLIST AND GLOSSARY**
>
> See Introduction on p. 7 for ideas about using the Wordlist at the end of each unit and the Glossary at the end of the book with your students.
>
> **REVIEW TEST**
>
> Go to esource.cambridge.org to print the Review test and for ideas about how and when to administer it.

RESEARCH PROJECT

> **Present an online English website**
>
> Divide the class into groups and tell them each group needs to research online English websites. They should compare different websites.
>
> Allow students class time to research the websites or they could do this for homework. Give students class time during the next lesson to create their presentations. They should use screenshots or technology in the classroom to show the other students what you can and cannot do on the sites.
>
> Students should give their presentations in the next lesson. Encourage students to try each other's websites outside of class time.

10 FREE TIME AND FASHION

UNLOCK YOUR KNOWLEDGE

👤 👥 Focus on the photograph. Ask: *Who's this?* about each person. Elicit the vocabulary for members of a family, e.g. mother, father, etc. Ask: *Where are they?* (in their house), *What's this?* (Point at various technology and other objects in the photograph).

Point to the questions. Ask a student to read each question aloud. Students work in groups and answer the questions. Monitor and help as necessary. Take feedback as a class.

> **Answers**
> 1 a and c
> 2 Answer will vary.

LISTENING AND READING 1

> **Learning objectives**
> - Use verb phrases to describe free-time activities – *go for a walk, bake cakes, have a picnic, do exercise, talk on the phone, go to the park, visit friends and family*
> - Notice different sounds of the letters *a*, *o* and *i* – (w<u>a</u>lk, b<u>a</u>ke, g<u>o</u>, d<u>o</u>, v<u>i</u>sit, exerc<u>i</u>se)
> - Understand descriptions of free-time activities
> - Use prepositions accurately in verb phrases and adverbials – *talk on the phone, do exercise at home*
> - Use sentence stress correctly in statements – *She talks on the phone with her friends.*
> - Ask about other people's free-time activities – *Do you go to the park?*
> - Describe the results of a survey about free-time activities – *Mariam and Anwar do exercise. Samira doesn't do exercise.*
>
> See p. 6 for suggestions on how to use these Learning objectives in your lessons.

> **Lead-in**
> Write *family* and *friends* in circles at the centre of two spidergrams on the board. Pretend to think for a moment then add the phrase *go to a restaurant* to the spidergram at the end of one of the lines coming from *friends*.

Elicit more ideas for things the students do with family and friends. Correct any mistakes with vocabulary to make accurate verb phrases, and encourage all ideas. If you like, you could use the spidergrams to review verb phrases. Ask students to write the completed spidergrams in their notebooks.

VOCABULARY: FREE TIME 1

1 🔊 10.1 👤 👥 Focus on the photographs of free-time activities. Play the audio for students to listen and read. Encourage students to follow the audio by pointing at each phrase in the book as they hear it. Drill the phrases. See p. 9 for advice on drilling. Check understanding using printable Flashcards 10.1. Go to esource.cambridge.org to print the flashcards.

Write the following on the board: *go _ _ walk, have _ picnic, talk _ _ the phone, go _ _ park*. Focus on the photographs and phrases in Exercise 1. Point at the gaps in the sentences on the board and elicit the missing words. Then erase everything except the nouns from the board. Encourage students to recall the phrases without looking in the book.

Demonstrate the next part of the exercise with a student. Point to a photograph and encourage a student to say the correct verb phrase. Then encourage the student to point at a photograph and say the correct verb phrase yourself. Students work in pairs. Monitor and correct any errors.

SOUND AND SPELLING: *o*, *a*, *i*

2 🔊 10.2 👤 👥 Focus on the words on rows 1–3. Ask: *Which letter is in all of the words in 1?* (*o*). Repeat for 2 (*a*) and 3 (*i*). Play the audio for students to listen and repeat. Model the phoneme /əʊ/ and then say the first word: *go*. Ask: *Can you hear /əʊ/?* Help students to understand the question by cupping your ear and using culturally appropriate gestures to indicate *Yes* or *No*. Repeat with each of the words: *phone* (yes), *do* (no). Elicit the sound that *o* makes in *do* /uː/. Point out the ticks ✓ and crosses ✗. Play the audio again. Students listen and tick or cross the words in lines 2 and 3. Go through answers as a class and drill the phonemes and words.

UNL⚪CK BASIC SKILLS TEACHER'S BOOK   135

> **Answers**
> 2 /ɔː/ walk ✓ bake ✗ talk ✓
> 3 /ɪ/   visit ✓ family ✓ exercise ✗

USING VISUALS TO PREDICT THE CONTENT

3 🔊 10.3 👤 Focus on the photographs in Exercise 4. Point at the photographs of the two people and ask: *What is his/her name?* (Emel, Saif), *Where is he/she from?* (Istanbul, Doha), *What's this?* (cakes, a smartphone). Read the sentences about Emel in Exercise 3 aloud. Focus on the options. Students work individually and circle the correct options. Then repeat for Saif. Do not confirm students' guesses yet. Say: *Listen and check.* Play the audio for students to listen, read, and check their answers. Go through answers as a class.

> **Answers**
> 1 c 2 b

READING FOR KEY INFORMATION

4 🔊 10.3 👤 Focus on verb phrases 1–8. Read the first verb phrase aloud. Say: *Emel or Saif?* in a questioning tone. Elicit the correct answer (Saif). Ask students to find the place in the text where this is mentioned (*I also talk on the phone.*). Encourage students to work quickly, underline the verbs in the text, and answer the questions. Students work individually. Play the audio again for students to check their answers. Go through answers as a class, asking students to show you the place in the text where they found the answer.

> **Answers**
> 3 E 4 S 5 S 6 S 7 E 8 E

LISTENING FOR DETAIL

5 🔊 10.3 👥 Ask students to cover the texts in Exercise 4. Focus on sentences 1–4 and point out the options. Say: *Listen and circle.* Play the audio. Students work individually and circle the correct options in the sentences. Students work in pairs and check their answers. Play the audio again and go through answers as a class.

> **Answers**
> 2 on Friday 3 at home 4 on the beach

ACADEMIC WRITING SKILLS

6 🔊 10.4 👤 Focus on the options under the line in sentence 1. Say: *go to a walk or go for a walk?* (for). Say: *Listen* and read the completed example aloud. Demonstrate circling the correct option under the line. Point to the next sentence and the options under the line. Students work individually and circle the correct options. Play the audio for students to check. Go through answers as a class. Then ask students to write the correct answers in the gaps. Monitor and check students' spelling.

> **Answers**
> 2 They usually do exercise <u>at</u> home.
> 3 We go <u>to</u> the park every Friday.
> 4 She always talks <u>on</u> the phone.

PRONUNCIATION FOR SPEAKING

7 🔊 10.5 👥👥👥 Focus on the five sentences. Point out the highlighted words and syllables. Say the sentences aloud, exaggerating the sentence stress. Say the highlighted words and syllables very loudly and clearly and the other syllables quietly. Play the audio for students to repeat. Drill the sentences.

SPEAKING AND WRITING

8 👥 👥👥👥 Tell students to turn to p. 208. Focus on the REMEMBER box. Drill the questions. Elicit questions for each of the activities in the left-hand column. Demonstrate the exercise with a student. Point to the space for a name and the column below. Say: *What's your name?* and write the name. Say: *Do you do exercise?* Elicit Yes or No. Demonstrate writing a tick for Yes or a cross for No. Students work in pairs and interview each other. They complete one part of the table each. Then students change partners. Continue until students have spoken to three other students. Monitor and correct any mistakes with vocabulary or pronunciation.

Now demonstrate the second part of the exercise. Focus on the speech bubble under the table. Point out the names (Mariam and Anwar, Samira). Read the sentences and point out the verb forms (*do* and *doesn't do*). Elicit the 3rd person verb forms for each of the verb phrases in the table (*do/does, go/goes, have/has, talk/talks*) Write these on the board.

Students work in groups of four and describe the results of their survey. Monitor and note any errors with vocabulary and grammar. Use the notes you made for feedback at the end of the exercise. See p. 8 for advice on conducting feedback on speaking activities.

LISTENING AND READING 2

Learning objectives

- Use common verbs – *chat online, sleep, wait, draw*
- Understand people describing their preferred free-time activities
- Use *and* and *or* to link ideas in positive and negative sentences – *I like taking photographs and drawing. I don't like talking on the phone or chatting online.*
- Describe preferences – *I like writing. She doesn't like waiting. They don't like drawing.*
- Spell verb + *-ing* forms accurately – *going, travelling, writing*
- Pronounce verb + *-ing* forms accurately – *drawing, watching, walking*

See p. 6 for suggestions on how to use these Learning objectives in your lessons.

Lead-in

You will need printable Flashcards 10.2, words and pictures separate. Go to esource.cambridge.org to print the flashcards.

Team pelmanism: Review the verb phrases using the flashcards. Then follow the procedure on p. 12.

With stronger classes you could do this with the word cards only. Cut the verb phrases in half and give one team the verbs and the other the object/complement that makes the verb phrase.

VOCABULARY: FREE TIME REVIEW

1 🔊 10.6 Focus on the words in the box and the incomplete verb phrases. Point to the completed example. Students work individually, reading and matching the verbs to make verb phrases. Go through answers as a class.

> **Answers**
> 2 <u>watch</u> TV 3 <u>travel</u> to different countries
> 4 <u>take</u> photographs 5 <u>buy</u> new clothes
> 6 <u>learn</u> new languages

FREE TIME AND FASHION · UNIT 10

PREPARING TO LISTEN

2 🔊 10.7 Focus on the photographs. Play the audio for students to listen and read. Encourage students to follow the audio by pointing at each verb in the book as they hear it. Drill the verbs. See p. 9 for advice on drilling. Check understanding by asking concept questions, e.g. *Do we sleep at night* (Yes)? *Do we sleep at university* (No)? *Do you draw in English class? What do you use to draw?* (a pencil), etc. See p. 7 for advice on concept checking.

Demonstrate the next part of the exercise with a student. Point to a photograph and encourage a student to say the correct word. Then encourage the student to point at a photograph and say the correct word yourself. Students work in pairs. Monitor and correct any mistakes with vocabulary or pronunciation.

LISTENING FOR MAIN IDEAS

3 🔊 10.8 Focus on the radio advertisement. Ask: *Is this a university radio show?* (Yes). *Do we have a radio show at this university?* (Your own answer). Ask: *When is this radio show?* (Tuesday at 4:30). Focus on the options. Play the audio. Students work individually and circle the answer. Check the answer as a class.

> **Answer**
> b free time

READING FOR DETAIL

4 🔊 10.9 Focus on the photographs. Point at the photographs of the two people and ask: *What is his/her name?* (Marta, Bilal). *What does he/she study?* (History/Chemistry). Say: *Read and listen.* Play the audio. Students listen and follow the text. Read the sentences about Marta aloud. Focus on the options. Point out the completed example. Ask students to find the place in the text where this information is given (I don't like baking or cooking.). Students work individually and tick ✓ or cross ✗ the activities for both texts. Go through answers as a class. Students say *Yes* or *No* and show you where they found the information in the text. For the *No* answers, elicit the correct information from students.

> **Answers**
> 1 chatting online and drawing
> 2 sleeping and travelling

UNL*O*CK BASIC SKILLS TEACHER'S BOOK **137**

> **NOTICE**
>
> Write these sentences on the board:
> 1 I study English ____ History.
> 2 I don't study Maths ____ Chemistry.
>
> Focus on the NOTICE box and point out the highlighted words. Elicit the missing words (1 *and*, 2 *or*) from the sentences on the board. Underline *don't*. Use + and – symbols to communicate the rules (+ *and* / – *or*).

GRAMMAR: LIKE + -ING

5 (◀)) **10.10** Write these jumbled sentences on the board: *1 I / emails / writing / like; 2 like / friends / we / meeting*. Focus on the table in the book. Play the audio for students to listen and read. Focus on the sentences on the board. Elicit the correct word order for each sentence (I like writing emails. We like meeting friends.). Ask: *What do I like?* (writing emails), *What do we like?* (meeting friends). Underline the + *-ing* in both sentences.

Focus on the highlighted letters in the table. Play the audio again and drill the sentences. Encourage students to create new sentences using the words in the box.

> **◉ Common student errors**
>
> **Verb form:** Arabic L1 students tend to use the bare infinitive after *like* instead of verb + *-ing*.
> *I like watch the sports news. I like go shopping with my friends. She likes cook for her family.*
> See p. 148 for tips on how to help students with **Verb form** errors.

> **NOTICE**
>
> Write these words on the board:
> takeing
> writeing
> traveling
> chating
>
> Focus on the NOTICE box and point out the highlighted letters. Elicit corrections for the spelling of each verb + *-ing* on the board. (See the NOTICE box in the Student's Book for corrected spellings.)

ACADEMIC WRITING SKILLS

6 (◀)) **10.11** Focus students on verbs 1–6 and the verb + *-ing* forms with missing letters. Students work individually and complete the exercise. Encourage students to count the number of missing letters in each word. Go through answers on the board as a class.

> **Answers**
>
> 2 waiting 3 writing 4 travelling 5 having 6 chatting

7 (◀)) **10.12** Focus on the words in the box. Point out the ticks ✓ and the crosses ✗. Focus on the completed example. Read the completed example aloud. Demonstrate writing on the line. Point at the second sentence and elicit the answer (*does not like*). Students work individually and write the affirmative and negative verbs on the lines. Monitor and check students' spelling. Play the audio for students to check. Go through answers as a class.

> **Answers**
>
> 2 do not like 3 likes 4 does not like 5 do not like 6 like

SOUND AND SPELLING: -ING

8 (◀)) **10.13** Focus on the words. Point out the highlighted letters in each word. Play the audio and drill the words. See p. 9 for advice on drilling.

SPEAKING

9 Tell students to go to p. 209. Focus on the survey. Point out the question: *What do you like doing in your free time?* Demonstrate reading through the survey and ticking or crossing each box. Students work individually and complete the survey about themselves. Monitor and help as necessary. You may wish to complete the survey yourself in preparation for the next part of the exercise.

Divide the students into groups of four. Demonstrate the exercise by describing your own likes and dislikes. Students tell the other members of their groups about themselves. Monitor and note any errors with vocabulary and grammar. Take feedback on what was the same and what was different in each group. Use the notes you made for feedback at the end of the exercise. See p. 8 for advice on conducting feedback on speaking activities.

> **Optional activity**
>
> Ask students to write sentences about their survey results in Exercise 9. Students swap notebooks and check each other's sentences for spelling.

LISTENING AND READING 3

Learning objectives

- Name a variety of clothes – *a coat, a jacket, a dress, a shirt, a scarf, a hat, trousers*
- Use the verb *wear* – *wear a coat and a scarf*
- Spell consonant clusters in clothing items accurately – *shirt, clothes, scarf, dress, trousers, jacket*
- Understand conversations about clothes
- Describe singular and plural objects – *These are my trousers. This is her sari.*

See p. 6 for suggestions on how to use these Learning objectives in your lessons.

Lead-in

Write these pairs of opposite adjectives on the board in a random order:

warm/cold, big/small, new/old, expensive/cheap, interesting/boring

Say: *I'm not hot. I'm …* Elicit: *cold*. Students work in pairs, matching the opposite words and writing the pairs of words down. Monitor and check spelling.

Follow up by asking pairs of students to give you an example with each pair of adjectives in the format: ___ *isn't* (adjective). *It's* (adjective). E.g. *Food isn't cheap. It's expensive*.

VOCABULARY: CLOTHES

1 (10.14) Focus on the photographs of items of clothing. Play the audio for students to listen and read. Encourage students to follow the audio by pointing at each item of clothing in the book as they hear it. Drill the words. See p. 9 for advice on drilling. Check understanding using printable Flashcards 10.3. Go to esource.cambridge.org to print the flashcards. You could also flick through the book and use pictures of people's clothing from other lessons.

Demonstrate the next part of the exercise with a student. Point to a picture and encourage a student to say the correct word. Then encourage the student to point at a picture and say the correct word yourself. Students work in pairs. Monitor and correct any mistakes with vocabulary or pronunciation.

FREE TIME AND FASHION — UNIT 10

Common student errors

Wrong word: Arabic L1 students often use the words *dress* or *dresses* instead of *clothes*.

All of the guests at the wedding wear new dresses.
We wear ordinary dress: a T-shirt and jeans.

See p. 148 for tips on how to help students with **Wrong word** errors.

2 Focus on the photographs and phrases with *wear*. Point to the tick boxes. Say: *Read and match*. Students work individually and match the phrases and photographs. Go through answers as a class.

Answers

1 c 2 a 3 b

NOTICE

Write: *I wear a trousers.* on the board. Say: *Yes or No?* in a questioning tone. Elicit correct answer (*No*). Correct the sentence and highlight *s* on *trousers*. Focus on the NOTICE box. Allow students a minute to read the information there.

LISTENING FOR MAIN IDEAS

3 (10.15) Focus on the photographs in Exercise 4. Point at the photographs and ask: *Who are they?* Encourage lots of ideas, but do not confirm anything. Read sentences 1–2 aloud. Focus on the options. Allow some time for students to read the options. Say: *Listen and tick*. Play the audio. Students work individually and circle the answers. Go through answers as a class.

Answers

1 clothes from different countries
2 winter clothes

READING FOR DETAIL

4 (10.15) Focus on the dialogue. Say: *Read and Listen*. Play the audio for students to listen and follow the dialogues. Focus on the sentences. Ask students to read the sentences. Read the first sentence aloud. Say: *Yes or No?* in a questioning tone. Elicit the correct answer (*Yes*). Ask students to find the place in the text where this information is given (M: *This is a nice dress.* Z: *It's a sari.*).

Students work individually and circle *Yes* or *No* for each sentence. Students work in pairs and check their answers. Then go through answers as a class. Students say *Yes* or *No* and show you where they found the information in the text.

> **Answers**
> 2 Yes
> 3 No (I don't like wearing trousers.)
> 4 Yes
> 5 No (I travel to Canada every winter holiday.)

ACADEMIC WRITING SKILLS

5 (♦ 10.16) Point at the completed example and then Exercise 1 and ask: *What word is this?* (shirt). Point at the second word. Ask: *What word is this?* (clothes). Point at the first space for a missing letter in the second word and elicit the missing letters (c, l). Students work individually and complete the words with the missing letters. Play the audio for students to check their answers. Write the answers on the board with weaker classes. Drill all the words. See p. 9 for advice about drilling.

> **Answers**
> 2 clothes 3 scarf 4 dress 5 trousers 6 jacket

GRAMMAR: THIS IS/THESE ARE

6 (♦ 10.17) Focus on the grammar table. Point out *a* on the singular nouns and ask: *How many?* (one). Point out the *s* at the end of the plural nouns. Draw or use flashcards to show that *jeans* and *trousers* are in fact single items, but have *s* at the end. Refer back to the NOTICE box on Student's Book p. 188 to remind students about these forms. Play the audio for students to listen and read. Check understanding. See p. 7 for advice on concept checking. Play the audio again for students to listen and repeat.

7 (♦ 10.18) Focus on the first sentence. Focus on the noun phrase (*an expensive bag*). Ask: *How many?* (one). Say: *Listen* and read the completed example aloud. Point out the next sentence. Students work individually and write the correct options. Play the audio for students to check. Go through answers as a class.

> **Answers**
> 2 These are my new shoes.
> 3 Are these his trousers?
> 4 Is this a jacket from Mexico?
> 5 These are their shirts.
> 6 This is my new coat.

SPEAKING

8 Tell students to turn to p. 209. Focus on the photographs of people a–c. Ask: *Where is he from?* (Students' guesses). *Is his/her country cold?* (No, it's warm/hot.). Ask similar questions about all of the pictures. Point at the items of clothing under the photos. Tell students to look and match the clothes with the people. Point out the REMEMBER box. Demonstrate the exercise by writing an appropriate letter in the first box. Students work in pairs and match the photographs of clothes to the people. Monitor and encourage students to say what they are thinking. Go through answers as a class. Ask pairs at random to tell you about each item.

> **Answers**
> Answers will vary.

> **Optional activity**
>
> Write these questions on the board. Elicit a possible answer to each one to check understanding. Drill the questions.
> 1 What clothes do you like?
> 2 What clothes don't you like?
> 3 Who do you go clothes shopping with?
> 4 Where do you go clothes shopping?
> 5 How often do you buy new clothes?
>
> Give each student in the class a number 1, 2, 3, 4, 5. Focus on the questions on the board. Say: *This is your question.* and point to the numbered questions. Check understanding by asking individual students to tell you their question.
>
> **Mingle**: Follow the procedure on p. 12.
>
> Ask students to note down the answers they receive. At the end of the activity students report back on what they heard, e.g. *Three people buy clothes at the shopping centre. Two people buy clothes at the market. Six people buy clothes online.*

WATCH AND REMEMBER

> **Learning objectives**
>
> - Understand what people like doing in their spare time – *We like baking. We have a picnic.*
> - Understand people discussing the clothes they wear – *I wear nice shirts.*
> - Practise discussing what clothes you like wearing, and what you like doing in your free time – *I never wear … / I like …*
>
> See p. 6 for suggestions on how to use these Learning objectives in your lessons.

FREE TIME AND FASHION — UNIT 10

> **Lead-in**
>
> Ask students to discuss, with a partner or in groups, any experience they have of cooking or baking. They can also discuss their favourite type of cakes.

PART 1

In Part 1, two families discuss what they like doing in their spare time.

BEFORE YOU WATCH

1 👤 Students match the photographs with the verb phrases and then write the verb phrase under each photograph. Monitor and check students' writing.

2 (🔊 10.19) Play the audio. Students listen and check their answers in Exercise 1. It might be useful to discuss the grammatical construction used, i.e. verb (+ article) + noun. Ask the class to think of other variations, using different nouns, e.g. *go for a meal*, *bake a potato*, *have a drink*.

> **Answers**
>
> 1 c 2 a 3 b

WATCH

3 ▶ 👤 Students read the sentences and options and predict their answers. Students watch the video and check their predictions.

> **Answers**
>
> 2 go online 3 walk 4 in the park

AFTER YOU WATCH

In stronger classes, Exercise 4 should be completed by students after watching Part 1. In weaker classes, students can watch Part 1 again and complete Exercise 4 or use the audio script at the back of the book.

4 👥 Students complete the sentences with words from the box. Students work in pairs and check their answers.

> **Answers**
>
> We <u>have</u> a picnic. We like <u>eating</u> fruit and <u>drinking</u> tea. We <u>walk</u> and we <u>talk</u>. We <u>take</u> photographs of the family. Omar <u>plays</u> in the park.

PART 2

In Part 2, a man discusses what clothes he likes to buy and wear.

BEFORE YOU WATCH

5 👤 Students match the pictures and write the words. Go through answers as a class.

> **Answers**
>
> a a shirt b a jacket c a shoe d a T-shirt

WATCH

6 ▶ 👤 Students read the questions and predict their answers. Students watch the video and check their predictions. Check students understand the difference between *always* and *usually*.

> **Answers**
>
> 1 likes 2 usually 3 T-shirts

AFTER YOU WATCH

7 👤👥 Students complete the gapped sentences. Students can repeat this exercise several times with different partners. Provide a model for the class if they find it difficult.

PART 3

In Part 3, students remember key information from the lesson and extend their vocabulary.

REMEMBER

8 ▶ 👤👥 Students complete the sentences with words from the box. Students work in pairs and check their answers. Go through answers as a class.

> **Answers**
>
> 1 milk, eggs 2 fruit, tea 3 shirts

MORE VOCABULARY: FOOD AND CLOTHES

9 Students match the words to the pictures. Students work in pairs and check their answers. Check the spelling of *biscuit*. Ask how the article before *egg* is different (i.e. it is *an* because *egg* begins with a vowel).

> **Answers**
> a tie b egg c biscuit

ASK AND ANSWER

10 Students ask and answer the question in pairs. Change pairs to give students more practice.

> **Optional activity**
> As a fun additional activity, and if appropriate in your context, students mime activities they like doing in their free time. The other students guess.

⊙ LANGUAGE FOCUS

> **Learning objectives**
> - Name six colours – *red, blue, white, black, green, yellow*
> - Understand conversations about clothes
> - Use *'s* to describe people's possessions – *my father's old hat, Paulo's new car*
> - Describe what children wear for school
> - Pronounce *s*, *sh* and *'s* (*clothe*s, *my brother's*, *school*, *student*s, *shop*)
>
> See p. 6 for suggestions on how to use these Learning objectives in your lessons.

> **Lead-in**
> You will need printable Flashcards 10.4. Go to esource.cambridge.org to print the cards. You need the sides with pictures only and some sticky tack.
> Review the names of the clothes taught in this unit.
> Stick the flashcards with the pictures only to the board and number them 1–10. Divide the class into two teams. Tell students they need to name the clothes and spell the word accurately to get the cards. Ask Team A to choose a card (1–10) and name and spell the word. If they make a mistake, stop them and offer the other team the opportunity to name the clothes and spell the word. If the team is successful, take the card from the board and give it to them. The activity is finished when all the cards have been awarded.

VOCABULARY: COLOURS

1 🔊 10.20 Focus on the colours. Elicit the words that students already know. Play the audio for students to listen and read. Encourage students to follow the audio by pointing at each word in the book as they hear it. Drill the colours. See p. 9 for advice on drilling. Check understanding by pointing at various coloured things around the classroom.

Demonstrate the next part of the exercise with a student. Point to a colour and encourage a student to say the correct word. Then encourage the student to point at a colour and say the correct word yourself. Students work in pairs. Monitor and correct any mistakes with vocabulary or pronunciation.

> **NOTICE**
> Focus on the NOTICE box. Allow students a minute to read the information there. Write: *She has a black new jacket* on the board. Say: *Yes or No?* in a questioning tone. Elicit correct answer (*No*). Correct the sentence.

GRAMMAR: ORDER OF ADJECTIVES

2 🔊 10.21 Focus on the photographs. Point at the photograph of the girl and ask: *What is her name?* (Li Na), *Where is she/he from?* (Shanghai), *How old do you think she/he is?* (Students' guesses: *I think she's …*). Tell students to look at the photograph, read the text and write the colours. Students work individually. Monitor and help as necessary. Play the audio for students to listen and check. Go through answers as a class.

> **Answers**
> new black big red

3 🔊 10.22 Focus on the options under the line in the first sentence. Focus on the first photograph. Say: *What is it?* (a dress) *Is it white or yellow?* (yellow) Say: *Listen* and read the completed example aloud. Demonstrate circling the correct option under the line. Point out the next photograph and the options under the line. Students work individually and circle the correct options. Play the audio for students to check. Go through answers as a class. Then ask students to write the correct answers in the gaps. Monitor and check students' spelling.

> **Answers**
> 1 beautiful white
> 2 new blue
> 3 old green

LISTENING FOR KEY INFORMATION

4 🔊 **10.23** 👥 Focus on the dialogues and point out the options. Say: *Listen, read and circle.* Play the audio. Students work individually and circle the correct options in the dialogues. Students work in pairs and check their answers. Play the audio again and go through answers as a class.

> **Answers**
> 1 blue 2 big 3 red

GRAMMAR: POSSESSIVE 'S

5 🔊 **10.24** 👤 Focus on the photographs in the table and play the audio. Encourage students to point at each picture as they hear the phrase. Play the audio again and focus on the words in the table. Drill the phrases. See p. 9 for advice on drilling.

Check understanding of the possessive 's. Indicate students around the classroom and things they have on their desks, e.g. *This is Mohammed. What's this?* (Hold up Mohammed's pen.). Elicit: *This is Mohammed's pen.* Write the sentences you elicit on the board.

Ask students to look at the dialogue in Exercise 4 and underline all the examples of possessive 's. (my sister's favourite dress; my brother's shoes; Lara's jacket).

> 👁 **Common student errors**
>
> **Form of possessives:** Arabic L1 students often use the wrong form of possessive 's when they talk about things that belong to particular people, e.g.
> *This is the house of Mohammed. The car of my friend is a Lamborghini.*
> The reverse form of the error is also made in cases where the *of* form of the possessive is required.
> *On the exam's evening I had a headache. I can see everything from my room's window.*
> Beginners cannot be expected to differentiate between the two types. Possession with *of* is not usually taught until a more advanced stage of learning. However, it is important to reinforce the idea that 's is used to refer to what people possess. You could use exercises with *whose* to reinforce this.
> Ask questions about the students' possessions in the classroom: *Whose bag is this? Whose mobile phone is this? Whose jacket is this?*

FREE TIME AND FASHION — UNIT 10

> Ask questions about photographs or a map in which the people are labelled: *Whose bag is red? Whose clothes do you like? Whose car is bigger? Whose house is near the library?*, etc.
> Encourage spoken and written answers in full sentences using names or relationships, e.g. *It is my friend's bag. That is Abdullah's mobile phone. Hamid's house is near the library.*

6 🔊 **10.25** 👤 Focus on the words under the line in the first sentence. Use the completed example to demonstrate the exercise. Read the completed example aloud. Point out the second sentence and the name under the line. Students work individually and form the possessives. Monitor and check students' use of apostrophes. Play the audio for students to check. Go through answers on the board as a class.

> **Answers**
> 2 Yasemin's 3 Paulo's 4 Raj's

LISTENING AND WRITING

7 🔊 **10.26** 👤 Focus on the photograph. Point at the photograph of the boy and ask: *What is his name?* (Akram) *Where is he from?* (Uzbekistan) *How old do you think he is?* (Students' guesses: I think he's …). Tell students to look at the photograph, read the text, and write the colours. Students work individually. Monitor and help as necessary. Play the audio for students to listen and check. Go through answers as a class.

> **Answers**
> Akram's trousers are <u>grey</u> and his shirt is <u>white</u>. He has a <u>nice blue</u> school bag and <u>new black</u> shoes.

SOUND AND SPELLING: s, sh

8 🔊 **10.27** 👥 Focus students on the words with highlighted letters. Ask: *What letters are these?* (s, ss, sh). Elicit the sound that *sh* makes /ʃ/. Play the audio. Students listen and repeat. Drill the words as a class. Go to p. 9 for advice on drilling.

> **Answers**
> /z/ clothes jeans bags my brother's
>   my teacher's Mohammed's
> /s/ school students dress
> /ʃ/ shirt T-shirt shop

SPEAKING

8 Tell students to turn to p. 209. Focus on the photographs. Tell students to choose a photograph and write notes on the clothes and the colours. Demonstrate the activity by writing short notes about a student in the class on the board (Mohammed, black T-shirt, blue jeans). Students work individually and make notes.

Divide students into pairs. Try to match students who have written about different photographs. Demonstrate the task. Describe the student you wrote notes about on the board, e.g. *This is Mohammed. His T-shirt is black. He wears blue jeans every day.* Students work in pairs and take turns to describe a photograph.

Monitor and note any correct use of language which has not been covered in the course so far as you monitor. Use the notes you made for feedback at the end of the exercise. See p. 8 for advice on conducting feedback on speaking activities.

Optional activity

Chain sentences: Follow the procedure on p. 11.
1 a shirt, a dress and a T-shirt
2 a red shirt, a green dress, a blue T-shirt
3 I like wearing a red shirt, a green dress and a blue T-shirt.

ACADEMIC LISTENING AND SPEAKING

Learning objectives

- Understand a conversation about free-time and clothes
- CT: Understand a survey
- Use tone correctly in questions – *What do you wear to university?*
- Conduct a survey and present the results

See p. 6 for suggestions on how to use these Learning objectives in your lessons.

Lead-in

You could prepare a short and simple text about your free time to share with your students. Alternatively, you could use this text:

In my free time, I like reading books. I go to the bookshop every week and buy one or two books. I also like driving. My family and I drive to the beach every Saturday. We go for a walk. In winter, I wear a hat, a coat and a scarf at the beach. It is very cold. My favourite coat is brown. It is very warm.

Tell students you are going to talk about your free time. Elicit questions from them, e.g. *What do you like doing? What do like wearing? Where do you go? Who do you meet? What do you buy?* Do not answer the questions. Write them on the board.

Read your text aloud to the students and ask them to make notes to answer their own questions. Tell them not to worry about spelling and grammar. Read your text aloud twice. Then ask students to share their notes with you. Reconstruct your text on the board as students share different parts of their notes with you.

PREPARING TO LISTEN

1 (10.28) Focus on questions 1–4 and ask a student to read them aloud. Point at the completed example by tracing the line from *What do you like doing in your free time?* to the correct answer. Students work individually to complete the exercise and then compare their answers in pairs. Play the audio for students to check. Go through answers as a class.

Check students understand the word *favourite*. Say: *I have three bags. A black bag, a brown bag and a blue bag. I usually use the blue bag. It is my favourite.* Talk to the students about some of their favourite things. Drill the word *favourite* and the question *What is your favourite colour?* Go to p. 9 for advice about drilling.

Answers

2 At home, I like wearing jeans. 3 I wear brown trousers and a shirt. 4 It's blue.

LISTENING FOR MAIN IDEAS

2 (10.29) Focus on the photograph. Point at the photograph and ask: *Who are they?* (Murat and Rafet). Read the sentence about Murat aloud. Focus on the options and point out the boxes. Allow some time for students to read the options. Say: *Listen and tick.* Play the audio. Students work individually and tick the answers. Go through answers as a class.

| Answer
| free time   clothes   favourite colours

LISTENING FOR DETAIL

3 🔊 10.29 👥 Focus on the sentences. Read the first sentence aloud. Say: *Yes or no?* in a questioning tone. Elicit the correct answer (No). Play the audio. Students work individually, reading the text and circling *Yes* or *No* for each sentence.

Students work in pairs and check their answers. Then go through answers as a class. Read out each sentence. Students say Yes or No. For the No answers, elicit the correct information from students.

| Answers
| 2 No (But I don't like cooking.)
| 3 Yes
| 4 No (At university, I wear… a white shirt.)
| 5 Yes
| 6 Yes

CRITICAL THINKING: UNDERSTAND

4 🔊 10.29 Focus on the words in the box and the student survey. Ask: *Whose survey is this?* (Murat's). Say: *Listen and read.* Play the audio. Demonstrate the exercise using the partially completed example in question 1. Students work individually and write the words from the box on the lines. Go through answers as a class.

| Answers
| 1 going to restaurants   2 jeans and a T-shirt   3 a shirt
| 4 green

5 Focus on the notes in Exercise 4. Ask: *Are these sentences?* (no). Demonstrate the exercise by writing notes about yourself on the board to answer the first question in the survey. Students work individually and complete the survey by making notes about themselves. Monitor and check students' spelling.

PRONUNCIATION FOR LISTENING

6 🔊 10.30 Focus on the four sentences and the main stress. Point out the highlighted words. Say the sentences aloud, exaggerating the sentence stress. Say the highlighted words very loudly and clearly and the other words quietly. Play the audio for students to repeat. Drill the sentence. Go to p. 9 for advice on drilling.

FREE TIME AND FASHION   UNIT 10

SPEAKING TASK

7 👥 Divide the class into Student As and Student Bs. Tell Student As to go to p. 202 and Student Bs to go to p. 205. Focus on the surveys. Demonstrate the exercise with a student. Ask the first question in Student As survey and then make notes on the student's responses on the board. Encourage extended responses. Students work in pairs and conduct the survey with a partner.

Monitor and note any errors with vocabulary and grammar. Use the notes you made for feedback at the end of the exercise. See p. 8 for advice on conducting feedback on speaking activities.

| Model answer
| A: What do you like doing in your free time?
| B: I enjoy sleeping. I also enjoy watching TV and reading books.
| A: What do you like wearing at home?
| B: I like wearing jeans and T-shirts. I also like wearing hats.
| A: What do you wear to university?
| B: I wear white trousers and a white shirt.
| A: What is your favourite colour?
| B: I like wearing green clothes, but my favourite colour is red.
| A: My friend's shirt is blue and his trousers are black.

Optional activity

Students prepare a short and simple text based on the ideas they wrote in Exercise 5. (See the example text below – it is the same one that was used in the Lead-in.)

In my free time, I like reading books. I go to the bookshop every week and buy one or two books. I also like driving. My family and I drive to the beach every Saturday. We go for a walk. In winter, I wear a hat, a coat and a scarf at the beach. It is very cold. My favourite coat is brown. It is very warm.

Tell students they are going to a listen to their partner and they should try to answer these questions about them. They should make notes. Write these questions on the board:

What do you like doing? What do you like wearing? Where do you go? Who do you meet? What do you buy?

Students work in pairs and take turns to read their text aloud to each other. Students make notes to answer the questions on the board. Then students use the notes they made to write a text about their partners. When they are finished, they compare texts and find out what was the same and what was different from the original.

ACADEMIC READING AND WRITING

Learning objectives

- Understand an advertisement for various student clubs
- Spell vocabulary learned in Unit 10 accurately
- Understand an email about a student club
- CT: Understand notes in relation to a model text
- CT: Create a student club and prepare notes for writing an email
- Use *and* and *also* to link ideas in writing
- Complete an email about a student club

See p. 6 for suggestions on how to use these Learning objectives in your lessons.

Lead-in

You will need printable Flashcards 5.3, 10.1 and 10.2. Go to esource.cambridge.org to print them.

Review the verbs and verb phrases. Elicit verb + *-ing* forms for each of the items on the flashcards, e.g. *reading books*, etc. Write these on the board.

Write the following adjectives on the board: *interesting, beautiful, new*.

Elicit their position in the verb phrases with verb + *-ing*, e.g. *reading interesting books*.

Tell students to choose two verb phrases and write a sentence with verb + *-ing*, e.g. *I like cooking and learning languages*. Students work in pairs and say their sentences.

USING VISUALS TO PREDICT CONTENT

1 👥 Focus on the photograph. Ask: *What do they like doing?* (playing chess). *Are they students or teachers?* (students). *Are they studying?* (No). *Where are they?* (University Chess Club). Focus on sentences (1–4) and point to the tick boxes. Point to the completed example and read it aloud. Ask: *Is this their free time?* (Yes). Students work in pairs and complete the exercise. Do not confirm their ideas until you go through the answers in Exercise 2. If appropriate for your context, ask students: *Are you in any clubs?* Write the names of the clubs on the board.

READING FOR KEY INFORMATION

2 🔊 10.31 👥 Focus on the flyer text. Ask: *Where is this from?* (a university). *What is it about?* (university clubs). *Who is it for?* (students). Play the audio and encourage students to listen and read, following the text line by line. Focus on the questions under the flyer text. Read the first question aloud and elicit the correct answer (*Tuesday 20th September*). Ask students to point out the place on the flyer where this information can be found (the first speech bubble at the top).

Students work individually and find the information in the flyer and write the answers to the questions. Monitor and help as necessary. Go through answers as a class, asking students to point out each place in the flyer where the information can be found.

> **Answers**
> 2 9:00–12:30 3 Yes 4 No 5 In Room 21 6 In Room 25

ACADEMIC WRITING SKILLS

3 🔊 10.32 👥 Write the vowels on the board: *a, e, i, o, u*. Point out the completed example. Ask: *What word is this?* (drawing). Point at number 2 and ask: *What word is this?* (baking). Point at the spaces for missing vowels and elicit the missing letters (a, i). Students complete the words with the missing vowels. Play the audio for students to check their answers. Go through answers as a class on the board.

> **Answers**
> 2 b<u>a</u>king 3 c<u>o</u>oking 4 r<u>e</u>ading 5 f<u>a</u>shion 6 cl<u>o</u>thes
> 7 l<u>e</u>arning 8 fr<u>e</u>e t<u>i</u>me

READING FOR DETAIL

4 🔊 10.33 👥 Focus on the email and then the sentences below it. Read the first sentence aloud. Say: *Yes or No?* in a questioning tone. Encourage students to scan the text and quickly find the answer. Elicit the correct answer (Yes) and ask them to show you where they found the information in the text (line 4: *To all new students*). Encourage students to read the sentences one by one and quickly scan the email to find the answers.

Students work individually, scanning and circling *Yes* or *No* for each sentence. Students work in pairs and go through their answers. Then go through the answers as a class. Read out each sentence. Students say *Yes* or *No* and show you where they found the information in the text. For the *No* answers, elicit the correct information from students.

> **Answers**
> 2 Yes 3 Yes 4 No (We like eating Japanese food. We go to a restaurant every month.) 5 Yes

FREE TIME AND FASHION — **UNIT 10**

CRITICAL THINKING: UNDERSTAND

5 Focus on the student notes. Ask: *Are these sentence or notes?* (notes). Focus on the verbs and ask: *Are these verbs with -ing?* (no). *Whose notes are they?* (Fiona's). Focus on the email in Exercise 4. Ask: *Who is it from?* (Fiona P.). Point at the first gap in the notes and encourage students to find the words in Fiona's email (*watching Japanese TV*). Demonstrate writing *watch Japanese* in the gap. Students work individually and complete Fiona's notes. If students write numerals rather than words in the notes, do not correct this in notes.

> **Answers**
> watch Japanese, Japanese, teachers, one, week, restaurant, month, 9, Tuesday

ACADEMIC WRITING SKILLS

6 Write these sentences on the board: *We like taking photographs. We like reading books.*

Focus on the example sentences in the book. Students read and review the uses of *and*. Students connect the two sentences on the board with *and*. (*We like taking photographs and reading books.*) Students work individually and write three full sentences using *and*.

> **Answers**
> 1 I like going to interesting places and taking beautiful photographs.
> 2 I like cooking interesting food and baking cakes.
> 3 I like computers and the internet.

CRITICAL THINKING: CREATE

7 Write: _____ *Club* on the board. Elicit different kinds of student clubs from the students (e.g. English Club, Book Club, etc.). If students cannot think of any ideas, then refer them to the flyer on p. 196. Tell students they are going to write about a student club. Put students into pairs to decide which kind of club they will write about. Ask students to tell you the clubs they are going to write about and write these on the board.

Focus on the space for their notes and the two questions in the book. With weaker classes refer back to Fiona's notes in Exercise 5. Students work in pairs and write notes about their student club.

> **Answers**
> Answers will vary.

WRITING TASK

8 Focus on the gapped email. Read the first gap in the email: *From: _____ @ camuni.ac.uk*. Elicit that this is an email address. Students complete it with their name. Students work individually and complete the email with their information and the information in the notes in Exercise 7. Monitor and help as necessary. Check students are using *and* correctly.

> **Answers**
> Answers will vary.

9 Students swap books and check each other's writing. Remind students to check the spelling.

> **Objectives review**
>
> See Introduction on p. 7 for ideas about using the Objectives review with your students.
>
> **WORDLIST AND GLOSSARY**
>
> See Introduction on p. 7 for ideas about using the Wordlist at the end of each unit and the Glossary at the end of the book with your students.
>
> **REVIEW TEST**
>
> Go to esource.cambridge.org to print the Review test and for ideas about how and when to administer it.

RESEARCH PROJECT

> **Conduct an online survey**
>
> Show the class a website where they can create a survey. (If this is not appropriate for your context, students could do the survey on paper.) Divide the class into groups and tell them each group needs to create a survey about free-time activities, clothes and people's favourites.
>
> Tell students that each group will give a 2–3 minute presentation using the information from the survey.
>
> Allow students class time to create the survey. They should share the survey online with their friends and family. (If this is not appropriate for your context, students could do the survey on paper around the university.) Give students class time during the next lesson to look at their results and plan their presentations. You could help them with ideas for how to present their results. Students should give their presentations in the next lesson.

HELPING STUDENTS WITH COMMON STUDENT ERRORS

Spelling:
Focus students on the spelling of challenging words by writing whole words on the board and pointing out any problematic sections such as consonant clusters (b**read**), vowel doubling (fr**ie**nd), or silent letters (the**re**). Present students with gapped words and elicit the correct letters to complete them. Conduct spelling tests and dictations using words your students have particular problems with. Encourage self-correction and peer correction rather than correcting any mistakes yourself. Write answers on the board and students correct their own work, or swap papers and check each other's work.

Sound and spelling:
Pronunciation problems can be focused on using lists of minimal pairs. If your students struggle with a particular sound, compile a list of words that differ only in the confused phonological element, e.g. long and short vowel sounds, /p/ and /b/, etc. for example: *leave, live; feel, fill; peak, pick; fees, fizz*. The internet can be a useful source of such lists. Use these words to familiarize students with the common spellings of the different sounds, and for drills and aural discrimination tasks. Ask students to work out the sounds of unknown words with the same spelling patterns, e.g. *peel, pill, leak, lick*.

Missing words:
When you hear students make this type of error, correct them by repeating their sentence whilst counting the words on your fingers. When you get to the missing word, wiggle the finger and pause, then continue to the next finger. Repeat, this time stopping at that finger and allowing the student to correct their mistake. Help the students as necessary and encourage them to repeat the whole sentence correctly. If this mistake occurs in writing, write similar sentences on the board using the ^ symbol to indicate where there is a missing word. Elicit the correction to the sentence on the board and then encourage the student(s) to self-correct their own writing.

Extra words:
When you hear students insert unnecessary words into sentences, take a note of the error. Create a short paragraph with a certain number of (e.g. five) instances of these extra words. Hand out copies of the paragraph or write it on the board. Tell students they have to find and delete five unnecessary words. Drill the correct sentences at the end of the activity.

Wrong word:
Wrong word errors often occur because of L1 interference. It's important to reinforce correct collocations in English. ***Verbs and nouns:*** You can use some of the flashcard activities such as Team pelmanism to reinforce correct collocation. Students match verbs to nouns or other complements to make verb phrases. Encourage students to personalize the language by making sentences including the collocations that are meaningful to them.
Prepositions: Since prepositions are very dependent on the overall meaning of the sentence, gapped sentences which contain the full context are the best way to focus on these. You can include a mixture of often confused prepositions. E.g. *I study _____ the University of Cambridge. English is _____ room 10. We study English _____ Mondays*. You can conduct these activities as written or aural/oral gap fills. Encourage self and peer correction in writing.

Word order:
Unscramble activities are helpful for reinforcing correct word order in sentences and questions (E.g. *I / at the shopping centre / new / clothes / buy*). If your students struggle with word order in statements and questions, provide a mixture of statements and questions in unscramble tasks:
I / can / a book / have / ?   can / I / a car / drive / .
Equally, tasks where students have to insert a word in the correct place in a sentence can also be helpful:
always   I go to the bank on Thursday.

Verb form / Noun form:
Students from many L1 backgrounds fail to make verbs agree with their subjects or use singular rather than plural subjects. You could include activities where students describe pictures of single people (He … / She …) and groups of people (They …), scenes with objects (There is / There are, a lot of bags / some people / a woman) etc. You can find images like these in the Student's Book and exploit them in this way, or find your own images. Encourage students to talk or write about the pictures. Encourage students to self-correct verb and noun form errors by repeating their sentence whilst counting the words on your fingers. When you get to the wrong form, wiggle the finger and pause, then continue to the next finger. Repeat, this time stopping at that finger and allowing the student to correct their mistake. Help the student as necessary and encourage them to repeat the whole sentence correctly.

Punctuation:
There are a variety of punctuation errors students may make. Activities which can be helpful to work on punctuation include presenting students with unpunctuated or wrongly punctuated sentences and paragraphs for correction, and (running) dictations in which students are given the opportunity to correct their own work against a correct text.

TEACHER'S NOTES FOR ADDITIONAL SPEAKING AND WRITING TASKS

SPEAKING TASK 1:
Students work with a student they do not usually talk to.

WRITING TASK 1:
Point out the *To*, *From* and *Subject* lines of the email.

SPEAKING TASK 2:
Ask students to bring in a photograph of their family.

WRITING TASK 2:
Students work in groups of three.

SPEAKING TASK 3:
Elicit what type of words are missing in the questions (subjects the other student studies).

WRITING TASK 3:
Elicit which words students will need to complete the email (*on*, *at* and *in*) in addition to the information on the timetable.

SPEAKING TASK 4:
Ask students to bring in a photographs from a family holiday (in another country if possible).

WRITING TASK 4:
Ask students to bring in a photographs from a family holiday (in another country if possible).

SPEAKING TASK 5:
Give students some time to prepare their ideas for this task by thinking of someone they know and their job. Help students with the vocabulary for jobs.

WRITING TASK 5:
Focus on 1–4. Elicit what type of words are missing for 1–4 (1 a month, 2 a month, 3 a subject, a month, 4 a teacher's name). Students complete the information. Focus on 5–8. Elicit which words are missing for the first gaps in 5, 6 and 7 (*he* or *she*). Focus on the Notice box on Student's Book p. 98 to help students complete the second gaps in 5, 6 and 7. Elicit what is missing from 8 (different answers are possible, for example *easy*, *on Wednesday* or *at 3 o'clock*). Students complete the information.

SPEAKING TASK 6:
If appropriate, ask students to bring in photographs of their family meals.

WRITING TASK 6:
Elicit some sentences students can write using the information in the pie chart, for example *Healthy people in Mexico eat a lot of rice and bread.*

SPEAKING TASK 7:
Students may need to prepare their ideas for this task by drawing a basic map. They should talk about the area near their home.

WRITING TASK 7:
Elicit what type of information students can write in the gaps at the beginning of each sentence (for example *is a* name of building).
Students can look at the text in Exercise 6 on Student's Book p. 143 to help them.

SPEAKING TASK 8:
Students may need to prepare their ideas for this task using an ideas map.

WRITING TASK 8:
Elicit what students can write in 1 (for example *one phone* or *three watches*). Focus on the Notice box on Student's Book p. 152 and elicit what type of words students are missing for each gap in 2 (for example *a lot* and *clothes*). Students complete 1–4.

SPEAKING TASK 9:
Divide students into groups of 3–4. Ask students to discuss the first question in their groups. Compare opinions as a class. Repeat for the other questions. You can add more questions which are especially relevant to your students.

WRITING TASK 9:
Ask students to write in their notebooks if they need more space. Elicit one or two sentences before students start writing. Monitor and check that students put the adverb in the correct place in their sentences. Students who finish early can compare answers in pairs and see if they agree or disagree.

SPEAKING TASK 10:
Ask students to think of a friend who they can talk about. They could also choose a family member or a classmate.

WRITING TASK 10:
Elicit some free-time activities before students start writing.

ADDITIONAL SPEAKING TASK 1

1 Work in pairs. Look at the questions. Ask and answer.

> What's your first name?
> What's your family name?
> How do you spell that?
> Where are you from?
> What's your phone number?
> What's your email?

2 Work in new pairs. Say.

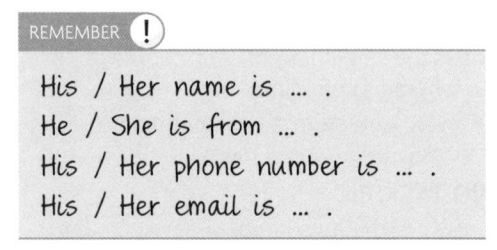

> **REMEMBER !**
>
> His / Her name is ... .
> He / She is from ... .
> His / Her phone number is ... .
> His / Her email is ... .

ADDITIONAL WRITING TASK 1

Look. Complete the email about Rashid Sharani.

> To: University Library   From: r.sharani@uni.co.sa
> Subject: Library card
>
> Hi,
> I'm a new student. I need a _____ .
> _____ is Rashid. _____ Sharani
> _____ Saudi Arabia. _____ 0443 020 894.
> _____ r.sharani@uni.co.sa
> I can come to the library on Monday.
> Thank you.
> Rashid

150 UNLOCK BASIC SKILLS TEACHER'S BOOK PHOTOCOPIABLE © Cambridge University Press 2017

ADDITIONAL SPEAKING AND WRITING TASKS

ADDITIONAL SPEAKING TASK 2

Ask and answer about a photograph of your family.

> **REMEMBER !**
>
> Who's this?　　　　　　　　His / Her name is … .
> How old is he/she?　　　　Their names are … .
> How old are they?　　　　　… years old.
> This is my … .

ADDITIONAL WRITING TASK 2

Complete the web page about your group.

```
••• www.cambridgeuniversity.uk/ourstudents
```

| Home | Our Class | Our Teachers | Our Students |

Welcome to English!

This is our class. _____ and _____ are friends. _____ is _____ years old and _____ is _____ years old.

Our teacher is _____ . _____ is from _____ . Our university is _____ old.

ADDITIONAL SPEAKING TASK 3

Work in pairs. Look at the questions. Ask and answer.

> What subjects do you study?
> What is your _____ class like?
> When is your _____ class?
> Who is your _____ teacher?

> **REMEMBER !**
>
> I study … .
> It's interesting / boring / easy / difficult.
> It isn't interesting / boring / easy / difficult.
> It's on (Monday) morning / afternoon.
> It's at … o'clock.
> Our teacher is Mr/Mrs/Dr … .

ADDITIONAL WRITING TASK 3

Read the timetable and complete the email.

subjects	day	time	room
Maths	Monday	9:00	6
IT	Tuesday	2:00	3
Japanese	Thursday	10:30	8

From: saeed.hassan@college.ac.ae   Reply   Forward
Subject: Your timetable

Dear Muhammed
This is our timetable for this week.
_____ is _____ .
_____ is _____ .
_____ is _____ .
See you in class!
Saeed

ADDITIONAL SPEAKING TASK 4

Student A: Ask questions about Student B's photograph. Student B: Answer Student A's questions.

REMEMBER !

What's this?
Where's this?
Who's this?
Is ... (hot / wet / dry / cold / interesting / boring)?
This is (London) in (the UK).
This is (my/our) ... .
Yes, it is.
No, it isn't.

ADDITIONAL WRITING TASK 4

Complete the text about your photograph(s).

This is _____ in _____ .
It is _____ . It is not _____ .
This is _____ .

ADDITIONAL SPEAKING AND WRITING TASKS

ADDITIONAL SPEAKING TASK 5

Talk about the job of someone in your family.

REMEMBER !

… is a … .
works with / in / on /at
travels / helps / meets / takes / reads / writes / starts / finishes
It is interesting / difficult / easy.

ADDITIONAL WRITING TASK 5

Write about your English classes and your teacher.
1 Classes start in _____ .
2 Classes finish in _____ .
3 The _____ exam is in _____ .
4 Our teacher is _____ .
5 _____ works _____ .
6 _____ starts work _____ .
7 _____ finishes work _____ .
8 Our English classes are _____ .

ADDITIONAL SPEAKING TASK 6

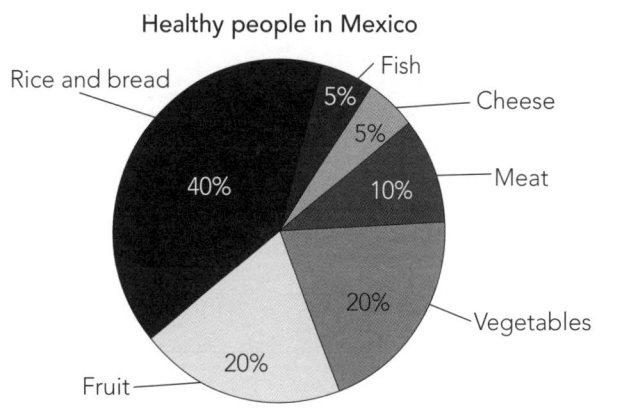

Talk about your family and food.

REMEMBER !

We have breakfast / lunch / dinner at … .	We eat / drink a lot of … .
We have … for breakfast / lunch/ dinner.	We eat / drink some … .
	We don't eat / drink a lot of … .

ADDITIONAL WRITING TASK 6

Write about healthy people in Mexico.
Healthy people in Mexico _____
_____
_____
_____
_____
_____
_____ .

Healthy people in Mexico

- Rice and bread 40%
- Fish 5%
- Cheese 5%
- Meat 10%
- Vegetables 20%
- Fruit 20%

UNLOCK BASIC SKILLS TEACHER'S BOOK PHOTOCOPIABLE © Cambridge University Press 2017

153

ADDITIONAL SPEAKING TASK 7

Talk about your house and your city.

> **REMEMBER**
>
> I live in ... .
> I live near a ... .
> There is a ... .
> There are a lot of ... .
> It is old / new / clean / big / small / busy / interesting.

ADDITIONAL WRITING TASK 7

Write about King Street.

There _____ on King Street.
There _____ near the _____ .
There _____ opposite the _____ .
There _____ .

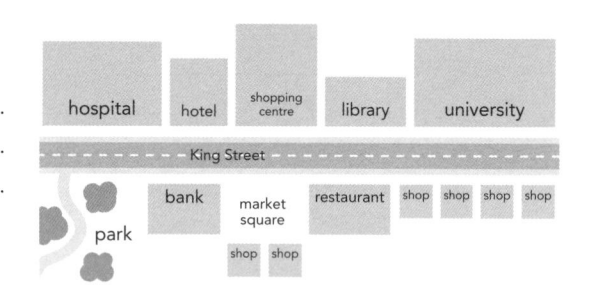

hospital | hotel | shopping centre | library | university

King Street

park | bank | market square | restaurant | shop | shop | shop
shop | shop

ADDITIONAL SPEAKING TASK 8

Talk about your family and shopping.

> **REMEMBER**
>
> We buy things in the shopping centre. / at the market. / on the internet.
> We spend a lot of money on ... .
> We buy ... every ... / once a ... / twice a day / week / month / year
> We buy ... every week.
> We usually pay ... .

ADDITIONAL WRITING TASK 8

Write about your things and what you buy.

1 I have _____ .

2 I spend _____ on _____ .

3 I buy _____ every _____ .

4 I pay _____ .

ADDITIONAL SPEAKING AND WRITING TASKS

ADDITIONAL SPEAKING TASK 9

Discuss the sentences.

This city is expensive.   English is difficult.   Video games are boring.

> **REMEMBER !**
>
> What do you think?
> I agree.
> I don't agree.
> That's right!
> I don't think so.

ADDITIONAL WRITING TASK 9

Write about your country. Use the words in the boxes.

people   women   children   men   adults   always   usually   often   sometimes   never

watch TV   play video games   write emails   cook   buy things online

_____
_____
_____
_____

ADDITIONAL SPEAKING TASK 10

Talk about your friend.

> **REMEMBER !**
>
> He / She likes … .
> He / She doesn't like … .
> …'s favourite colour is … .
> He / She likes wearing … .

ADDITIONAL WRITING TASK 10

Write about your and your family's free time.

My family like _____ . We also like _____ . We don't like _____ .

My _____ . _____ also _____ .

UNL**O**CK BASIC SKILLS TEACHER'S BOOK PHOTOCOPIABLE © Cambridge University Press 2017   155

VIDEO SCRIPTS

UNIT 1

▶ Unit 1 Meeting people Part 1. My name's Saif.
Saif: Hello. My name's Saif. I'm from Saudi Arabia. This is my city, Riyadh. I'm a teacher.
Carlos: Hi. I'm Carlos. I'm from Mexico City, in Mexico. I'm a student.
Elaine: Hi. My name's Elaine. I'm from the UK. This is my city, London. I'm a teacher. Nice to meet you.

▶ Part 2. He's in the library.
Narrator: He's Demir. He's from Ankara, in Turkey. He's a new student. He's in the university library. His first name is Demir – D E M I R. His family name is Topuz – T O P U Z.

▶ Part 3. Remember
Where is Saif from?
Where is Carlos from?
What's her job?
What's his family name?

UNIT 2

▶ Unit 2 People and things
 Part 1. My family has three cars.
Hachiro: This is Japan. I'm Hachiro. I like books. This is my grandfather, my father and my brother. I have one brother. My brother is six years old. My grandfather is 71 years old. This is my grandmother. She's 66 years old. And this is my mother and my father. My mother and father have two cars. My grandfather has one car.

▶ Part 2. I have one camera.
Sheila: My name is Sheila. My family name is Smith. I'm from the USA. I have one daughter. Her name is Anna. And I have one son. His name is David. They're at university. Look, I have one camera!
David: I'm David. I have one mobile phone.
Anna: I'm Anna and I'm a student. This is my computer. I have one computer here. And this is our house. We have one computer here … and we have one television here. And I have one television here. We have two televisions – my television and a family television. This is my father, James. He has one mobile phone and he has one computer here. We have three computers – my computer, his computer and a family computer. And my mother has one bag! Her camera is in the bag!

▶ Part 3. Remember
How many brothers does Hachiro have?
How many computers do the Smith family have?
How many televisions do the Smith family have?

UNIT 3

▶ Unit 3 University life Part 1. I'm a student.
Mira: Hi, I'm Mira. I'm a student in Abu Dhabi, in the UAE. I study Business.
Faisal: Hello, my name is Faisal. I'm a student in Jeddah, in Saudi Arabia. I study IT. It's interesting!
Fathima: Hello. My name's Fathima. I'm from Muscat, in Oman. I study Japanese. It's difficult!
Emma: Hello. I'm Emma. I'm from Dublin, in Ireland. I study Chemistry. It isn't easy.

▶ Part 2. When's your class?
Narrator: When's your class?
Mira: My Business class is on Wednesday morning. My class is at eight o'clock.
Narrator: Where's your class?
Mira: It's in room 42.
Narrator: What floor is it on?
Mira: It's on the third floor.
Narrator: When's your class?
Faisal: My IT class is on Monday afternoon at three o'clock.
Narrator: Where's your class?
Faisal: It's in room 21.
Narrator: What floor is it on?
Faisal: It's on the fourth floor.
Narrator: When's your class?
Fathima: My Japanese class is on Tuesday morning.
Narrator: What time is your class?
Fathima: It's at nine o'clock.
Narrator: Where's the class?
Fathima: It's in room 82.
Narrator: What floor is it on?
Fathima: It's on the second floor.
Narrator: When's your class?
Emma: My Chemistry class is on Friday afternoon.
Narrator: Where is it?
Emma: It's in room 18.
Narrator: What floor is it on?
Emma: It's on the first floor.
Teacher: Please look at your new Chemistry timetable. There are some changes this week. Your Chemistry classes are on Monday, Tuesday, Wednesday and Thursday. The class on Monday is in room 1. It isn't in room 8. It's easy. The class on Tuesday is not in room 12. It is in room 22. The class on Wednesday is not in room 23. It is in room 13. The class on Thursday in room 5 on the first floor is very interesting. Don't be late! Do you have any questions?

▶ Part 3. Remember
What does Mira study?
What does Fathima study?
What does Faisal Study?
What does Emma study?

UNIT 4

▶ Unit 4 Different countries Part 1. Where's this?
Narrator: Hello Maryam. Nice to meet you.
Maryam: Nice to meet you too.
Narrator: Where are you from?
Maryam: This is Doha, in Qatar.

VIDEO SCRIPTS

Narrator: What's it like in Doha?
Maryam: It's warm and dry.
Narrator: Who's this?
Maryam: This is my brother, Ali.
Narrator: And where's this?
Maryam: It's in Doha. It's the 'Pearl'.
Narrator: Is it new?
Maryam: Yes, it is. It's a new city. It's beautiful and clean … and very expensive.
Narrator: Hi Antonio, where's this?
Antonio: This is Mexico City, in Mexico.
Narrator: Is it big?
Antonio: Yes, it is. It's very big. It's new! And it's old. This is the palace.
Narrator: And who's this?
Antonio: This is Mr Garcia. He's very busy.

▶ Part 2. What's it like?
Narrator: Hello Mohammed.
Mohammed: Hi.
Narrator: Where are you from?
Mohammed: I'm from Muscat, in Oman.
Narrator: What's this?
Mohammed: It's the fort in Muscat. It's very old.
Narrator: Is Muscat old?
Mohammed: There are new places and there are old places. There are beautiful places too.
Narrator: What's this?
Mohammed: It's the palace. It's hot and dry in Oman.
Narrator: Hello Nicola. Where's this?
Nicola: It's London, in the UK.
Narrator: What's it like in London?
Nicola: It's wet and cold.
Narrator: And who's this?
Nicola: This is me!
Narrator: Hello Min-seo. Where are you from?
Min-seo: I'm from Seoul, in South Korea. This is the palace. And this is the fort.
Narrator: Is it cold in Seoul?
Min-seo: It's very cold in Seoul!

▶ Part 3. Remember
What's the 'Pearl'?
Where is it hot and dry?
Where is it wet and cold?
Where is it very cold?

UNIT 5

▶ Unit 5 Work Part 1. What are their jobs?
A: Who's this?
B: This is Neil.
A: Is he a pilot?
B: Yes, he is. He travels to different countries and he meets a lot of people.
A: What's it like?
B: It's interesting.
A: Who's this?
B: This is Aadab.
A: Is she a nurse?

B: No, she isn't. Her name is Dr Aadab Nazari. She's a doctor. She helps people.
A: What's it like?
B: It's difficult.
A: Who are they? Are they photographers?
B: Yes, they are. They take photographs of interesting people.
A: What's it like?
B: It's a nice job!
A: And who's he?
B: He's an actor. It's a very nice job!
A: Who's this?
B: He's a waiter. He's very busy this evening.
A: Who's he?
B: He's a driver. He meets interesting people.

▶ Part 2. When does it start?
Narrator: Hello William. Where are you from?
William: I'm from the UK.
Narrator: Are you a doctor?
William: No, I'm not. I'm a dentist.
Narrator: When does your holiday start?
William: It starts in January.
Narrator: Where is it?
William: It's in Switzerland.
Narrator: Hi Saad. Where are you from?
Saad: I'm from Saudi Arabia.
Narrator: Are you a police officer?
Saad: No, I'm not. I work in an airport. I work in Riyadh.
Narrator: Where is your holiday?
Saad: It's in Jeddah.
Narrator: When does your holiday start?
Saad: It starts in June.
Narrator: Hi Safiya. Where are you from?
Safiya: I'm from Dammam, in Saudi Arabia.
Narrator: Where do you study?
Safiya: I study in London, in the UK.
Narrator: What do you study?
Safiya: I study Biology.
Narrator: When is the first day of university?
Safiya: It's in September.

▶ Part 3. Remember
Look at Neil. What's his job?
Is Aadab a nurse?
When is the holiday for William?
When is the holiday for Saad?

UNIT 6

▶ Unit 6 Food and health Part 1. What do you eat?
Narrator: What's your name?
Gamze: My name's Gamze. I'm a student. I study History. I'm from Istanbul, in Turkey.
Narrator: When do you get up?
Gamze: I get up early. I get up at seven o'clock. And I have breakfast at seven thirty.
Narrator: What do you have for breakfast?
Gamze: I drink coffee. A lot of people in Turkey drink tea for breakfast, but I drink coffee. A lot of people in

Turkey eat bread for breakfast. I don't eat bread. I eat salad with cheese and olives.

Narrator: Do you walk to university?

Gamze: No, I don't. I go to university by bus. But some people in Istanbul walk to university.

Narrator: What do you have for lunch?

Gamze: For lunch we eat bread and drink tea. Bread and tea are cheap. The name of this bread in Turkey is 'simit'. I have lunch with my friend Oya.

Narrator: What do people in Turkey have for dinner?

Gamze: A lot of people in Turkey eat meat for lunch or dinner. Some people in Istanbul have a big and expensive dinner. They eat meat for dinner too. I have dinner with Oya. For dinner we eat noodles. We're students, and noodles are cheap!

Narrator: When do you go to bed?

Gamze: I go to bed late. I'm a student!

Narrator: What's your name?

Kashif: I'm Kashif. I'm from Dubai. I'm a bank manager. I work there. It's an interesting job.

Narrator: When do you get up?

Kashif: I get up early and go to work. Dubai has a lot of markets.

Narrator: What do you eat?

Kashif: I eat a lot of fruit. It's good for you. And I eat a lot of vegetables. I eat some fish. But he eats a lot of fish! And I eat dates. People in the UAE eat a lot of dates. They're good for you. I'm hungry! Let's have lunch. We eat fish and vegetables for lunch.

▶ Part 2. We eat a lot of fruit and vegetables.

Amy: My first name is Amy. Our family name is Brown. We're from the UK. I eat a lot of fruit and vegetables. I drink tea and we drink green tea. My grandfather drinks a lot of coffee with milk and sugar. It's not good for you. He goes to the market. He eats vegetables. And a lot of bread and cheese.

▶ Part 3. Remember
What does Gamze eat for breakfast?
What does Kashif eat a lot of?
Where does the grandfather go?

UNIT 7

▶ Unit 7 Places
Part 1. There are a lot of interesting places.

Rashid: I live in the UAE. In Dubai there is a famous tall building. The name of the tall building is Burj al-Arab. And there are beaches and parks. There are a lot of shops and a big shopping centre. There are a lot of interesting fish in the shopping centre! There are beautiful, expensive hotels. There are a lot of fish in the hotel too! There's an airport. It's beautiful! This is the metro station in the airport. There are interesting metro stations. Some trains go over the bridge to the hotel. And there are good hospitals in the UAE too. We have a lot of things in the UAE!

Ji-woo: I live in Incheon in South Korea. There are a lot of tall office buildings and a big park in my city. I walk to work and I go over the bridge. I live near some beautiful beaches. And there's a big car factory in my city. There are a lot of new cars and some big boats!

▶ Part 2. Where's Green Park?

A: Excuse me, where's Green Park?

B: It's on Old Street.

A: Where's that?

B: Go over the bridge. Turn right. Go straight on. Then turn left. There's City Park. Turn right. Turn left at Queen's Park. Queen's Park is big. Turn right. Turn left. Then turn right. Then turn left. There's Green Park.

A: I'm sorry. Could you say that again, please?

B: Of course! Go over the bridge. Turn right. Go straight on. Then turn left. There's City Park.

A: OK.

B: Turn right. Turn left at Queen's Park.

A: Queen's Park?

B: Yes. Turn right. Turn left. Then turn right. Then turn left. There's Green Park. Green Park is beautiful and interesting.

A: Thank you very much.

B: You're welcome.

▶ Part 3. Remember
What is famous in Dubai?
Where are the fish?
What is in the factory?
What's Green Park like?

UNIT 8

▶ Unit 8 Spending
Part 1. What's on your shopping list?

Narrator: Hello Tom. What's on your shopping list?

Tom: I buy bread twice a week. I buy fruit, vegetables and meat once a week.

Narrator: What fruit do you buy?

Tom: I buy bananas. I eat a lot of bananas.

Narrator: How much are they?

Tom: I buy five bananas. They're one pound. I buy a newspaper once a day.

Narrator: Do you pay for the bananas and newspaper by cash?

Tom: Yes, I do.

Narrator: How much is a newspaper?

Tom: It's one pound.

Narrator: Hello Luca. Where are you from?

Luca: Hi! I'm from Italy.

Narrator: What's on your shopping list?

Luca: I buy fruit twice a week.

Narrator: How much is it?

Luca: A bag of apples is three euros.

Narrator: What fruit do you buy?

Luca: I buy a lot of apples. And I buy some peaches.

Narrator: Hello Eric. What's on your shopping list?

Eric: I buy milk twice a week. I buy fruit and vegetables once a week. I buy some food on the internet. And I buy some food at the market.

Narrator: How much are the apples?

Eric: The apples are six dollars for three bags.
Narrator: Do you buy a newspaper?
Eric: No, I don't. I read the newspaper on my tablet.

▶ Part 2. How many tablets do you have?
Narrator: Hello Aiysha. How many tablets do you have?
Aiysha: I have one tablet. I buy a new tablet once a year.
Narrator: How much is it?
Aiysha: It's two thousand dirhams.
Narrator: Do you pay by bank card or by cash?
Aiysha: I pay by card.
Narrator: Hi Adam. Is this your laptop?
Adam: Yes, it is. I work in a clothes shop.
Narrator: How many laptops do you have?
Adam: I have one laptop. I buy a new laptop once a year.
Narrator: And how many clothes do you have?
Adam: I have a lot of clothes! I buy new clothes once a month.
Narrator: Hello Zhou.
Zhou: Hi.
Narrator: How many computers do you have?
Zhou: I have one computer.
Narrator: And how many video games do you have?
Zhou: I have one hundred video games.
Narrator: How often do you buy video games?
Zhou: I buy one twice a month.
Narrator: Are they expensive?
Zhou: No, they're not. They're cheap.
Narrator: Hi Salem. How much is a coffee?
Salem: It's ten dirhams.
Narrator: Do pay by cash or bank card?
Salem: I pay by card.

▶ Part 3. Remember
Look at Tom. What's on his shopping list?
Look at Luca. What's on his shopping list?
Look at Aiysha. What does she buy?
Look at Salem. What does he buy?

UNIT 9

▶ Unit 9 Technology
   Part 1. Do you have any good apps?
Narrator: Hi Mike, where are you from?
Mike: I'm from London, in the UK.
Narrator: Do you have any apps on your smartphone?
Mike: Yes, I do.
Narrator: What app do you like?
Mike: I like this app. It can buy food.
Narrator: Are you hungry?
Mike: Yes, I am!
Narrator: Hello Sarah, who's this?
Sarah: This is my brother, Paul.
Narrator: Where are you and your brother from?
Sarah: We're from Paris, in France.
Narrator: Do you have any good apps on your smartphone?

Sarah: Yes, I do. I have an app for reading English newspapers online. It can download the news. It can help you learn new words.
Narrator: Paul, do you have any good apps?
Paul: This is a nice app. It can take photographs and it can save the photographs.
Narrator: Hello Aliyah. Where are you from?
Aliyah: I'm from New York, in the USA.
Narrator: Who's on your phone?
Aliyah: This is my mother.
Narrator: Where's your mother?
Aliyah: She's in the USA too. She's in Chicago. Do you have family or friends in a different city? This app can help you. It can call your family and friends. My mum has it too.
Aliyah: Hi mom!
Mother: Hi Aliyah!
Narrator: Good morning, Sam.
Sam: Good morning!
Narrator: Where are you from?
Sam: I'm from London, in the UK.
Narrator: Do you have any good apps on your smartphone?
Sam: Yes, I do. Buy this app! It's good for you!

▶ Part 2. Do you have a USB drive?
Shop assistant: Good morning.
Sophie: Good morning. Excuse me, do you have a USB drive? I need a big one.
Shop assistant: Yes, we have a lot of USB drives. Here you are.
Sophie: Is it good?
Shop assistant: Yes. It's very big. It can save a lot of photographs or a lot of work.
Sophie: I need it for my work. How much is it?
Shop assistant: It's three pounds.
Sophie: Two USB drives, please.
Shop assistant: That's six pounds.
Sophie: Can I pay by card?
Shop assistant: Of course.
Sophie: I'm sorry. How do you use the USB drive?
Shop assistant: Do you have a laptop?
Sophie: Yes. Here you are.
Shop assistant: Look.
Sophie: Thank you! Let's go home and start work! I have a lot of work! I can save my work on my new USB drive. And I have a lot of emails to read! My computer can download emails but it can't read emails!

▶ Part 3. Remember
What can this app do?
What can this app do?
What can this app do?
What can the computer do?

UNIT 10

▶ Unit 10 Free time and fashion
Part 1. What do you like doing in your free time?
Chris: I like cooking interesting food with my son, Robert. We don't bake cakes. Cakes are difficult! We bake biscuits. Biscuits are easy! We go online with the tablet to look at different things to make. Then we walk to the shop to buy the food. We like going for a walk. We buy milk and eggs.
Let's start. We use the tablet. Here are the eggs. Here's the milk. I like talking and baking with my son. Here are the biscuits!
Narrator: Hi Rashid.
Rashid: Hi. This is my wife Talihah and my son Omar.
Narrator: What do you like doing in your free time?
Rashid: We have a picnic. We like eating fruit and drinking tea. We walk, and we talk and we take photographs of the family. Omar plays in the park.

▶ Part 2. Do you like buying new clothes?
Narrator: Hello Peter. Do you like buying new clothes?
Peter: Yes, I do. I like wearing nice clothes at work.
Narrator: What do you wear at work?
Peter: I wear nice shirts. My favourite colours are blue and white. And I wear a nice tie. I like blue ties and red ties.
Narrator: Do you wear a jacket?
Peter: Yes, I usually wear a jacket at work. I like black or blue jackets.
Narrator: What shoes do you like?
Peter: I always wear black shoes.
Narrator: Do you wear T-shirts?
Peter: No, I never wear T-shirts.
Narrator: You look very nice with your white shirt, your blue tie and your blue jacket.
Peter: Thank you!

▶ Part 3. Remember
What do Chris and Robert buy?
What do Rashid, Talihah and Omar eat and drink in the park?
What does Peter wear?

ACKNOWLEDGEMENTS

The publishers are extremely grateful to the following people for reviewing this course during its development. The course has benefited hugely from your insightful comments and feedback.

Ashwaq Al-Jahlan, Princess Noura University, Saudi Arabia; Peggy Alptekin; Dr. Wafa Aws, Dar Al Uloom, Saudi Arabia; Anil Bayir, Izmir University, Turkey; Patrick Boylan, King Abdulaziz University, Saudi Arabia; Pauline Chahine, Qatar Armed Forces, Qatar; Esengul Hasdemir, Atilim University, Turkey; Dr Anwar Jamal, Kuwait University, Kuwait; Megan Putney, Dhofar University, Oman; Tracy Quayat, Princess Noura Univeristy, Saudi Arabia; Katherine Rick, Lincoln College, Saudi Arabia; Hussein Saeed, Jubail Industrial College, Saudi Arabia

CODE FOR TESTS

The code for the *Unlock Basic Skills* tests is:

UBStests-7102

Instructions for e-Source and the code for the course audio and video, Presentation Plus, and additional printable material are on the inside of the front cover.

The authors and publishers acknowledge the following sources of copyright material and are grateful for the permissions granted. While every effort has been made, it has not always been possible to identify the sources of all the material used, or to trace all copyright holders. If any omissions are brought to our notice, we will be happy to include the appropriate acknowledgements on reprinting and in the next update to the digital edition, as applicable.

Cover Photography by David Kirkland/Perspectives/Getty Images; (woman): Jenny Acheson/Stockbyte/Getty Images; (whiteboard): Nemida/iStock/Getty Images Plus/Getty Images.

p. 54: Hill Street Studios/Blend Images/Getty Images.

Corpus

Development of this publication has made use of the Cambridge English Corpus (CEC). The CEC is a multi-billion word computer database of contemporary spoken and written English. It includes British English, American English, and other varieties of English. It also includes the Cambridge Learner Corpus, developed in collaboration with the University of Cambridge ESOL Examinations. Cambridge University Press has built up the CEC to provide evidence about language use that helps to produce better language teaching materials.

Typeset by emc design ltd.